DISCARD

BETHANY
COLLEGE
LIBRARY.

P9-DNB-985

DISCARD

The Regulation of
International Banking

The Regulation of International Banking

RICHARD DALE

Woodhead-Faulkner · Cambridge
Prentice-Hall, Inc., Englewood Cliffs, New Jersey

Library of Congress Cataloging-in-Publication Data

Dale, Richard.
    The regulation of international banking.

    Includes bibliographies and index.
    1. Banks and banking, International—Law and
legislation.   2. Banks and banking, International.
I. Title.
K1066.D35   1985   341.7'51   85–20532
ISBN   0–13–771254–5

© Richard Dale 1984

Woodhead-Faulkner Ltd, Fitzwilliam House, 32 Trumpington Street,
Cambridge CB2 1QY

This American edition published 1986 by Prentice-Hall, Inc., Englewood Cliffs,
New Jersey 07632

Conditions of sale
All rights reserved. No part of this publication may be reproduced, stored in a retrieval
system or transmitted, in any form or by any means, electronic, mechanical, photocopying,
recording or otherwise, without the prior permission of the publishers.

First published November 1984

ISBN   0 85941 261 X   (Woodhead-Faulkner edition)
ISBN   0–13–771254–5   (Prentice-Hall edition)

10 9 8 7 6 5 4 3 2 1

ISBN   0-13-771254-5   01

Prentice-Hall International (UK) Limited, *London*
Prentice-Hall of Australia Pty. Limited, *Sydney*
Prentice-Hall Canada Inc., *Toronto*
Prentice-Hall Hispanoamericana, S.A., *Mexico*
Prentice-Hall of India Private Limited, *New Delhi*
Prentice-Hall of Japan, Inc., *Tokyo*
Prentice-Hall of Southeast Asia Pte. Ltd., *Singapore*
Editora Prentice-Hall do Brasil, Ltda., *Rio de Janeiro*
Whitehall Books Limited, *Wellington, New Zealand*

Designed by Geoff Green
Phototypeset by Hands Fotoset, Leicester
Printed in Great Britain by St Edmundsbury Press, Bury St Edmunds, Suffolk
American liaison: Margaret Rizzi

Contents

341.751
Diss r

Preface

The third world debt crisis that erupted in the summer of 1982 has focused attention on the explosive growth of multinational banking and of the Eurocurrency markets through which the bulk of international lending has been routed. The emergence of global banking networks straddling numerous jurisdictions poses special policy problems for national supervisory authorities. In particular, uneven regulatory practices can lead to a situation in which banks are drawn to the most permissive regimes. Furthermore, the proliferation of offshore banking centres competing for international banking business poses a continuing obstacle to regulatory co-ordination at a time when the increasing interdependence of banks and banking systems points to the need for a global approach to the problems of bank safety and soundness.

This book examines the 'prudential' implications of the growth of multinational banking and assesses the policy response of national supervisory authorities to this phenomenon. The overall conclusion is that a fragmented regulatory structure is no longer appropriate to the global banking system that has emerged since the early 1970s and that the present approach to co-ordination of national regulatory practices is no substitute for a formal framework of international law in this area.

Research for this study was undertaken during my tenure of a Rockefeller Foundation International Relations Fellowship. I would like to thank, in addition to the Rockefeller Foundation, both the Brookings Institution and the School of Advanced International Studies at Johns Hopkins University, Washington, DC, to which I was affiliated as a visiting scholar during the period of my fellowship.

I would also like to express my gratitude to: the Group of Thirty for allowing me to use in Chapters 6 and 7 some material originally published as a Group of Thirty Monograph, *Bank Supervision Around the World* (1982); the editors of the *Banker* and the *Columbia Journal of World Business* for permission to use extracts from articles that have appeared in their publications; and Martinus Nijhoff, Publishers, for permission to adapt material originally published by them in *International Lending in a Fragile World Economy* (1983).

Richard Dale

1 *The Growth of Multinational Banking*

One of the more remarkable financial developments since the Second World War has been the rapid expansion not merely of international bank lending but of multinational banks servicing such business from offices spread across the globe. While the growth of international lending can, perhaps, be readily explained by means of conventional economic analysis, it is less easy to account in these terms for the proliferation of foreign banking offices and their host financial centres. Indeed, multinational as distinct from international banking may more accurately be described as an artifice born of regulatory anomalies than as a natural economic phenomenon rooted in comparative advantage. The impact of force-fed multinational banking structures on the safety of banking and on the effectiveness of international supervisory co-operation forms the main subject-matter of this book.

International banking has always tended to attract controversy on account of its supposed riskiness. In 1875 a director of London and Westminster Bank said in evidence before the UK Select Committee on Banks of Issue that 'speaking for the London and Westminster Bank we hold . . . that the public entrust us with large deposits and large funds and that the security of our property should be here on the spot and not broadcast all over the world'.[1] Similarly, in 1921, the Chairman of the London City and Midland Bank, when reaffirming his bank's opposition to foreign branching, asserted that 'we have no present intention of deviating from this policy which . . . gives greater security to our domestic depositors by restricting our activities to their home fields'.[2]

On the other hand, the acknowledged risks of international lending induced some banks, after the First World War, to move in the opposite direction. One motive for the establishment of foreign banking offices at this time was evidently the 'desire on the part of the parent banks to relieve themselves of the risks which are more serious in the financing of foreign than of domestic business'.[3] Accordingly, both Lloyds Bank and London and Westminster Bank organised their operations in continental

1

Europe as subsidiaries, so as to sever legal liability and thereby protect themselves against what we might now call country risk – the risk that adverse political or economic developments in the host countries concerned might prevent local borrowers from meeting their external obligations.[4]

Behind this controversy over foreign operations lie some pertinent issues, the topicality of which can hardly be said to have diminished with the passage of time. Should ordinary depositors be exposed to risks incurred in far-off countries of which they have no knowledge? If banks are to conduct extensive international operations, should these be structured in such a way as to protect depositors with the parent institution? Do the risks involved in international banking require special regulatory measures and, if so, who should apply them and what form should they take? To what extent should national authorities co-ordinate their regulatory activities and should there be an agreed framework of international law in this area?

Today the status and stability of multinational banking have emerged as a major policy issue. This has come about as a result of the rapid growth of international trade and capital flows, the growing tendency for domestic banks to conduct their international operations from offices established in other countries (it is this practice, indeed, which distinguishes multinational from international banking) and the spectacular expansion of the Eurocurrency markets, that is, the markets in currencies deposited outside their country of issue. During the same period, successive oil crises have highlighted the pivotal role of multinational banks as intermediaries between surplus and deficit countries at a time of increasing balance of payments disequilibria. Finally, the global debt crisis that erupted in the summer of 1982 has focused attention on the growing interdependence of national banking systems, while also raising doubts about the adequacy of the existing regulatory framework for international lending.

Against this background, this book will examine the structure and stability of the multinational banking sector, the current scope of international supervisory co-operation and the desirability of new initiatives aimed at safeguarding the international banking system. Throughout, multinational banking is understood to mean banking business conducted not from a bank's home base but from dependent establishments located in foreign centres. Many of the safety or prudential issues relating to multinational banking apply more generally to international banking, but multinational banks pose a special regulatory problem for the very reason that they straddle numerous national jurisdictions. It will further be argued that the co-existence of global banking networks knowing no jurisdictional boundaries and a fragmented nation-based regulatory structure can itself become an independent source of international financial instability. The main policy focus here is therefore on multinational rather than international banking, although much of the analysis is applicable to both kinds of activity.

It should be emphasised from the outset that there are several layers to the bank safety problem, not all of which receive equal treatment in this book. Broadly speaking, bank stability can be considered at three different levels: the potential for external disturbances, which may take the form of credit, interest rate or other shocks; the capacity of banks to withstand such disturbances, as measured, for instance, by capital and liquidity ratios; and the ability and willingness of national or international authorities to provide support in the event that individual institutions or the system as a whole should experience severe financial strains. The analysis presented here is concerned primarily with the latter two levels, although clearly an appropriate policy response in these areas must take account of the economic environment in which banks are expected to operate.

This first Chapter traces the recent explosive growth of multinational banking in the context of more general financial trends, and advances the argument, elaborated in Chapter 2, that such expansion is to an important extent a by-product of disparities in domestic financial regulation. This conclusion, as will be shown, has adverse implications for the scope and effectiveness of international supervisory co-operation and for the overall stability of a highly integrated global banking system.

THE EXPANSION OF INTERNATIONAL LENDING

International bank lending can be classified according to three basic critera, namely: the residence of the bank, the residence of the borrower and the currency denomination of the loan. The residence of a bank may be determined by reference to the country in which the bank office is physically located ('location' method) or to the country in which its parent bank has its headquarters ('charter' method). For the purpose of analysing the growth of multinational banking it is generally more appropriate to use the location method, although for supervisory purposes the charter method may be more suitable.[5]

Bank lending may be described as 'international' when it is cross-border, that is, when the lending bank and the borrower reside in different countries. In such cases lending will also be cross-currency, that is, denominated in a currency foreign either to the lender – in which case the bank's claim is said to be a Eurocurrency loan – and/or to the borrower. The great bulk of present day international bank lending is in the form of Eurocurrency credits serviced by banking offices located in the major Eurocurrency centres such as London, Luxembourg and Singapore.

International lending in its broadest sense need not necessarily be cross-border, however. For instance, foreign currency loans by US banks to US residents may for some purposes be categorised as international claims, as may all loans extended by foreign offices of US banks to local residents.[6] In the first case the lending is cross-currency but not cross-border, while in the case of the local currency claims of foreign offices it is neither. This last example highlights the difference between the charter and location methods of determining a bank's country of residence: from the point of view of the parent bank such 'local' lending may be considered cross-border (and even cross-currency) although from the perspective of a narrow residency test it is not.

International lending, then, broadly defined, may be viewed as consisting of all claims of domestic bank offices on residents of foreign countries, plus all claims of foreign bank offices on local residents or residents of other foreign countries, plus all claims of domestic bank offices on domestic residents denominated in foreign currencies. In other words, international lending may be cross-border, cross-currency and/or booked through a foreign bank office, any one of these elements being sufficient to confer on the loan an international status.

On the other side of the balance sheet bank deposits may also be classified according to the residence of the bank, the residence of the depositor and the currency denomination of the deposit. Deposits placed with banks resident (in a location sense) outside the country in whose currency the deposit is denominated are generally considered to be Eurocurrency deposits. However, the residence of the depositor is also relevant here, since some statistical sources, notably the Bank for International Settlements (BIS) exclude banks' foreign currency positions *vis-à-vis* residents from their definition of the Eurocurrency market.[7] Finally, non-resident deposits, whether denominated in foreign or domestic currency, may have a special significance in so far as they are subject to separate regulatory arrangements (see, for instance, the discussion of US International Banking Facilities on pages 30–32).

Unfortunately, available banking statistics are subject to a number of comparability problems which make it virtually impossible to construct a comprehensive and consistent picture of international banking activity over a period of time. Different sources (or the same source at different times) may have different geographical coverage, use the location or charter method to determine the residence of banks, report data gross or net of interbank claims, employ a residency and/or currency test in compiling banks' international claims and liabilities, and adopt a concept of 'banking' which may or may not include broader categories of depository institution.[8] Nevertheless, since the present purpose is to identify broad trends and since, as it happens, the observed trends are largely independent of the choice of data, it is unnecessary to become deeply involved in these and other statistical difficulties.

Tables 1 to 3 highlight respectively three key features of international banking activity in recent years. First, new international lending, Eurocurrency assets and Eurocurrency liabilities have all been growing at

Table 1 Indicators of International Banking and Lending Growth

	1. Eurocurrency Assets, Total	2. Eurocurrency Claims on Non-Banks	3. Eurocurrency Market, Net Size	4. Deposit Banks' Foreign Assets	5. Deposit Banks' Foreign Liabilities	6. Net New International Bank Lending	7. Net New International Bank Lending to Non-Oil LDCs
US Dollars (bn)							
1966	20.3	2.8	17.4	51.8	61.3	NA	NA
1973	187.6	38.7	132.0	354.5	384.7	31	10
1980	751.2	193.5	575.0	1,711.3	1,777.8	165.0	41*
Average Annual Rates of Growth (%)							
1966–80	29.4	35.4	28.4	28.4	27.2	NA	NA
1966–73	37.4	45.6	33.6	31.6	30.0	NA	NA
1973–80	21.9	25.8	23.4	25.2	24.4	27.0	26.5†

Notes: * 1979; † 1973–79.
Sources: Columns 1–3, BIS Annual Reports; Columns 4 and 5, IMF, International Financial Statistics; Columns 6 and 7, BIS and IMF *International Capital Markets* (Occasional Paper), September 1980. Columns 4 and 5 refer to IMF 'world' aggregates (all countries).
Reproduced from A.K. Swoboda, 'International Banking: Current Issues in Perspective', *Journal of Banking and Finance*, September 1982.

Table 2 Growth of Selected 'World' Economic Series

	Annual Growth Rates (%)		
	1966–1973	1973–1980	1966–1980
World money	10.2	12.9	11.5
Consumer prices			
(world index)	5.6	12.7	9.2
Value of exports	9.2	25.2	14.3
Total world reserves			
(gold at SDR35 per ounce)	11.1	12.8	12.0
Total world reserves			
(gold at market prices)	16.4	19.9	18.2
Memorandum item			
Deposit banks' foreign assets	31.6	25.2	28.4
Deposit banks' foreign liabilities	30.0	24.4	27.2

Source: Quoted in A.K. Swoboda., 'International Banking'.

Table 3 Bond Versus Bank Financing (US$bn)

	1971–73	1979	1980	1981	1982
Net international bank lending	27.0	125.0	160.0	165.0	95.0
Net international bond financing					
(Eurobond plus foreign bond issues)	8.0	28.0	28.0	36.5	58.5
Less double counting due to bank					
purchases of bonds	–	8.0	8.0	6.5	8.5
Total net bank and bond financing	35.0	145.0	180.0	195.0	145.0

Source: World Bank and BIS data.

annual rates well in excess of 20 per cent. Secondly, the growth of these banking aggregates has since 1966 been much more rapid than that of global economic series such as estimated world money supply, the value of international trade and official reserves. Thirdly, the volume of new international bank lending has recently been much larger than direct international financing in the form of bond issues, although the trend was interrupted in 1982/83 when bank lending was sharply curtailed in the wake of the international debt crisis.

The foreign offices (branches and subsidiaries) of domestic banks have also played an important and, in recent years, increasingly dominant role in the explosive growth of international bank lending. Table 4 outlines the US experience up to 1978, the interesting point being that whereas in 1964 domestic offices accounted for over two-thirds of total international claims of US banks, by 1978 this proportion had fallen to little more than one-fifth. The expansion and distribution of US banks' overseas branches that has accompanied this shift from 'onshore' to 'offshore' lending is shown in Table 5.

Again, data deficiencies make it impossible to present a comprehensive global picture of the growth of multinational banking since the 1960s. However, Table 6 provides data on the present structure of multinational banking classified both by the country of origin ('home

Table 4 International Claims of American Banks (US$bn)

	1964	1969	1973	1978
International claims held by:				
US offices	10.6	10.5	16.8	78.0
Foreign branches	3.8	32.2	106.5	270.6
Foreign subsidiaries	0.3	1.7	9.7	19.3
Total	14.7	44.4	133.0	367.9

Source: John Sterling, 'Competitive Advantage', p.412a.

Table 5 Foreign Branches of US Banks

Host Area	1961	1970	1978
United Kingdom	11	37	56
France	3	15	21
Germany	3	21	22
Switzerland	0	11	8
Netherlands	0	9	7
Other Europe	4	32	60
Other Latin America	52	109	85
Japan	14	14	32
Hong Kong	2	10	31
Other Far East	11	57	69
Middle East	4	10	30
Africa	7	13	16
Caribbean	4	89	188
Panama	8	26	19
Singapore and Malaysia	5	14	26
Total	128	467	670

Source: based on Diane Page and Neal Soss, *Some Evidence on Transnational Banking Structure*, US Comptroller of the Currency, 1980, pp.21–23.

country') of the parent bank and by the foreign office's country of residence ('host country').[9] Looked at from the point of view of the home country, the interesting question, given the rapid growth of international lending, is why domestic banks have chosen to establish foreign banking networks to service this business. From the point of view of the host financial centres, the more relevant issue is why foreign banks should have chosen to locate themselves in one centre rather than another. These questions, which are fundamental to the problem of bank regulation, are given preliminary attention below and considered more fully in Chapter 2. First, however, it is necessary to consider what, if anything, is new about the growth of multinational banking and the international lending business with which it is associated.

It has been noted that international bank lending comprises three distinct strands: cross-border loans; cross-currency loans; and loans booked at foreign banking offices (the multinational aspect). It was also noted that the growth of international banking is closely linked to the expansion of the Eurocurrency deposit market through which inter-

Table 6 Multinational Banking Presence, 1978–79

	Banking Institutions	Branches	Subsidiaries	Affiliates
(a) By Country or Region of Origin				
United States	151	800	113	244
United Kingdom	25	961	86	54
France	19	228	37	126
Germany	21	55	16	115
Switzerland	13	32	18	30
Netherlands	6	109	20	25
Other Europe	86	407	54	282
Canada	8	222	34	39
Japan	23	127	–	–
Australia and New Zealand	8	550	7	10
Latin America (excl. Caribbean)	34	125	4	27
Other Asia	52	589	9	10
Middle East	43	153	13	111
Africa	31	17	–	66
Total	520	4,375	440	1,232
(b) By Host Country or Region				
United States	–	304	46	59
United Kingdom	–	406	35	195
France	–	108	21	116
Germany	–	85	13	73
Switzerland	–	31	32	46
Other Europe	–	245	86	159
Booking centres *	–	803	88	169
Other America	–	365	22	83
Middle East	–	331	14	52
Africa	–	264	46	202
Other	–	1,433	37	78
Total	–	4,375	440	1,232

Note: * Caribbean area, Panama, Singapore, Malaysia, Bahrain, Channel Islands.
Source: quoted in R.M. Pecchioli, *The Internationalisation of Banking: The Policy Issues*, OECD, 1983, p.60.

national loans are typically funded. The question to be addressed here is whether these characteristics of international bank lending are a recent (post-Second World War) development or whether they represent merely the continuation of longer-term historical trends.

Cross-border, cross-currency and even 'Eurocurrency' bank lending can be traced back to the Renaissance period and the international activities of the Medici and Fugger banking houses.[10] However, these banks can hardly be considered to be depository institutions in the modern sense (for instance, the Fugger's loan portfolio was funded for the most part by its owners) and much of their international lending was in the form of trade financing rather than medium-term credits. Even so, it is interesting to observe that the international operations of these houses, and particularly cross-border loans to sovereign borrowers, appear to have played a major part in their eventual downfall.[11]

The nineteenth and early twentieth centuries witnessed a rapid expansion of international and multinational banking based on the far-flung colonial banking networks of Britain, France and, to a lesser extent, Germany and Holland.[12] However, the activities of these banks were confined largely to trade finance and local currency business, there being virtually no other cross-border or cross-currency lending at this time. During the inter-war period the foreign branching of US banks, made possible by the Federal Reserve Act of 1913, paralleled the activities of the colonial banking networks.[13] In particular, offices of US banks were established in Latin America to conduct dollar-denominated trade financing on behalf of local borrowers. However, reflecting a series of major defaults in the 1920s and 1930s, the scale of US multinational banking had declined sharply by the beginning of the Second World War, while the colonial banking networks were gradually unwound or disposed of in the years after 1945, offsetting the expansion of multi-national banking elsewhere.

Until the 1930s longer-term international lending was largely in the hands of merchant banks which, however, acted as underwriters and arrangers of bond issues rather than as lenders in their own right.[14] In this sense the Second World War may be said to mark a watershed in the pattern of international financing. In the earlier period banks generally refrained from cross-border sovereign lending, while private investors were large-scale purchasers of bonds issued by the governments of developing countries. In the subsequent period these roles were reversed, with the banks displacing private investors as the primary lenders to sovereign borrowers.

It has been claimed that the origins of the Eurocurrency deposit market can be traced back to the late nineteenth century. In any event, banks in most European countries accepted deposits in a variety of currencies immediately prior to the First World War and in the 1920s.[15] On the other hand, there is no evidence that these deposits were used to fund banks' international lending, while in some instances they appear to have been converted into local currency and covered in the forward exchange market.[16] The modern evolution of the Eurocurrency market may be said to have begun in the early 1950s when the Soviet Union, allegedly fearing that the United States might block its dollar reserves, decided to deposit dollars in a Soviet-owned Paris bank, Banque Commerciale pour l'Europe du Nord (known as 'Euro-bank' – hence the term Eurodollars).[17] In September 1957 the market was given a major stimulus on the demand side when the UK authorities imposed a ban on sterling credits to finance trade between third countries, the result being that London-based banks began to bid for dollars as a new source of funding for this business.[18] It is significant that the post-war development of the Eurocurrency market should have begun in the first place in anticipation of a US regulatory initiative and in the second place as a positive response to UK restrictions on the use of sterling; for it is a basic contention of this book that both multinational banking and the Eurocurrency market on which it feeds are to a large extent the creation of national regulatory arrangements.

In summary, the various strands of modern international banking can, taken separately, be traced back to well before the Second World War and in several instances far beyond. In this sense there is nothing 'new' about international banking, even if its recent growth has been unprecedented. On the other hand, the *combination* of these individual strands in a single integrated banking operation has no historical parallel. Today, international bank lending is typically conducted by bank offices operating from financial centres outside the lending bank's country of origin as well as the borrowing entity's country of residence. Such loans are typically denominated in a currency foreign both to the host financial centre and to the borrower, while the bank's own funding is based on similarly extraneous Eurocurrency deposits. In short, the activities of the modern 'offshore' banking office have no apparent connection with the centre in which it is located. This is a situation far removed from the old colonial banking networks and other traditional forms of international trade financing, where the locus of the bank's operations was determined either by the currency in which it transacted (for instance, London in the case of international sterling business) or the country whose trade it financed. Viewed in this way, modern international and, more specifically, multinational banking is both qualitatively and quantitatively different from anything that has preceded it.

A variety of explanations can be offered for the rapid growth of international bank lending since the 1960s. On the demand side, the extraordinary expansion of international trade has generated a corresponding need for international financing, while even before the first oil crisis developing countries had launched into expansion programmes requiring heavy resort to external funding. The OPEC crisis of 1973 is, however, widely regarded as a turning-point for international commercial bank lending. Since that date bank credits have played a dominant role in financing aggravated balance of payments disequilibria, while the proportion of international claims in banks' total claims has doubled.[19]

Supply-side explanations for the growth of international bank lending are less clear-cut, although the decline in 'spreads' (the gross margin between banks' lending and borrowing rates) that occurred during the 1970s suggests that increased demand for credits is by no means the whole story.[20] It has been suggested that banks' perception of country risk may have diminished,[21] that their international activities represent a conscious move in the direction of risk diversification[22] and/or that the new technology of syndicated loans, involving floating interest rates, the parcelling out of credit risks and shared information,[23] has lowered the effective cost of international lending. Finally, it is sometimes argued that the depositing of surplus OPEC funds in the Eurocurrency markets has left the recipient banks little alternative but to re-lend these funds as Eurocurrency credits to sovereign borrowers. In its simplest form this last argument betrays an over-compartmentalised view of domestic and international financial markets, but there can be little doubt that the ready availability of OPEC funds has facilitated the expansion of banks' international loan portfolios.

While unfettered market responses to a changing global economic environment may provide the main explanation for the growth of international bank lending, there is one important aspect of this process which is not so easily accounted for. Banks have in recent years (until the debt crisis erupted in 1982) shown a greater willingness to lend to developing countries than at any time in the past, while private investors, who were extremely active purchasers of third world bond issues prior to the First World War and in the 1920s, have tended to shun such debt issues. Put another way, it is paradoxical that investors should be prepared to lend indirectly via the international banking system to countries they would not consider lending to directly. It has been suggested that banks can benefit from economies of scale in information not available to private investors, that individuals cannot impose conditions on foreign borrowers and that the risk/return calculus for banks has been transformed by the IMF's supportive role as a conditional lender to distressed sovereign borrowers. However, none of these factors provides an entirely convincing explanation for the displacement of direct by indirect international financing and it may be that, following the national banking reforms of the 1930s, private investors believe that banks enjoy the implicit support of national authorities and are therefore safer than their balance sheets alone would suggest.[24]

THE DEVELOPMENT OF INTERNATIONAL BANKING

Whereas the growth of international bank lending may, subject to this last qualification, be viewed as a market phenomenon, rather different explanations must be sought for the parallel expansion of multinational banking networks.[25] Certainly, market forces have in many instances induced banks to conduct their international business from foreign establishments rather than from their home base. Foreign retail banking business can, of course, be developed only in this way while financial services in the corporate finance, investment management, leasing and financial consultancy areas may also require a locally based physical presence. It is well recognised, too, that banks have tended to follow their corporate clients abroad both to service their needs there and to protect existing home-based relationships. In addition, large-scale lending to borrowers resident in a particular country may demand a strong local presence for marketing, client liaison, information-gathering and loan-monitoring reasons. More generally, marketing considerations may dictate that a bank office should be located in the same or a broadly similar time zone as its clientele.

On the other hand, wholesale international banking is unusual among internationally traded services in that it matters little from an economic or practical point of view where the service is provided. A borrower need not be concerned where a loan is arranged, booked or even advanced since funds can be transferred promptly and without cost to wherever they may be needed via established international clearing mechanisms. Given today's global telecommunications network, institutional and other large-scale depositors may be similarly indifferent (country risk considerations apart) as to the locus of their deposits. From the bank's point of view, too, national differences in personnel and property rental costs are unlikely to be a decisive factor in the location decision, given the dominance of funding over all other costs. Furthermore, the modern technique of loan syndication reduces the need for direct client contact so far as participant banks are concerned. The key relationships here are between the borrower and the lead manager (or management group) on the one hand, and the lead manager and participant banks on the other. Given the lead manager's intermediary role participant banks may, regardless of their location, engage actively in the loan syndication business via telexed communications with syndicate managers. In this sense, too, international banking is a disembodied activity in which physical presence can be divorced from the service provided.

Because conventional economic factors rate relatively low in a bank's location decisions, the structure and scale of multinational banking are highly sensitive to regulatory differences between national jurisdictions. As noted above, syndicated Eurocurrency credits, which constitute the bulk of international bank lending, are frequently serviced from financial centres that have little apparent connection with the borrower, the lending bank's country of origin or the currency denomination of the loan; for in a market fostered by regulatory anomalies rather than natural economic forces, participants establish themselves in those centres offering the most favourable regulatory environment.

The key regulatory anomaly to be considered in this context is the asymmetrical treatment of domestic and foreign currency deposits for reserve purposes. Most national authorities impose compulsory reserve requirements on banks' domestic currency liabilities as a lever by which to control their money supply, and where (as is generally the case) these reserves must be held as interest-free or low-yielding deposits with the central bank, the requirement amounts to an implicit tax on domestic currency banking business. Foreign currency deposits are, on the other hand, typically exempt from reserve requirements, the rationale being that international banking business can in this way be encouraged without jeopardising control of the domestic money supply. This dual regulatory regime confers on offshore or Eurocurrency banking business an artificial cost advantage. The extent of the advantage depends on the level both of reserve requirements and of nominal interest rates, the latter representing the opportunity cost of holding interest-free deposits (see Table 7).

Table 7 Cost Advantage of Offshore Banks Relative to Domestic Banks

Reserve Requirement (%)	Average Interest Rate on Assets (%)						
	6	7	8	9	10	11	12
2	0.12	0.14	0.16	0.18	0.20	0.22	0.24
3	0.18	0.21	0.24	0.27	0.30	0.33	0.36
4	0.24	0.28	0.32	0.36	0.40	0.44	0.48
5	0.30	0.35	0.40	0.45	0.50	0.55	0.60
6	0.36	0.42	0.48	0.54	0.60	0.66	0.72
7	0.42	0.49	0.56	0.63	0.70	0.77	0.84

Source: Robert Z. Aliber, Hearings before the Subcommittee on Domestic Monetary Policy and the Subcommittee on International Trade, Investment and Monetary Policy of the Committee on Banking, Finance and Urban Affairs, House of Representatives, 96th Congress, First Session, 1979, p.89.

Asymmetrical monetary regulation may therefore be said to have given the international banking system a bias in favour of external financial intermediation. In other words, banks are in general better off conducting their international lending business outside the country in whose currency the business is denominated. The magnitude of this distortion has, furthermore, tended to increase over time as the rise in world interest rates has raised the cost of having funds tied up in interest-free or low-yielding mandatory reserves. The increasing opportunity cost of holding such reserves may also help to explain the secular decline in spreads on Eurocurrency credits, since as short-term rates rise funds will tend to flow from the domestic to the Eurocurrency markets.[26]

Another form of monetary regulation that has, at least in the past, given a powerful stimulus to offshore banking is the control of domestic interest rates. For instance, under the US Banking Act of 1933 the Federal Reserve is authorised to impose limits on US deposit rates. Whenever Regulation Q, through which this authority is exercised, has held domestic deposit rates well below other money market yields, US deposits have moved offshore while US banks have simultaneously expanded their offshore operations to recapture these funds.[27] Since 1970, however, short-term deposits of over $100,000 have been exempt from Regulation Q so that interest rate distortions are no longer an important factor in the Eurodollar market. On the other hand, interest rate controls on non-resident domestic currency deposits imposed periodically by Switzerland and West Germany in order to discourage capital inflows have contributed to the growth of external markets in Swiss francs and Deutschmarks. In addition, Japan's continuing elaborate controls on domestic deposit rates have encouraged the expansion of the Euroyen market. Finally, it may be noted that interest rate cartels in domestic markets operate in the same direction as official controls.

While the avoidance of domestic monetary regulation provides the basic inducement for going offshore, the choice of venue for conducting international banking business is determined by a variety of other regulatory considerations. On the fiscal side, exemption of non-resident foreign currency deposits from local withholding taxes is a precondition for large-scale Eurocurrency funding, the payment of withholding tax being for this purpose equivalent to an interest-free loan by the depositor. Similarly, the imposition of local stamp duties or transfer taxes on international loan instruments may inhibit syndicated credit business. Finally, the corporation tax applicable to a bank's own profits clearly has a major bearing on where business is conducted and loans are booked.

Bank secrecy laws may also influence the siting of international banking operations. Such laws protect the borrowers, the bank and, most importantly, the depositor who, for fiscal or other reasons, may wish to remain outside the regulatory purview of national authorities. Looked at from the non-resident depositor's point of view, the absence of local withholding tax, when coupled with guaranteed anonymity, may be equivalent to a substantive tax benefit that lowers his required rate of return.

The scope and severity of local prudential regulations is another factor to be considered in the location decision. As discussed below (see Chapter 3) such regulations seek to limit the risks incurred by banks to a socially acceptable level. To the extent that foreign banking offices fall outside the regulatory control of the home supervisory authority, a bank may be able to establish its chosen risk profile by operating from a permissive jurisdiction. For instance, the decision of West German and Swiss banks to pass much of their international business through Luxembourg subsidiaries in the 1970s and early 1980s can be attributed in part to their desire to escape the strict limitations on financial gearing imposed by their home authorities.

Regulations introduced for balance of payments reasons have in the past had an important influence on the location of international banking operations. Indeed, foreign exchange regulations provided the original stimulus for the post-1945 expansion of the Eurocurrency markets. It was noted above that restrictions on the sterling financing of third country trade introduced by the United Kingdom in 1957 helped to establish the Eurodollar market in London. The shift to offshore dollar financing was further encouraged by a succession of US balance of payments controls imposed from 1965 to 1974, the combined effect of which was to move the locus of international dollar financing from New York to London and other foreign centres. Reflecting this development, the number of foreign branches of US banks increased nearly four-fold between 1964 and 1973, while in the same period the share of US banks' total foreign assets held by their foreign branches rose from 26 per cent to 80 per cent (see Table 4). Following the removal of controls in 1974 there was a sharp increase in foreign lending booked to US banks' domestic offices, but by then the offshore dollar lending business was firmly entrenched and no longer depended on US balance of payments restrictions for its continued growth. Today foreign exchange controls play a relatively minor role in determining the scale and geographical location of Eurocurrency banking business, since restrictions on outward capital flows have been widely liberalised while the free transfer of foreign currency deposits between non-residents (the basic precondition for the existence of a local Eurocurrency market) is allowed in virtually all developed countries.

Nevertheless, the *threat* of foreign exchange controls can be a potent force in the Eurocurrency markets. We have already seen that fear of a US freeze on Soviet dollar deposits contributed to the early development of the Eurodollar market. At the same time, most commentators have taken the view that dollars placed outside the United States are in general more vulnerable to confiscation or controls on transferability than dollars deposited within the United States, thereby accounting for the observed interest rate premium on Eurodollar deposits over equivalent US domestic investments.[28] However, the relative security of domestic versus Euromarket deposits has been obscured by recent political initiatives as well as by the uncertain legal status of Eurocurrency deposits. The Iranian assets freeze imposed by the United States in November 1980 extended to Iran's Eurodollar deposits held with foreign branches of US banks, although the legality of this extra-territorial reach was never tested.[29] In contrast, the freeze on Argentinian assets applied by the United Kingdom in April 1982 was territorial rather than national in scope, embracing branches and subsidiaries of foreign banks in London but excluding the overseas offices of UK banks.[30] Given the demonstrated propensity of both home and host country authorities to interfere with free transferability for political reasons, and the controversy over the legal situs of Eurocurrency deposits for this purpose, it is far from clear that deposits can be considered safer in one jurisdiction than another. On the other hand, the value of anonymity in international financial dealings has been enhanced, a consideration which may favour those centres offering the protection of secrecy laws and untraceable fiduciary accounts.

So far it has been suggested that international banking is unusually sensitive to regulatory disparities and that there are in practice a wide variety of non-market factors influencing the location of such business. It follows naturally that the development of international financial centres should, like multinational banking itself, be viewed primarily as a response to the regulatory environment. This proposition is further elaborated in Chapter 2 with reference to a number of financial centres whose status rests to an important extent on local regulatory advantages.

Some preliminary explanation of the services provided by international financial centres is, however, in order.

INTERNATIONAL FINANCIAL CENTRES

Broadly speaking, international financial centres can fulfil three kinds of function.[31] First, they can be net suppliers of capital to foreign borrowers, this for instance being the traditional role of London in its nineteenth century heyday as a financial centre. Secondly, the capital exporting function can be distinguished from (although very often it goes hand in hand with) an intermediary or *entrepôt* role in which both foreign borrowers and lenders utilise the centre's domestic financial markets. Here the international financial centre may be viewed as having a comparative advantage in financial intermediation because of the breadth and efficiency of its own financial markets, with the result that 'lenders and borrowers from other regions transfer to that market their gross demands and supplies, not just excess demand and supply'.[32]

The third category may loosely be described as the 'offshore' centre (such centres traditionally being islands located 'offshore' from the mainland and hence outside its jurisdiction) and has been brought into being by the 'new' international bank lending based on the Euro-markets. The distinguishing characteristic of the offshore centre is that it provides an intermediary service for foreign borrowers and lenders which, however, utilises not the domestic financial markets of the centre concerned but rather the external markets in foreign currencies – that is, the Eurocurrency markets. Since lending and borrowing take place outside the centre's own financial market the service provided is here one of external financial intermediation. Of course, major international financial centres may combine the capital exporting, *entrepôt* and offshore functions.

Within the general category of offshore centre a further distinction is sometimes drawn between functional centres and paper or shell centres.[33] A functional centre by this definition is one in which banks have a physical presence, where actual deposit-taking and lending take place and where the concentration of financial activity is due to the centre's natural advantages such as geographical location and the availability of local expertise. A paper or shell centre, on the other hand, is characterised as one in which business is booked but not transacted, where banks do not need to have a physical presence and where the magnet for financial activity is the avoidance of taxes and other regulations rather than the centre's comparative advantage in external financial intermediation. According to this distinction, functional centres are a product of their environment whereas paper centres can in principle be located anywhere, for which reason they are much more sensitive to regulatory changes.

It must be doubted, however, whether this is a very realistic description of the world of offshore banking. As will be seen in Chapter 2, several centres which might be supposed to enjoy important natural advantages (for instance Frankfurt or Tokyo) have been prevented by regulatory impediments from attracting large-scale offshore banking business. At the same time, active 'functional' centres such as Singapore have proved to be highly sensitive to changes in the regulatory environment. Furthermore, even among the so-called functional centres it is possible to identify various kinds of specialisation that reflect the particular regulatory characteristics of the centre concerned: for instance, there are funding centres where deposits are collected and then transmitted to other centres via the interbank market, and lending centres where loans to final borrowers are arranged and disbursed. Given this situation, banks may wish to establish themselves in several offshore centres in order to exploit the regulatory advantages of each, while funds may similarly be routed through a number of such centres with a view to capturing the distinctive regulatory benefits of each along the way.

In summary, it is unrealistic to draw a hard and fast distinction between functional/natural and paper/artificial centres since all offshore centres are sensitive in varying degrees to regulatory differences, not only among themselves but also between themselves and the country whose currency is used in the external intermediation process. In other words, a centre such as Luxembourg is sensitive to its regulatory position *vis-à-vis* both West Germany (the country of issue for Luxembourg's predominantly Euro-Deutschmark business) and other offshore centres, particularly those within the same or a similar time zone. Furthermore, because of the unique mobility of multinational banking, such natural advantages as Luxembourg or any other offshore centre may enjoy can very easily be outweighed by regulatory considerations.

It is sometimes suggested that Eurocurrency or offshore banking, because it is largely unregulated, represents a victory for market forces over attempts by national authorities to constrain and tie down the activities of commercial bankers. A leading American banker has expressed this viewpoint as follows:

> 'National borders are no longer defensible against the invasion of knowledge, ideas or financial data. The Euro-currency markets are a perfect example. No-one designed them, no-one authorised them, and no-one controlled them. They were fathered by controls, raised by technology and to-day they are refugees, if you will, from national attempts to allocate credit and capital for reasons which have either little or nothing to do with finance and economics.'[34]

However, a very different case can be put. National authorities regulate banking for monetary, prudential, fiscal, competitive and other reasons. To the extent that legitimate national policy goals in these areas can be thwarted by banks rerouting business through offshore centres, serious concerns may arise. Control over the domestic money supply may be weakened, taxes may be avoided, evaded or paid to foreign revenue authorities and official attempts to safeguard the banking system may be frustrated. Indeed, concerns of this kind recently prompted the US authorities to permit the establishment of a novel form of banking unit – the International Banking Facility or IBF – designed to re-incorporate some portion of the runaway Eurodollar market into the US domestic banking system (see page 30). The introduction of IBFs at the end of 1981 may or may not prove to have been a turning-point in the secular expansion of the Eurodollar market, but it cannot be expected that this initiative will of itself resolve the complex policy problems associated with the existence of offshore banking.

This book is concerned with prudential issues, that is, those bearing on the safety and stability of multinational banking. From this perspective the proliferation of offshore financial centres offering regulatory concessions to their banking clientele carries with it two kinds of danger. First, banks may not only escape their home-based regulatory net but in doing so may gravitate to the least regulated financial centres. Secondly, and more importantly, attempts such as are now being made to co-ordinate national supervisory activities in this area may be jeopardised by the underlying competitive tension that necessarily exists among national supervisory authorities trying at one and the same time to safeguard their domestic banking systems and to protect their share of international banking business. The need for and obstacles to effective international supervisory co-operation are matters taken up again in Chapter 7.

NOTES

1.   A.S.J. Baster, *The Imperial Banks* (London, P.S. King & Son, 1929), p.220.
2.   Cited in George W. Edwards, *International Trade Finance* (New York, Pitman & Sons, 1925), p.174.
3.   Edwards, *International Trade Finance*, p.130.
4.   Edwards, *International Trade Finance*, p.166.
5.   The 'charter' approach consolidates a bank's worldwide operations and reports them according to the location of the head office. Currently the United States and the United Kingdom are the only countries that make such data available, although other countries in Western Europe intend to collect data on this basis as part of the concerted move towards consolidated supervision. See Group of Thirty, International Banking Supervision and Risk Study Group, Appendices to *Status Report*, September 1981, pp.27, 48.
6.   For instance, the US inter-agency *Country Exposure Lending Survey* (Washington, DC, Federal Financial Institutions Examination Council) includes as international claims lending by US banks to US residents in non-national currencies.
7.   For a discussion of different definitions of the Eurocurrency market see John Sterling, 'Competitive Advantage in Bank Euro-currency Lending,' PhD thesis, Johns Hopkins University, 1980, Chapter I.
8.   See Sterling, 'Competitive Advantage'. As from January 1984 the IMF has extended its statistical coverage of international bank lending: see IMF *Survey*, 9 January 1984, p.1.
9.   The number of affiliates indicated in Table 6 involves some double-counting because a single banking establishment may be an affiliate of several participating banks.

10. For details see Raymond de Roover, *The Rise and Decline of the Medici Bank, 1397–1494* (Cambridge, Mass., Harvard University Press, 1963).

11. See Robert-Henri Bautier, *The Economic Development of Medieval Europe* (New York, Harcourt Brace Jovanovich, 1971).

12. By 1910 England had 32 colonial banks with head offices in London and 2,104 branches in the colonies; France had 18 colonial banks with 104 branches; Germany 13 with 70 branches and Holland 16 overseas banks with 68 branches. See Clyde Phelps, *The Foreign Expansion of American Banks* (New York, Ronald Press, 1927), p.20.

13. By the end of 1920 American banks had 181 foreign branches. See Phelps, *Foreign Expansion*, p.131; also Frank M. Tamagna and Parker B. Willis, 'United States Banking Organisation Abroad', *Federal Reserve Bulletin*, December 1956, pp. 1284–99.

14. For details of the earlier foreign bond financing regime see William H. Wynne, *State Insolvency and Foreign Bondholders*, Volume 2: *Case Histories* (New Haven, Yale University Press, 1951).

15. Oscar Altman, *Foreign Markets for Dollars, Sterling and Other Currencies*, IMF Staff Papers, December 1961.

16. See Paul Einzig, *A Dynamic Theory of Forward Exchange* (London, Macmillan, 1961), pp.420–25, 432–33.

17. See Sterling, 'Competitive Advantage', Chapter III, for the postwar evolution of the Eurocurrency market.

18. For details see 'The UK Exchange Control: a Short History', *Bank of England Quarterly Bulletin*, September 1967, pp. 245–60.

19. See R.M. Pecchioli, *The Internationalisation of Banking: the Policy Issues* (Paris, OECD, 1983), p.19, Table 3.

20. The average spread on syndicated medium-term credits to non-oil developing countries fell from around 1¾ per cent in 1975–77 to under 1 per cent in 1979–80 before rising slightly over 1 per cent in 1981–82. In the 18 months to mid-1984 spreads again rose to nearly 1¾ per cent in the context of large-scale reschedulings. See R.B. Johnston, *Banks' International Lending Decisions and the Determination of Spreads on Syndicated Medium-Term Credits*, Bank of England Discussion Paper No. 12, September 1980, p.22; also, *Financial Market Trends* (Paris, OECD, June 1984), p.45.

21. This interpretation of the growth of international lending has, however, been challenged. See Kengo Inone, *Determinants of Market Conditions in the Eurocurrency Market – Why a 'Borrower's Market?* BIS Working Papers, No. 1, April 1980, pp.16–19.

22. See A.E. Fleming and S.K. Howson, 'Conditions in the Syndicated Medium-Term Euro-credit Market', *Bank of England Quarterly Bulletin*, September 1980, p.314.

23. Fleming and Howson, 'Conditions in the Syndicated Medium-Term Euro-credit Market'.

24. On this point see A.K. Swoboda, 'International Banking: Current Issues in Perspective', paper presented at the Ente Einaudi Conference on International Banking: its Market and Institutional Structure, Perugia, September 1981, pp. 27–31.

25. For a summary analysis of the growth of multinational banking see Pecchioli, *The Internationalisation of Banking*, pp.51–67 and references cited therein.

26. For an analysis of spreads in international lending see Johnston, *Banks' International Lending Decisions*.

27. See Janet Kelly, *Bankers and Borders: The Case of American Banks in Britain* (Cambridge, Mass., Ballinger, 1977), pp.93–99.

28. See, for instance, Robert Z. Aliber, 'Exchange Risk, Political Risk and Investor Demand for External Currency Deposits', *Journal of Money, Credit and Banking*, May 1975. Interestingly, however, there appears to be no material yield differential between Eurodollar deposits and deposits placed with US International Banking Facilities; see note 35, Chapter 2.

29. See Roberts Owen and Lori Damrosch, 'The International Legal Status of Foreign Government Deposits in Overseas Branches of US Banks', *University of Illinois Law Review*, 1982, No.1.

30. 'Emergency Laws (Re-enactments and Repeals) Act 1964: Argentine Republic', Bank of England Notice, 13 April 1982.

31. The classification presented here follows Gunter Dufey and Ian Giddy, *The International Money Market* (New Jersey, Prentice-Hall, 1978), pp.35–40.

32.   C.P. Kindleberger, *The Formation of Financial Centers: A Study in Comparative Economic History* (Princeton, NJ, Princeton University Press, 1974), p.10.
33.   See, for instance, Ian McCarthy, *Hosting Offshore Banks: Benefits and Costs* (Washington, DC, International Monetary Fund, May 1979), pp.5–9.
34.   Remarks of Walter Wriston, Chairman of Citibank, cited in David Wise, 'International Banking Facilities and the Future of Offshore Banking', *The Fletcher Forum*, Volume 6, No. 2, Summer 1982, p.299.

2 Regulating the Euromarkets

The growth of multinational, and especially offshore, banking has both highlighted the need for co-operation among national regulatory authorities and given rise to tensions which tend to frustrate moves towards such co-operation. Offshore financial centres compete among themselves for multinational banking business by offering monetary, fiscal and other regulatory concessions to the banks they host. Onshore financial centres whose currencies are actively employed offshore often resent the 'externalization' of their financial markets with the resulting loss of domestic jobs, tax revenues, and regulatory control. Moreover, these centres have become increasingly concerned that the emergence of rapidly expanding external markets in their own currencies can greatly complicate the task of domestic monetary policy.

To understand the conflicts of interest that may arise in this area it is necessary to examine in some detail the regulatory framework of multinational banking in the major financial centre countries. This Chapter focuses on monetary, fiscal and other non-prudential regulations, although as previously emphasised and subsequently demonstrated (see Chapter 7), the way in which these matters are handled has a direct bearing on the effectiveness of international supervisory co-operation. Particular attention is given here to US regulatory arrangements, since the dollar is the dominant vehicle currency for offshore banking purposes.

THE UNITED STATES

The United States is a major focus for international financial activity. In the first place, for much of the period since the Second World War it has been a net exporter of capital to the rest of the world. Secondly, New York is a major *entrepôt* financial centre, the unrivalled depth and sophistication of whose financial markets have encouraged both foreign borrowers and lenders to use its intermediary services. And thirdly, a number of its states (notably New York, California and Illinois) are hosts to a large number of foreign-owned banking establishments engaging for the most part in domestic wholesale and retail banking. In recent years, successive OPEC crises have greatly increased the gross flow of funds into and out of New York, reflecting its enhanced role as an *entrepôt* centre balancing the needs of surplus and deficit currencies.

On the other hand, the United States has been unusual among Western industrial countries in that, prior to the introduction of International Banking Facilities at the end of 1981, it did not attract a significant volume of offshore or Eurocurrency banking business. For instance, at the end of 1980 US banks' external claims payable in foreign currencies totalled $6.1 billion,[1] representing little more than 1 per cent of the net Eurocurrency market as measured by the Bank for International Settlements. The regulatory explanation for the virtual absence of Eurocurrency banking is straightforward: although interest on US bank deposits is statutorily exempt from the general 30 per cent withholding tax applicable to interest and dividends paid to non-residents, the Federal Reserve's mandatory reserve requirements imposed under Regulation D have always applied uniformly to domestic bank deposits regardless of currency denomination. In other words, the asymmetry in monetary regulation that has encouraged the growth of external currency markets elsewhere did not exist in the United States prior to 1982, domestic and foreign currency business being for this purpose 'taxed' in a non-discriminatory manner. The policy basis for the US decision to discourage the growth of domestic Eurocurrency business in this way was indicated by the Federal Reserve in 1973 and again in 1975. In response to a bank's enquiry it was on both occasions stated that issuance of foreign-currency-denominated time deposits by member banks at their offices in the United States would not be in the public interest because development of the practice 'could, at times, pose an increased threat to the international stability of the dollar'.[2]

While the US regulatory climate has until recently prevented the emergence of an indigenous offshore banking industry, it has operated in the opposite direction by providing a forceful stimulus to the expansion of the Eurodollar market outside the United States. In summarising the main regulatory considerations here it should be stressed that two kinds of incentive are involved: first, US controls may shift the situs of dollar-based *international* lending from onshore to offshore centres; and secondly, incentives may be created to route *domestic* lending through the Eurodollar market. In the first case there is external intermediation of international dollar business, and in the second case external intermediation of domestic dollar business – a process known as 'round-tripping'.

Between 1965 and 1974 a variety of balance of payments controls encouraged US banks to conduct their international lending business from outside the United States.[3] The Voluntry Foreign Credit Restraint

Program limited the amount of foreign loans a bank could make from home offices to foreigners but did not apply to loans advanced from foreign branches. The Foreign Direct Investment Program, by requesting and then requiring US companies to limit the amount of capital they exported from the United States, also had the effect of shifting the financing of US direct investment abroad to the Eurodollar market. Finally, the Interest Equalization Tax increased the interest cost on long-term loans to foreigners, thereby encouraging foreign branches of US banks to engage in long-term dollar lending abroad.

During the 1960s interest rate ceilings on US bank deposits imposed under the Federal Reserve's Regulation Q (which does not apply to foreign branches) also encouraged a switch from onshore to offshore dollar financing. Every time deposit rates bumped up against their regulatory limit, banks began to experience deposit run-offs as savers sought higher-yielding investments such as commercial paper. Accordingly, during periods of tight money US banks would bid for Eurodollars through their foreign branches, which then channelled these funds to their parent institutions for on-lending in the US domestic market. Unlike US balance of payments controls, therefore, Regulation Q provided an incentive for round-tripping, i.e. the use of US banks' foreign branches as a funding base for their domestic lending.

A more general stimulus to the Eurodollar market has been provided by the non-interest-bearing mandatory reserve requirements imposed by the Federal Reserve on banks' deposit liabilities. In 1918 the Federal Reserve ruled that foreign branch deposits were exempt from such requirements while until 1969 US banks' borrowings from their foreign branches were not considered to be 'deposits' or reservable liabilities. Under these circumstances differential monetary regulation as between offshore and onshore dollar deposits offered US banks a continuing incentive to fund both their international and their domestic business from outside the United States.

Section 19 of the Federal Reserve Act prohibits member banks from paying interest on domestic demand deposits, which for this purpose were defined as deposits payable within 30 days (in 1980 the maturity limit was lowered to 14 days, and in 1982 to seven days – see page 29). Foreign branch deposits are exempt from this prohibition and since 40–50 per cent of non-bank Eurodollar deposits are of less than 30 days' maturity (and 20 per cent of less than eight days' maturity)[4] it is clear that the interest rate prohibition on demand deposits has provided a strong inducement for depositors to place their dollar funds in London and other offshore centres rather than in the United States.

Finally, US tax laws have tended to encourage the offshore booking of international dollar loans. In particular, New York City and New York State each levy a local income tax on banks within their jurisdiction without any credit or deduction being allowed in respect of foreign withholding tax. The combined burden of these taxes is nearly 25 per cent; this, on certain assumptions, can mean a final cost advantage to loans booked through a foreign branch of over two percentage points.[5]

First Responses to Emerging Concerns

In these various ways the US regulatory framework had the unintended effect of driving a growing volume of dollar business offshore, part-icularly to London, where the number of foreign branches of US banks increased from 11 to 37 between 1961 and 1970. Between 1964 and 1970 the proportion of US banks' foreign loans booked to their foreign branches soared from 29 per cent to 74 per cent.[6] This shift to offshore banking began to be of concern to the US Federal Reserve, for two reasons. First, it was felt that the larger US banks' privileged access to the Eurodollar market via their London branches enabled them, by round-tripping, to ride out periods of domestic monetary restraint at the expense of smaller US banks. Secondly, the process of round-tripping itself was viewed as inimical to domestic monetary control.

The Federal Reserve's somewhat contradictory response to these concerns was in 1969 to permit smaller US banks to tap the Eurodollar market at low cost by setting up shell branches or book-keeping entities in Nassau, and at the same time to discourage round-tripping by extending reserve requirements for the first time to domestic borrowings from the Eurodollar market. Specifically, from September 1969 a 10 per cent marginal reserve requirement was imposed on US banks' borrow-ings from their foreign offices, borrowing by US member banks from unaffiliated banks outside the United States, and loans extended directly to residents by the foreign offices of member banks.[7] Subsequently, in June 1970, short-term time deposits of over $100,000 were exempted from the Regulation Q interest rate ceilings, the exemption being extended to wholesale time deposits of all maturities in May 1973. From this point onwards, Regulation Q ceased to be a major influence on the Eurodollar market.

Despite the implementation of these measures, the US authorities became increasingly disturbed during the 1970s at the continuing uncontrolled expansion of the Eurodollar market. Their concern centred on the competitive position of US banks *vis-à-vis* foreign-based banks, the ability of foreign banks in offshore centres to lend directly to US residents without attracting reserve requirements (thereby circumvent-ing the 1969 restrictions on round-tripping), the emergence of a large pool of money-like Eurodollar liquid assets and the broader monetary and prudential implications of unregulated offshore dollar lending. However, they faced an apparently intractable policy dilemma in that any unilateral attempt to tighten control over US banks' foreign branches would be calculated to undermine their competitive position, thereby pushing offshore dollar business into the hands of foreign-owned banks.

Under these circumstances, US policy-makers were confronted with three options if they wished to correct the regulatory bias in favour of the Eurodollar market. They could further deregulate domestic banking, for instance by lowering or removing reserve requirements, or by paying market interest rates on reserves; they could tighten the regulatory requirements on foreign branches of US banks as part of an internationally co-ordinated move towards regulation of the Eurocurrency markets; or they could devise some means of separating domestic and international banking business and establishing within the United States regulation-free international banking that would otherwise be conducted offshore.

In the event initiatives were taken in all three directions, although, because of the need for legislative action and international consultations, no concrete measures emerged until 1980–81. Meanwhile, the Federal Reserve used moral suasion as well as interpretative rulings in an attempt to limit both offshore dollar placements and also the monetary feedback effects of Eurodollar operations. In a series of statements[8] it indicated that it would be inappropriate for a member bank to solicit or encourage the placement of deposits by US residents at its foreign branches unless such deposits were placed to serve a definite, necessary purpose outside the United States. It further issued an interpretative ruling to the effect that foreign branch deposits guaranteed by the head office of a US member bank are subject to Regulations D and Q, the stated rationale being that 'a customer who makes a deposit that is payable solely at a foreign branch assumes whatever risk may exist that the foreign country might impose restrictions on withdrawals', and that a deposit guaranteed by a foreign branch's head office 'enjoys substantially the same rights as if the deposit had been made in a US office of the bank'.[9] In other words, while the Federal Reserve was anxious to ensure that US banks enjoyed competitive parity with foreign banks when operating offshore, it was unwilling to allow offshore dollar deposits to become perfect substitutes (in a risk sense) for domestic dollar placements. When the Bank of California tried to evade this ruling in 1981 the Federal Reserve promptly tightened its regulations, noting that 'the purpose of foreign branches of US banks is to conduct a foreign and international business and not to function as a substitute for domestic banking facilities'.[10]

The Federal Reserve also tried to close off the remaining Eurodollar round-tripping loophole by seeking the co-operation of foreign central banks. At the April 1980 meeting of central bank governors in Basle, Paul Volcker, Chairman of the Federal Reserve Board, delivered a personal letter to each of his colleagues asking them to support President Carter's anti-inflation programme by keeping the growth of their banks' lending to US residents within the 6–9 per cent range being applied to US domestic banks:

'I would greatly appreciate it if you could find the opportunity by whatever means you consider appropriate, to urge the municipal banks in your country, whether or not they have branches or agencies in the US, to support our programme and to limit their loans to US residents in line with the objectives of the special credit restraint programme.'[11]

Significantly, this unusual move followed the defeat of US attempts to enlist international support for the imposition of reserve requirements on all Eurocurrency deposits (see below). Significantly, too, the central banks of Switzerland, West Germany, France and the United Kingdom were reported to be cool in their response; only the Bank of Canada and the Bank of Japan offered more than token support.[12]

Finally, the Federal Reserve began to take account of US residents' Eurodollar holdings in formulating its domestic monetary policy. In redefining the US monetary aggregates in February 1980 it included within the broader measure of the money supply, M2, overnight Eurodollars held by US non-bank residents at Caribbean branches of US banks.[13] However, this move did not altogether resolve uncertainties over the monetary status of residents' Eurodollar holdings in other centres where a maturity breakdown is not available.

Towards Control of the Euromarkets

Piecemeal measures apart, the US authorities had become convinced by the end of the 1970s that something radical needed to be done to check the expansion of the Eurodollar market. Of the three options noted above – domestic deregulation, co-ordinated international regulation, or separation of domestic and international banking business within the United States – the Federal Reserve strongly favoured the second. Closing the regulatory differential in this way between onshore and offshore banking would preserve and possibly enhance US banks' competitive position, restore full monetary control to the Federal Reserve and impose a uniform order on the international banking system.

An initiative had been taken in this direction as early as March 1973, when a ministerial meeting of the Group of Ten agreed to study the impact of the Eurocurrency markets and particularly 'the possible need for reserve requirements comparable to those in national banking markets'.qr The first OPEC crisis and subsequent financial disturbances disrupted this line of investigation and nothing further was heard until the issue re-emerged in 1979. In April of that year the Federal Reserve Chairman of the time, Mr William Miller, launched a strong US initiative aimed at securing international agreement on the need for reserve requirements on Eurocurrency deposits. As a result of this, two committees were set up under the auspices of the Bank for International Settlements: one (the Larre Committee) to study the macro-economic implications of the Euromarkets, the other (the Axelrod Committee) to study the specific US proposal for reserve requirements.

With regard to the latter, the basic choice was between a territorial scheme, where each participating country imposed reserve requirements on the Eurocurrency liabilities of all locally based banks, and an extraterritorial arrangement, under which each participating country imposed requirements on the Eurocurrency liabilities of its own banks' head offices, branches and affiliates, no matter where located. Since there are more actual/potential centres hosting foreign banks than actual/potential centres providing the headquarters for their own multinational banks, the first option required the co-operation of many more countries than the second. The US proposal therefore favoured the extraterritorial approach, but also suggested that each participating country should impose reserve requirements on the local offices of banks headquartered in non-participating countries.[15] The Federal Reserve's discussion paper argued that although banks of non-participating countries operating in those countries would be exempt from agreed reserve requirements they would 'not be well-known internationally and non-resident depositors, for a variety of reasons, are not likely to take the risk of placing large amounts of funds with them'.[16] Minimum reserve requirements would be the same for all Eurocurrency deposits, regardless of currency denomination, but individual countries would retain the freedom to adjust the reserve requirements on local currency domestic deposits held by residents. On the other hand, non-resident local currency deposits would possibly have to be subject to the international reserve requirement in order to 'avoid disruptive attempts by any individual country to capture Eurocurrency business'.[17]

A variant of the Federal Reserve's proposal was also taken up in Congress. A bill sponsored by Representative Leach (HR 3962 or 'The Eurocurrency Market Control Act of 1979') would have required the Federal Reserve to impose reserve requirements on foreign offices of US banks once countries which together exercised jurisdiction over banks with a combined total of not less than 75 per cent of all Eurocurrency deposits had been persuaded to adopt comparable requirements.[18]

The official US proposal was initially backed by West Germany, which had suffered the same monetary feedback effects from Euro-Deutschmark activities in Luxembourg as the United States had experienced from Eurodollar operations in London and elsewhere (see page 41). However, the Bundesbank became less enthusiastic when it realised that it did not have the legal authority to impose extraterritorial reserve requirements on West German banks' important foreign subsidiaries. Since any amendment to the Bundesbank's basic law would have invited other, less welcome, legislative changes which might threaten its independence, the West German central bank decided to press instead for consolidated capital ratios, which would require merely an amendment of the statutes of the Banking Supervisory Office in Berlin.[19]

Having lost the active support of the Bundesbank, the US reserve requirement proposal was overwhelmingly defeated when it finally came before the central bank governors' meeting at Basle in April 1980. The Bank of England and the Swiss National Bank led the opposition,[20] the main arguments for rejection being legal difficulties, the danger of interfering with the recycling of oil funds, potential damage to national banking business, prospective new anomalies arising from differential reserve requirements as between the Euromarkets and the domestic markets of countries which had never applied reserve requirements, and the probable removal of Eurocurrency business to 'exotic' centres.[21] The Basle *communiqué* issued that month was correspondingly vague on the subject of the Eurocurrency markets. The governors noted that 'differences in competitive conditions between domestic and international banking that arise out of official regulations and policies stimulate growth of international bank lending in general', and that Eurocurrency operations can create monetary feedback problems. The governors accordingly undertook to 'continue efforts already being made to reduce the differences in competitive conditions, fully recognising the difficulties arising from differences in the national structure and traditions of banking systems'.[22]

Deregulation

While the ill-fated international negotiations over regulation of the Euromarkets were proceeding, progress was being made in the complementary field of the deregulation of US domestic banking. Following a prolonged period of legislative indecision, approval was given in March 1980 to the Depositary Institutions Deregulation and Monetary Control Act, the main purpose of which was to iron out certain competitive inequalities between US banks and domestic savings institutions while extending the range of deposit-taking entities subject to the Federal Reserve's minimum requirements.

The Monetary Control Act also had important implications for the competitiveness of US-based banks *vis-à-vis* the Eurodollar market. It initiated the phasing out of Regulation Q interest rate ceilings over a period of six years and, while extending reserve requirements to all US-based banks (including branches of foreign banks), reduced the regulatory bias in favour of offshore banking by permitting a general lowering of reserve ratios. At the same time, the Federal Reserve, in implementing the Monetary Control Act, imposed the same average 3 per cent reserve requirement on Eurodollar borrowings as it applied to non-personal domestic time deposits, the stated rationale being that 'this action will eliminate any artificial incentive through the reserve requirement structure that favours raising funds offshore as compared with the domestic market'.[23] The Monetary Control Act also authorised the Federal Reserve to impose minimum reserve requirements on loans made directly to US residents by non-US offices of foreign banks having offices in the United States. Such authorisation enabled the United States to close the final loophole permitting Eurodollar round-tripping; but the Federal Reserve has so far declined to exercise this power, on the grounds that imposing reserve requirements on a US banking office based on the activities of its foreign parent would be both legally and politically controversial.[24] Indeed, in one respect the Monetary Control Act has added to the problem of round-tripping since by imposing reserve requirements on US offices of foreign banks it has created incentives for some foreign banks (depending on their precise tax status)[25] to book US loans offshore. Furthermore, given the Federal Reserve's difficulties in obtaining data on such lending, it is uncertain to what extent US domestic credit policies are being circumvented in this way.

As part of its programme for implementing the Monetary Control Act, the Federal Reserve established a new type of time deposit with a minimum maturity of 14 days (in place of the previous 30 days) on which interest could be paid. The declared purpose of this move was 'to help improve the ability of domestic depositary institutions to compete with banking offices located abroad and with short-term domestic issues'.[26] On the other hand, the fact that around 20 per cent of Eurodollar liabilities to non-banks are of less than eight days' maturity (see page 23) suggests that the interest rate prohibition on domestic deposits of under 14 days' maturity continued to distort the relative attractiveness of offshore and onshore deposits. Accordingly, in 1982 the Federal Reserve reduced the minimum maturity for all time deposits to seven days, partly on the grounds that this would enable US banks to compete more effectively with the Eurodollar market.[27]

Finally, the Monetary Control Act, by authorising the imposition of reserve requirements on non-member banks, also broadened the Federal Reserve's existing power to impose such requirements on the foreign offices of US banks. Already, in June 1979, the Board had asserted its authority to impose reserve requirements on deposits at foreign branches of member banks under section 25 of the Federal Reserve Act, and in Congressional hearings of July that year Governor Wallich stressed the need to extend that power:

'We do think our reserve requirement authority over banks in the international sphere should be broadened. We have that power with respect to member banks and affiliates, and branches of member banks. It should be extended to branches of US banks that are not members, as is provided, for instance, in HR 7 [The Monetary Control Act].'[28]

The Federal Reserve's evident determination to extend its authority to impose reserve requirements on US foreign branches was presumably related to national discussions then taking place on the possibility of a concerted move towards control of the Eurocurrency markets. It may also be taken as an indication that US initiatives in this direction have not yet run their full course.

International Banking Facilities

Prior to the passage of the Monetary Control Act and in the context of stalled international negotiations over Eurocurrency reserve requirements, the US Federal Reserve became interested in a third approach to repatriating offshore dollar business – that of establishing within the United States regulation-free International Banking Facilities (IBFs). In the late 1970s the New York banking community, backed by the state authorities, had determined that New York's status as an international financial centre could be considerably enhanced by creating a free banking zone for international banking business, in much the same way that *entrepôt* trading centres allow imported goods to be stored and processed for re-export without attracting local taxes. Specifically, it was felt that if the tax and regulatory restrictions which had driven the Eurodollar market offshore could be lifted in respect of transactions between non-residents, much of the *entrepôt* banking business that had gone abroad could be repatriated to the United States. New York State accordingly enacted legislation in June 1978 authorising the establishment of International Banking Facilities in New York City and granting such facilities exemption from New York State and City taxes.[29] However, activation of this scheme was made conditional on the Federal Reserve's agreement to exempt IBF deposits from reserve requirements and interest rate restrictions.

For their part, Federal Reserve Board staff expressed some reservations about the IBF proposal, which were given voice in two discussion papers.[30] It was noted that 'the principal advantage of IBFs appears to be in the possibility that, over time, banks in the US may be able to use them to promote the role of US locations as international banking centres *and thereby increase the share of US banks in international finance*' (emphasis added).[31] It was also pointed out, however, that 'foreign banks could be expected to respond to limit any erosion of their market share, *and authorities abroad might support their efforts by reducing taxes on earnings from international banking activity, or easing regulatory constraints or both*' (emphasis added).[32] The staff studies also expressed concern that IBFs could create monetary control problems by accentuating the existing leakage between the offshore and onshore banking sectors.

Mr Anthony Solomon, as President of the Federal Reserve Bank of New York, was more explicit in his support for IBFs:

> 'More importantly, from a policy perspective, I can see a direct advantage in authorizing IBFs as a way to back up our efforts to achieve uniform treatment of the various pieces of global dollar banking. When a substantial share of what is now Eurocurrency business is done from a US base, it will be made transparent to others that the United States has tangible, unassailable interests in making a common approach to regulation. Sooner or later, a consensus will be built recognizing the need for negotiations to achieve uniform treatment of

international banking markets. Countries will inevitably differ on the goals of regulation and the types of regulatory instruments that should be used. But our position in those negotiations can only be strengthened when, through IBFs, one important part of the overall Euromarket is located within this country. Authorizing IBFs would send a clear message that we take seriously the need for new approaches to organizing and controlling the Euromarkets and that we are prepared to move ahead with new initiatives.'[33]

The Federal Reserve's conversion to the IBF cause must therefore be viewed within the broader context of international negotiations over the Euromarkets. On the other hand, it was recognised that the proposal had some merits in its own right. The United States stood to benefit from improved supervisory control over its own banks' international operations as well as from some modest increase in local employment and federal tax revenues; both US banks and their customers would be able to reduce their exposure to country risk; and by enabling US banks to draw directly on the name of their head office they could expect to attract foreign deposits at lower interest rates and thereby increase their share of the international loan market (although in view of subsequent developments this might be considered a dubious advantage). By November 1980 the Federal Reserve had indicated its approval in principle for the IBF proposal and, using powers conferred or at least clarified by the Monetary Control Act, established with effect from 3 December 1981 a new category of 'IBF time deposits' exempt from Regulation D reserve requirements and Regulation Q interest rate ceilings.

Essentially, an IBF is a separate record-keeping entity within a US domestic banking office, segregating the international business of that office from its domestic business.[34] An IBF can accept dollar or foreign currency deposits from foreign residents, make loans to foreign residents and engage in interbank transactions with other IBFs free of state and local income taxes (where the necessary legislation has been passed), reserve requirements and interest rate limitations. However, these freedoms are counterbalanced by a number of constraints which the US authorities believed to be necessary in order to minimise the risks of leakage between the domestic and international dollar markets, whether through a shift of foreigners' domestic transaction balances to IBFs (thereby distorting the monetary aggregates) or through foreign companies borrowing from IBFs and relending the funds to US affiliates (the familiar round-tripping problem).

To reduce the risk that IBFs might attract transaction balances, non-bank customers (only) are subject to a minimum transaction size of $100,000 and a minimum two-day maturity/notice of withdrawal on their deposits. IBFs may not issue certificates of deposit (CDs) or other bearer instruments since it would be difficult to prevent their transfer to US residents. Finally, to avert the dangers of round-tripping a 'use of proceeds' test is applied: regulations require written notification to non-bank IBF customers that deposits and loans are to be used only to support offshore operations, and there is a further requirement that foreign affiliates of US corporations formally acknowledge that notification.

The IBF experiment is therefore a compromise between the authorities' desire on the one hand to place US-based banks on an equal regulatory footing with offshore centres and on the other hand to prevent damaging monetary feedbacks into the US domestic banking system. The end result is that IBFs suffer serious regulatory disadvantages *vis-à-vis* their offshore counterparts (notably with respect to minimum maturities, CD issuances and the prohibition on business with US residents) while creating additional opportunities for monetary leakage. At the same time the inducement that was widely expected to attract offshore depositors to IBFs – lower perceived country risk – has apparently not materialised, there being no discernable yield differential between IBF and Eurodollar deposits.[35]

The halfway-house nature of the IBF experiment suggests that it is a poor second best to the Federal Reserve's preferred regulatory solution to the Euromarket problem. It is possible that some further relaxation of IBF restrictions will occur in the light of experience but in that event the Federal Reserve has to bear in mind the warning of its own staff study to the effect that foreign banks could be expected to retaliate against any erosion of their market share, possibly supported by their national banking authorities. A similar warning was given recently by a director of the West German Bundesbank:

> 'In a global perspective, the [IBF] measures taken by the United States might in the long run turn out to be counterproductive. Since they tend to perpetuate and possibly enlarge Euromarket type inequalities, other large countries might be tempted to 'retaliate' and follow the US example. *This could provide artificial incentives to international banking on a global scale and permit borrowers and depositors to utilize the facilities 'crosswise': domestic US banking business might begin to emigrate at an even faster pace into other financial centres with highly attractive new IBFs, while the United States might increasingly attract regular domestic banking business from other industrial countries'* (emphasis added).[36]

This statement, from a central banker close to the international negotiations over regulation of the Euromarkets, underlines the dangers of a self-defeating competitive erosion of monetary and prudential disciplines as national authorities seek to protect their own monetary and banking systems. Also of particular interest in the context of this discussion is the possibility, referred to above, that one kind of multinational banking based on the external intermediation of international lending via the Euromarkets could be displaced by another based on the external intermediation of domestic lending. In other words, offshore banking could become a mechanism for reciprocal round-tripping, thus inflicting mutual monetary damage on all concerned.

Since the dilemma posed by competing national interests in a financially interdependent world presents parallel difficulties in the field of prudential regulation, there are broader lessons to be learned from the wrangle over regulation of the Euromarkets. These are considered in Chapter 7.

CANADA

Non-resident foreign currency deposits are not subject to the minimum reserve requirements applicable to all other deposits placed in Canada. Encouraged by this exemption, as well as close financial linkages with the United States, a significant volume of Eurodollar business is hosted by Canada, amounting at the end of 1981 to over $50 billion. Local tax laws do not favour the booking of US loans in Canada, and the bulk of Eurodollar deposits are used to fund Canadian banks' involvement in the international syndicated credit market as well as net capital imports into Canada. The Bank Act of 1980 imposes reserve requirements on foreign currency deposits in Canada held by Canadian residents, but not on non-residents' Canadian dollar deposits with the foreign offices of Canadian banks. This exemption is intended to protect Canadian banks' share of the $2.5 billion offshore market in Canadian dollars. The recent expansion of Canadian banks' foreign business, including the growing proportion of assets booked abroad, has been attributed in part to the circumvention of domestic reserve requirements and other regulations.[37]

WESTERN EUROPE
Belgium

Although they possess the necessary powers, the Belgian authorities do not in practice impose minimum reserve requirements on domestic deposits. At the same time non-residents' deposits, of whatever currency denomination, are exempt from the 20 per cent Belgian with-holding tax. There are, therefore, few monetary or fiscal impediments to Belgium's Eurocurrency business, which at the end of 1981 stood at over $65 billion. In the absence of reserve requirements on domestic deposits there is little incentive for the development of an active offshore market in Belgian francs, although residents of Belgium are believed to hold a significant volume of local currency deposits in Luxembourg.

France

The French authorities have consciously discouraged France's development as a conventional *entrepôt* financial centre through the application of foreign exchange controls, while actively promoting Paris as a Euromarket centre. This policy stance is the precise opposite of that favoured by West Germany (see below). Participation in Eurocurrency business is encouraged by the exemption of non-resident foreign currency deposits from domestic withholding taxes, reserve requirements and interest rate ceilings. At the end of 1981 Paris-based banks' foreign currency liabilities amounted to some $132 billion, making Paris the second largest Euromarket centre after London.

The French authorities have discouraged the emergence of a large-scale market in Eurofrancs (for instance, French residents cannot hold such deposits).

Italy

Italy, like France, separates offshore and onshore banking by means of extensive exchange controls. Non-resident foreign currency deposits are not subject to reserve requirements while non-resident banks' domestic and foreign currency deposits are exempt from the usual 20 per cent withholding tax. At the end of 1981 Italian banks' foreign currency liabilities stood at just under $47 billion, representing a three-fold increase since 1974 when there was a sharp reduction in Italy's Euro-currency business in the aftermath of the Bankhaus Herstatt collapse (see page 156). The market in Eurolira is minimal.

Luxembourg

Luxembourg's status as an international financial centre is based wholly on its ability to attract Eurocurrency business, which at the end of 1981 stood at over $82 billion, representing some 10.5 per cent of total Euro-currency deposits. This business revolves around a series of bilateral connections which have enabled Luxembourg to exploit to its own advantage regulatory disparities *vis-à-vis* the countries concerned.[38]

By far the most important connection is with West Germany. Of Luxembourg's 100 foreign-owned banks, 29 are subsidiaries of West German banks; the Deutschmark accounts for around 50 per cent of Luxembourg banks' foreign currency liabilities; and Luxembourg interest rates for Deutschmark rollover credits ('Luxibor') are increasingly used as reference rates. In addition, syndicated loans arranged in West Germany are frequently booked in Luxembourg.

Geographical proximity to and cultural affinities with West Germany apart, the attractions of Luxembourg as a Euro-Deutschmark centre are three-fold. First, by routing either domestic or international lending business through their Luxembourg subsidiaries, West German banks can avoid the costly minimum reserve requirements applied by the Bundesbank. Secondly, the relatively liberal 33:1 maximum gearing ratio imposed by the Luxembourg authorities has enabled West German banks in Luxembourg to expand their balance sheets much more rapidly than they would be permitted to do within West Germany. And, finally, Luxembourg's bank secrecy laws, although designed to protect the banks' customers, may also be used by West German banks to operate beyond the surveillance of their home authorities. Against this background it may be assumed that the Bundesbank had Luxembourg very much in mind when it reported in 1979 that 'international lending by German banks is increasingly carried out through foreign subsidiaries because foreign regulations are in some cases significantly less stringent or nonexistent and particularly because of the lack of minimum reserve requirements and the less strict rules governing bank supervision'.[39]

The West German authorities' frustrations over the Luxembourg connection were partly responsible for their joint proposal with the United States for Eurocurrency reserve requirements, their subsequent move towards consolidated supervision of domestic banks (discussed in Chapter 5) and their recent support for regulatory harmonisation within the EEC. For their part, the Luxembourg authorities have responded by promoting fee-based banking services which are not constrained by the need to adhere to consolidated capital ratios.

Luxembourg also benefits from a strong Swiss connection, hosting seven banks of Swiss origin and attracting over 20 per cent of Switzerland's fiduciary investment business. Fiduciary funds placed in Switzerland are channelled on to Luxembourg because the Grand Duchy imposes no withholding tax and Luxembourg banks are subject to liberal capital ratio requirements. However, the Swiss authorities' introduction of consolidated accounting with effect from 1981 has threatened this business and the Luxembourg authorities have therefore attempted to attract non-bank deposits directly both by strengthening their own bank secrecy laws and by liberalising the laws covering fiduciary deposits. In particular, under a recent Luxembourg law fiduciary accounts no longer have to be included in banks' balance sheets as contingent liabilities and are also excluded from any calculation of banks' capital ratios.[40] Luxembourg is also hoping to benefit from the imposition of withholding tax or stamp duties on Swiss fiduciary deposits, should the Swiss legislature eventually agree to such a move. All in all, the relationship between the Swiss and Luxembourg authorities has a strong competitive element – which is one reason why Switzerland has been reluctant to sign a double taxation agreement with Luxembourg.

Luxembourg also has a special connection with Belgium within the framework of the Belgium–Luxembourg Economic Union. Luxembourg's bank secrecy laws, together with the absence of withholding taxes, present obvious opportunities to Belgian residents, who are widely believed to have placed the equivalent of several billion dollars in Luxembourg banks in recent years, thereby evading their own country's 20 per cent withholding tax.

The above bilateral relationships do not, of course, provide a complete picture of Luxembourg's international banking business. For instance, Luxembourg benefits from a Nordic connection which is based not only on regulatory disparities[41] but also on Nordic countries' desire to tap the Euro-Deutschmark market as a means of funding their balance of payments deficits. Furthermore, Luxembourg appears to be attracting an increasing volume of primary (non-interbank) Eurocurrency business from OPEC and wealthy individuals. On the other hand, it remains an interesting example of a financial centre whose authorities have consciously sought to extract benefits for their local banking community from the regulatory restrictions imposed on banks in neighbouring countries. Moveover, since it is far from being a tax haven for banks themselves (corporation tax stands at 48 per cent) the Grand Duchy has been able to benefit directly from higher fiscal revenues as well as from the fact that the banking sector employs 5 per cent of the local working population. Luxembourg therefore has just as much interest in preserving offshore banking as, say, West Germany has in eliminating it. In the words of the Deputy Commissioner of Banking, 'the future of Luxembourg depends in part on the future of the Euromarkets'.[42]

The Netherlands

The Netherlands does not impose reserve requirements on domestic deposits and exempts foreign currency deposits from withholding taxes. The official attitude to the Eurocurrency market is ambivalent, and it has been officially indicated that 'the authorities do not wish, in the absence of coordinated international regulation of the Eurocurrency markets, to put the Dutch banking system at a competitive disadvantage'. Accordingly, 'banks are free to supply funds in domestic and foreign currency to foreign banks and other nonresidents and they may thus contribute to the growth of the Euro-guilders and other Euro-currency markets'.[43] At the end of 1981 Dutch banks' foreign currency liabilities amounted to nearly $54 billion, while the Euroguilder ranks below the Euro-French franc in market size.

Switzerland

Switzerland, like West Germany, has traditionally been a net exporter of capital and also a conventional *entrepôt* centre hosting international banking business denominated in its domestic currency. However, unlike West Germany, Switzerland can also claim to be an important Eurocurrency centre, particularly if account is taken of Swiss banks' large-scale business in fiduciary deposits.

The Swiss regulatory environment has a direct bearing on the country's international financial status. On the monetary side, the authorities rely largely on foreign currency swaps to influence domestic liquidity and do not therefore impose reserve requirements on domestic banks, except occasionally in respect of non-resident Swiss franc deposits. From a fiscal point of view the most important restrictions are, briefly: a standard 35 per cent withholding tax applicable to both resident and non-resident bank deposits of any currency denomination, with an exemption for deposits of under one year's original maturity held by domestic or foreign banks; and a stamp duty of 0.3 per cent levied on the face amount of syndicated loans booked in Switzerland to non-resident borrowers.[44] Finally, depositors enjoy the bank secrecy protected by Article 47 of the Banking Law, which makes it a criminal offence for a bank employee, representative of the Banking Commission or auditor to divulge confidential information relating to a bank customer.

The stamp duty charged on syndicated loans has prevented Switzerland from becoming a major Eurocurrency lending centre. However, funds may be channelled through the interbank market for on-lending to final borrowers in other financial centres, while in some cases loans may be arranged in Switzerland and booked in, say, Luxembourg. On the other side of the balance sheet, the 35 per cent withholding tax on non-bank deposits prevents Switzerland from being a primary funding centre for conventional Eurocurrency business. This particular restriction is largely responsible for the rapid development of an alternative funding route in the form of 'fiduciary transactions', which are defined under Swiss law as follows:

> 'Investments and credits effected or granted by the bank in its own name but at the exclusive risk and account of the customer in conformity with written instructions. The principal assumes the foreign exchange, transfer and dealer credit risk and is entitled to the entire proceeds from the transaction; the bank merely earns commission.'[45]

When a Swiss bank (or foreign bank in Switzerland) accepts a fiduciary deposit from a non-bank customer it acts as agent, not as principal, and by redepositing the funds outside Switzerland enables the fiduciary depositor to avoid the 35 per cent withholding tax which is not applied to foreign source income. The depositor may prefer this pass-through to a direct placement in the Euromarkets because he is afforded the full protection of the Swiss bank secrecy laws. The Swiss bank, while taking a commission of, say, ½ per cent for the service (this may be viewed as the price paid for secrecy), does not include the fiduciary account in its balance sheet and is thereby permitted to expand its business without fear of infringing domestic capital ratio requirements.

Fiduciary deposits may be placed by residents and non-residents and be denominated in Swiss francs or foreign currency. Non-resident fiduciary accounts in foreign currencies, which are in effect if not in form Swiss-based Eurocurrency deposits, amounted at the end of 1982 to around $80 billion; well in excess of Switzerland's non-fiduciary international banking business. Commission earned by banks on this disguised Eurocurrency activity is of the order of $400 million annually, suggesting why Switzerland has been one of the strongest opponents of the US Federal Reserve's proposal for uniform Eurocurrency reserve requirements. However, the scale of fiduciary business, as well as its uncertain legal status, has recently caused some concern at the Swiss National Bank which is seeking to curb its growth (see page 124).

Despite the absence of domestic reserve requirements, the Swiss franc
has emerged as the third most important Eurocurrency behind the
Deutschmark, claiming approximately 7.5 per cent of the total Eurocurrency market. The explanations for this are: first, the 35 per cent Swiss
withholding tax, which has encouraged both residents and non-
residents to place Swiss franc deposits offshore, either directly or
through fiduciary accounts; secondly, Swiss banks' willingness to pay
more for Swiss franc deposits at their offshore subsidiaries owing to the
latters' freedom from domestic capital ratio requirements (the recent
adoption of consolidated accounts, however, has removed this
incentive); and finally, official control of banks' medium-term borrowing
rates which limits the returns on domestic savings deposits relative to
those available on offshore investments.[46]

The United Kingdom

Prior to the First World War London was pre-eminent both as a large-
scale net exporter of capital to the rest of the world and as a provider of
sterling intermediation services. Subsequently London's international
status declined along with the UK economy, but even after the Second
World War it remained an important *entrepôt* centre, providing sterling
trade finance within Europe and the old sterling area. In 1957 the British
authorities, actuated by a balance of payments crisis, imposed new
restrictions on the international use of sterling, a move which prompted
British banks to shift from sterling to dollar financing. From this point
onwards, while losing its residual status as a sterling-based financial
centre, London developed its Eurocurrency business to the point where
at the end of 1981 British banks reported over $400 billion of foreign
currency liabilities, representing more than one-third of the total Eurocurrency market as calculated by the Bank for International Settlements.
Sterling lending was renewed after the abolition of UK exchange controls
in October 1979 but remained at a modest 5–6 per cent of total international lending.

London's new role as the hub of the Eurocurrency market can be
considered a natural sequel to its former status as a sterling financial
centre, but this transformation has also been fostered by a highly
favourable regulatory climate.[47] Banks operating in the United Kingdom
are not subject to any reserve requirements, credit controls, interest rate
ceilings or withholding taxes in respect of their Eurocurrency business,
offshore banking activity being largely separated from onshore banking
for regulatory purposes. In general, UK tax laws have also tended to
favour London as a booking centre. UK banks have a tax incentive to
undertake foreign lending subject to high foreign withholding taxes
through their head offices in London rather than through their overseas
branches, while under a number of double taxation agreements a UK tax
credit may be available even where a foreign government has waived its

right to levy withholding tax (this treatment of 'tax-spared' loans is, however, under review).[48] On the other hand, UK *branches* of foreign banks may have an incentive to book loans funded from London at tax haven centres in the Caribbean and elsewhere, for which purpose the UK Inland Revenue applies a standard $5/64$ imputed profit to any intra-bank transfer of funds from London.[49]

While the United Kingdom has benefited from being a prime location for Eurocurrency business, it has not been unduly embarrassed in a monetary sense by activity in the Eurosterling market. Largely because banks in the United Kingdom are required to hold only ½ per cent of their eligible sterling liabilities as non-interest-bearing deposits at the Bank of England, there has, since the abolition of UK exchange controls in 1979, been virtually no differential between Eurosterling and domestic sterling interest rates. As the Bank of England has itself pointed out: 'In this respect, the [Eurosterling] market is different from those in, for example, Eurodollars or Euro-Deutschmarks, where domestic reserve requirements mean that the cost of intermediation domestically is significantly greater than in the Euromarkets; the consequent interest rate differential encourages use of the Eurocurrency.'[50]

Against this background the Bank of England has taken the view that neither on prudential nor on monetary grounds is international regulation of the Eurocurrency markets necessary or desirable. In a speech delivered in 1976 the present Deputy Governor of the Bank, Mr C. W. McMahon, said that he could not see a need for the introduction of new forms of prudential control over the Euromarkets at the international level and went on to argue that, from a monetary point of view, the Euromarkets 'are very largely an alternative channel for, rather than a net addition to credit flows that would take place in some form or another in any event.'[51] Mr McMahon's conclusion, which may be taken to reflect general Bank of England thinking on this issue, was as follows:

'All these considerations lead me to reject the analysis which suggests that the Euromarkets have had a major impact on the volume of world credit, and hence the main case for global control over Euromarket activity. But I also question the practicability of the controls that have been advocated. Many variants have been suggested but most involve the imposition of internationally agreed reserve requirements in some form to be held against Eurocurrency deposits. Their initial effect would be to reduce the profitability of Eurocurrency operations to the banks, which would react by raising their lending rates or lowering the rates paid on deposits, in either case tending to reduce the volume of lending through the controlled areas of the Euromarkets.

But this would not necessarily mean a slower expansion of world credit. The effect would more probably be to induce the banks to divert a large part of their business through alternative channels, perhaps particularly through brass-plate companies established in offshore banking centres outside the scope of the control. In principle, this avoidance of control could be prevented by more elaborate controls – of the Bardepot type – on foreign currency borrowing by residents of the control area. But there is a danger in piling control on top of controls, which could have a severe impact on international financing to the extent that it was in fact successful.'[52]

During the discussions in 1979–80 regarding Eurocurrency reserve requirements, the Bank of England's objections to any international initiative prevailed and the US proposal was dropped, at least for the time being. However, the Bank's argument that controls imposed by the major financial powers would be circumvented by the rerouting of Eurocurrency business through unregulated channels deserves particular attention, for it illustrates a fundamental characteristic of international banking, already noted in Chapter 1: namely, its unique mobility and therefore unusual sensitivity to regulatory differentials between financial centres. The policy implication is that regulatory reforms, whether of a monetary, fiscal or prudential nature, must be co-ordinated on a global basis if they are to be effective; the corollary being that competitive considerations pose a constant threat to international co-operation in this area.

The same point emerges from the Bank of England's response to the introduction of International Banking Facilities in the United States. Commenting in 1982 on the possible shift in Eurocurrency business arising from this move, Mr McMahon gave the following warning:

> A major danger is, perhaps, that the establishment of IBFs in the US may prompt similar developments in other countries, particularly Japan and Germany. This might lead to undesirable competition in fiscal laxity, and in that case some offshore centres might feel the draught more seriously.'[53]

The conclusion to be drawn from the above is that while unilateral or less-than-global regulation invites circumvention, unilateral deregulation invites competitive retaliation. In either case both national and collective goals can be frustrated by the competitive process, strongly suggesting a need for a supranational order for international banking.

West Germany

In marked contrast to most other European financial centres, West Germany is a significant *entrepôt* centre of the traditional kind, allowing foreign borrowers and lenders relatively free access to its domestic financial markets but hosting only a modest volume of Eurocurrency business. During the 1970s, West Germany was a major net exporter of capital and the Deutschmark became an important Eurocurrency, second only to the US dollar. In all these respects West Germany's international financial status has much in common with that of the United States.

The authorities have deliberately discouraged the development of an active Eurocurrency market within West Germany.[54] This has been achieved through the application of non-interest-bearing minimum reserve requirements to both non-resident and resident deposits with a maturity of less than four years, whether denominated in domestic or foreign currencies. The most important condition for the emergence of a Euromarket centre, namely the asymmetrical monetary regulation of domestic and foreign currency banking, is therefore notably lacking and at the end of 1981 West German banks' foreign currency liabilities totalled less than $25 billion – around 2 per cent of the total Eurocurrency market as reported by the BIS.

On the other hand, the Bundesbank has not been able to prevent the emergence of a large-scale external market in Deutschmarks, for the very reason that stringent monetary reserve requirements (averaging in recent years around 9 per cent on wholesale time deposits) have provided a strong inducement for Deutschmark banking business to be conducted offshore. Periodic restrictions on interest payable on non-resident Deutschmark deposits within West Germany, imposed in order to discourage capital inflows, have in the past further stimulated the growth of the Euro-Deutschmark market. The point has now been reached where the external Deutschmark claims and liabilities of West Germany's domestic banking system have been dwarfed by the external intermediation of international lending business denominated in Deutschmarks and conducted through offshore centres such as London and Luxembourg.[55] Apart from that, a large and increasing proportion of Euro-Deutschmark business represents the routing of domestic lending through offshore centres in order to avoid domestic reserve require-ments. The importance of this round-tripping activity can be gauged from the fact that in recent years approximately one-third of Euro-Deutschmark assets have consisted of claims on West German residents, the great bulk of these being held by the Luxembourg subsidiaries of West German banks.[56] Furthermore, it seems that the Bundesbank is powerless to prevent this credit leakage; in the first place because it has no direct legal authority over domestic banks' foreign subsidiaries (which are therefore beyond the reach of domestic reserve require-ments), and secondly because any restrictions imposed on West German banks in this area would merely invite their displacement by foreign banks.[57]

From the above it may be understood why West Germany should share with the United States a distinctly jaundiced view of the Eurocurrency markets. Towards the end of the 1970s, moreover, the Bundesbank became increasingly concerned over what it termed the 'over-recycling' of the OPEC surpluses through the Euromarkets and the lack of prudential supervision in this area. In its 1979 Annual Report, the Bundesbank commented on the need for co-ordinated regulation as follows:

'The accelerated expansion of both the Euromarkets and traditional foreign lending activities, together with the risks this involves, has given a new impetus to the discussion of the possibilities of exercising better control over international banking. Germany's special interest in this subject is explained on the one hand by the fact that international lending by German banks is increasingly carried out through foreign subsidiaries because foreign regulations are in some cases significantly less stringent or non-existent and particularly because of the lack of minimum reserve requirements and the less strict rules governing bank supervision. On the other hand, the Deutschmark plays such an important role today in Euromarket transactions that it appears prudent to carefully examine the consequences of unchecked growth and to adopt appropriate measures where necessary. But it has often been found that effective measures can only be introduced jointly with other countries and that such measures must be based on a uniform assessment of these markets.'[58]

Reflecting these concerns, the United States and West Germany undertook a joint initiative in 1979 aimed at securing international agreement on the need for a uniform Eurocurrency reserve requirement.[59] When these negotiations broke down, in early 1980, the United States went ahead with its unilateral introduction of regulation-free IBFs. The West German authorities parted company with the United States at this point, taking the view that IBFs would merely add to the competitive tensions and anomalies in the international banking system. The Bundesbank's President, Herr Otto Pohl, expressed this view as follows:

'Once these deliberations [on Euromarket controls] proved to be leading nowhere the US authorities pushed forward with their initiative against the objections of some of their partner central banks, stating openly that this "could strengthen our hand in international discussions of how offshore markets should be treated". The implications of such unilateral action have yet to become clear . . . the question may be asked what would be the consequences if similar offshore facilities were introduced in other major countries? Large-scale cross-country borrowing could lead to a situation where such privileged borrowing would constitute the normal channel of intermediation, at least for all banks and non-banks whose size and standing would give them access to such facilities. It is only natural that suggestions have been made to facilitate the location of international banking operations in Germany. But it will surprise no one that a central bank which has always viewed the activities of the Euromarkets and the growing international role of the Deutschmark with considerable caution is not exactly enthusiastic in its response to such suggestions.'[60]

At present, then, although West Germany and the United States share common concerns about the Euromarkets, they have been unable to secure international agreement on reform and have sharply differing views on how best to respond to the breakdown of negotiations on this issue. Whereas the United States has moved towards unilateral deregulation of international banking business, West Germany is seeking to apply more stringent prudential controls to its own banks' Eurocurrency operations with a view to curtailing their activity in this area (see Chapter 3). Nevertheless, there were signs in mid-1984 that the Bundesbank might be reconsidering the question of Eurocurrency reserve requirements in response to the excessive international bank lending that contributed to the global debt crisis.[61]

THE ASIAN–PACIFIC REGION

Competition for international banking business among the Far Eastern financial centres has become increasingly intense.[62] Hong Kong and Singapore are traditional rivals in this field but in 1979 Manila introduced its own 'offshore banking units' (OBUs) through appropriate deregulatory legislation, followed in 1983 by Taiwan. Tokyo has also been considering the introduction of offshore banking facilities along lines similar to those already adopted by the United States.

Japan

The attitude of the Japanese authorities to the evolution of Tokyo as an international financial centre has been ambivalent, mainly because freedom of capital movements runs counter to Japan's long tradition of tightly regulated domestic financial markets.[63] Nevertheless, an amendment to the Foreign Exchange and Foreign Trade Control Law, which took effect from December 1980, liberalised the exchange control regime and thereby laid the foundation for a considerable expansion of Tokyo's role as a yen-based *entrepôt* centre. Even so, the combination of a 20 per cent withholding tax on private non-resident bank deposits, a minimum reserve requirement of 0.25 per cent on all deposit liabilities to non-residents and elaborate controls on domestic yen interest rates, has encouraged non-resident borrowers and lenders to bypass domestic banks in favour of the Euroyen market. According to unofficial calculations, this market (including Hong Kong and Singapore) expanded from the equivalent of $10 billion at the end of 1980 to $50 billion in mid-1983, suggesting that domestic regulation faces a growing threat from the shift to external intermediation.[64]

Although regulatory impediments, in the form of withholding tax and minimum reserve requirements, have curbed the growth of Eurocurrency activity in Tokyo, there is a considerable local interbank market in dollars. Foreign currency business has also increased as a result of the liberalisation of exchange controls, and at the end of 1981 Japanese banks reported foreign currency liabilities of over $87 billion, 90 per cent of which were in dollars. However, a major part of Japanese banks' reported dollar borrowings are for the purpose of dollar import financing as well as for general purpose or 'impact' loans to resident companies. In contrast, Japanese banks' dollar syndicated loan business is typically conducted from their foreign branches. Bearing in mind the 'domestic' nature of Tokyo's existing Eurocurrency activity, the emergence of a broader based offshore banking industry would appear to be dependent on a more favourable regulatory environment.

Following the introduction by the United States of IBFs, the Japanese Ministry of Finance began in 1980–81 to consider the possibility of a Japanese free banking zone. Extensive international consultations took place and a draft scheme was prepared by Mr Takashi Hosomi, President of Japan's Overseas Economic Co-operation Fund. This aimed to establish in Tokyo US-type International Banking Facilities for trans-actions between non-residents denominated in both yen and dollars. The proposal was, however, strongly opposed by the Bank of Japan on the grounds that deregulation of the offshore sector was incompatible with a highly regulated domestic financial system. In particular, the central bank, in common with the smaller regional banks, was unhappy about the possible implications for regulated domestic interest rates. Accordingly, the Hosomi proposal was shelved in 1982 after prolonged debate.[65]

The offshore banking issue may nevertheless be revived before long. A recent study sponsored by the Ministry of Finance concluded that gradual deregulation of domestic interest rates is inevitable, since funds will otherwise be moved on an ever-increasing scale into unregulated sectors such as the Euroyen market.[66] At the same time the Governor of the Bank of Japan indicated in mid-1983 that the IBF proposal might be reconsidered as and when interest rate controls had been phased out over a period of years.[67] A programme for relaxing such controls over a period of 'a few years' was subsequently announced in mid-1984 as part of a financial deregulation package agreed with the US authorities and aimed at strengthening the yen's role as an international currency.[68] In the meantime, the Japanese authorities appear to be encouraging a gradual development of offshore banking business in the form, for instance, of foreign-currency loan syndications managed from Tokyo.[69]

Singapore and Hong Kong

Singapore has certain natural advantages as an international financial centre, which include its strategic location in a rapidly developing region of the world and the fact that its time zone permits business to be conducted with Sydney, Tokyo, Hong Kong, the Middle East and Western Europe on the same business day. However, the emergence of Singapore as one of the leading offshore banking centres also provides a startling example of the role of regulation (or, as in this case, deregu-lation) in determining the situs of international banking activity.[70] For it may be said that by deliberate and comprehensive deregulation of the offshore banking sector, the Singapore authorities have created, within the time-span of a few years, the dominant source of international funding in South-East Asia.

The Asian currency market (the Singapore equivalent of the Euro-currency market) was instituted in 1968 when the Singapore branch of the Bank of America was licensed to set up a special international department to handle the transactions of non-residents. Subsequently, formal regulations were introduced for the licensing of such Asian Currency Units (ACUs), involving the segregation of non-resident banking business in special accounting units. ACUs were exempted from exchange controls and over the next few years the following regulatory concessions were introduced: in 1968 the 10 per cent with-holding tax on interest income from non-resident foreign currency deposits was abolished; in 1972 ACUs were exempted from the 20 per cent liquidity ratio applicable to foreign currency deposits; and in 1973 the corporate tax on net income from offshore lending was reduced from 40 per cent to 10 per cent. Also during this period, various stamp duties were abolished and permission given for the issuance of Asian dollar certificates of deposit to non-residents and other ACUs. Finally, in June 1978 exchange controls were lifted and ACUs authorised to deal with Singapore residents (though only in foreign currency).[71]

Reflecting this wholesale deregulation of offshore banking, the numbers of ACUs rose from one in 1968 to 120 in 1981, while the Asian currency market (overwhelmingly in the form of US dollars) expanded to over $85 billion, the initial surge being followed in 1975–81 by an average annual increase of around 35 per cent. The Asian currency market, like the Eurocurrency market of which it is part, is dominated by interbank transactions, with non-bank participants accounting for approximately 15 per cent of the deposit business and just over 20 per cent of all lending.[72] OPEC investors, for instance, evidently prefer to place their deposits with London banks which then redeposit such funds in Singapore, while on the asset side funds are typically channelled on to banks in other centres such as Hong Kong. In this sense Singapore may be regarded as a staging post for interbank funds rather than a centre intermediating between final borrowers and lenders, although syndi-cated loans to Asian-Pacific borrowers have become a significant factor in recent years.

Until 1981 Hong Kong, in direct contrast to Singapore, was essentially a lending centre where syndicated credits to non-resident borrowers were arranged and booked, although funded from outside. The explan-ation for these two divergent but complementary financial roles lay in local tax laws.[73] Until 1982 Hong Kong applied a 15 per cent withholding tax to non-residents' foreign currency deposits whereas Singapore exempts ACUs from its own withholding tax, thereby creating a strong fiscal incentive to deposit in Singapore. On the other hand, Hong Kong exempts offshore lending from its local profits tax while Singapore until 1982 taxed offshore banking profits at a concessionary rate of 10 per cent, the effect of this differential being to favour Hong Kong as a centre for syndicated credit business. Furthermore, withholding tax is not deductible from interest paid by a Hong Kong branch to the head office or any other branch of the same bank. This means that banks can, by establishing offices in both centres, enjoy the fiscal advantages of each, accepting deposits in Singapore and channelling the funds to Hong Kong for on-lending to final borrowers.

The complementary relationship between Hong Kong and Singapore was, however, terminated abruptly in February 1982 when Hong Kong's Financial Secretary announced the abolition of withholding tax on all foreign currency deposits, the stated aim being 'the enhancement of Hong Kong's position as an international financial centre'.[74] This move clearly challenged Singapore's hitherto unrivalled position as a regional funding centre but since the Singapore authorities could not accept with equanimity a substantially smaller share of the offshore banking business a competitive response was widely anticipated. This came in Singapore's March 1983 Budget which, for a five-year period, exempted from tax (hitherto charged at 10 per cent) income derived from loan syndications arranged in Singapore.[75]

Other Asian–Pacific Centres: Australia, the Philippines, Taiwan

Australia has virtually no offshore banking business and maintains a closed financial system to which foreign banks are denied access. In early 1984 a committee chaired by the managing director of the State Bank of New South Wales proposed that Sydney should become an offshore banking centre rivalling Singapore and Hong Kong.[76] The committee calculated that if 80–100 OBUs were established in Australia, the federal government could collect up to US $100 million annually in extra revenue. The authors' conclusion was that Sydney could eventually become the world's third largest financial centre after New York and London, if the government was prepared to introduce the necessary banking legislation.

The Philippines emerged as an offshore banking centre in 1979 after the enactment of legislation authorising the establishment of OBUs. By the end of 1982 Manila hosted 27 OBUs with aggregate deposit liabilities of nearly $5 billion.

Taiwan In 1983 the Finance Ministry and central bank formulated proposals for the introduction of OBUs with the stated aim of establishing Taiwan as a regional financial centre. In November 1983 legislation was approved exempting OBUs from local taxes, exchange controls, capital and reserve requirements and interest rate controls.

Bahrain

Bahrain is a host financial centre to dollar-based offshore banking business; it also provides intermediary services in regional currencies to neighbouring Gulf states.[77] The Bahrain Monetary Agency had identified the potential for an offshore centre in 1974, influenced both by the favourable experience of Singapore and also by the numerous regulatory constraints imposed by other Gulf countries on banks' local operations, including in several cases the requirement that foreign banks operate as joint ventures with local partners. More generally, an adviser to the Bahrain Monetary Agency noted that 'the growth of the international Eurocurrency market and satellite communications had combined to free banking from direct physical constraints on its sphere of activity, although time zones still favoured some geographical specialization'.[78] Accordingly, in 1975 the Monetary Agency began to license OBUs which could conduct all kinds of banking business with non-residents of Bahrain (and also with the Bahrain government), free from withholding or corporation tax and from reserve or liquidity requirements, but subject to a $25,000 annual licence fee.

By the end of 1982 Bahraini OBUs had attracted nearly $60 billion in deposits, just under one-third of which were denominated in regional currencies (mainly Saudi riyals). The regional currency deposits are typically lent back to their countries of origin, a form of round-tripping which (as elsewhere) has created some tension *vis-à-vis* the home authorities concerned. The Bahrain Monetary Agency took the view that OBUs could undercut other banks in the region because of the latter's 'greed and inefficiency'. Kuwait and the United Arab Emirates became sufficiently concerned that their own bank regulations were being bypassed to take steps to discourage the offshore use of their currencies; however, a large volume of Saudi riyal business continues to be routed through Bahrain OBUs which, being free of Saudi reserve and liquidity requirements, enjoy a cost advantage over Saudi-based banks. Given the Saudi authorities' reluctance to allow use of the riyal for international loans, this business, too, consists largely of lending back to Saudi residents.[79] Meanwhile, the fact that Bahrain has failed to attract large-scale official deposits from the other Gulf states is indicative of the mixed feelings in the region towards the 'Bahrain connection'.

The Caribbean Offshore Centres

Of the major Caribbean financial centres, Panama is alone in its development as an important regional centre providing dollar-based intermediary services to Latin America. Its role as an offshore banking centre began in 1970 with the enactment of Cabinet Decree No. 238.[80] This statute, which was drafted in consultation with experts from the IMF, provided comprehensive regulatory exemptions for banks engaging solely in transactions with non-residents. Between 1970 and 1981 foreign currency deposits increased exponentially from $218 million to $42 billion, although there was a levelling off in 1982/83, reflecting, no doubt, both the introduction of IBFs in the United States and regional concerns associated with the Latin American debt crisis.

In contrast to Panama, the Bahamas and the Caymans are mere shell centres. The US Federal Reserve began to allow US banks to establish Caribbean shell branches in 1969 with a view to enabling smaller regional banks to gain access to the Eurodollar market at low cost.[81] Since under this arrangement the primary loan documentation is maintained at the US bank's head office, where the business of the shell branch is also managed, the Caribbean location is purely notional. By the end of 1981 US branches in the Bahamas and Caymans had total assets of nearly $150 billion, representing approximately one-third of total overseas branch assets of US banks.

Because US banks' operations in the Bahamas and Caymans amount to little more than segregated accounting units they have already proved vulnerable to the introduction of IBFs.[82] On the other hand, bank secrecy for depositors (recently strengthened in the Caymans in response to efforts by the US Internal Revenue Service to penetrate offshore banking secrecy) provides shell branches with one competitive advantage over IBFs. In addition, shell branches, unlike IBFs, can accept funds from US residents – subject to compliance with the Federal Reserve's request that these be related to an international purpose – and can make loans to US residents subject to Regulation D reserve requirements.

CONCLUSION

The above survey reinforces certain points made in Chapter 1 concerning the location and scale of multinational banking; crucially, the determining role played by regulatory discrepancies and the consequent competition to attract business through fiscal, monetary and prudential deregulation. There is, moreover, an additional tension between the offshore centres and those countries, notably the United States and West Germany, whose currencies are used in offshore operations.

Given the competitive strains and conflicts of interest involved, the pursuit of international co-operation in bank regulatory matters is beset with difficulties. As one central banker has put it:

'Historically rooted differences in domestic financial structures and institutional arrangements, opposing economic policy principles and preferences, and diverging national interests – which do not necessarily coincide in issuing, host and mere user countries of Eurocurrencies – make it a rather complex task to achieve international agreement on uniform harmonization procedures, even if such efforts were confined to the most relevant areas of concern.'[83]

It may also be noted that those countries, such as the United States, which object to large-scale offshore use of their currencies have little negotiating leverage in the matter and may therefore feel obliged to resort to domestic deregulation in order to reduce competitive irregularities between domestic and offshore markets. As Mr Anthony Solomon, President of the Federal Reserve Bank of New York, explained when justifying the introduction of IBFs:

'When a substantial share of what is now Eurocurrency business is done from a U.S. base, it will be made transparent to others that the United States has tangible, unassailable interests in shaping a common approach to regulation.'

However, such initiatives, at least in the short run, strengthen the deregulatory bias already inherent in an international banking system based on competing financial centres.

Finally, it should be apparent from the discussion above that monetary and prudential regulation of the Euromarkets are overlapping issues. Those who advocate greater competitive equality between domestic and Eurocurrency markets may have in mind prudential and/or monetary objectives, while prudential and/or monetary constraints may be used to achieve greater competitive equality between the two markets.[84] Given such interdependence it is probable that the prudential problems which are the main subject matter of the present work can only be resolved as part of a broader reform of the regulatory framework in which offshore banking is conducted.

NOTES

1. Regulations Affecting International Banking Operations (Paris, OECD, 1982), p.76.
2. OECD Regulations Affecting International Banking Operations, 1982, pp.86–87.
3. For details see Janet Kelley, *Bankers and Borders: the Case of American Banks in Britain* (Cambridge, Mass.: Ballinger, 1977), Chapter 5.
4. See Henry C. Wallich, 'Why the Euromarket Needs Restraint', *Columbia Journal of World Business*, Volume 14, No.3, Fall 1979, p.18.
5. See Thomas Horst, 'Taxation of International Income of Commercial Banks' in Gary Hufbauer, ed., *The International Framework for Money and Banking in the 1980s* (Washington, DC, Georgetown University Law Centre, 1981).
6. Janet Kelley, *Bankers and Borders*, p.105.
7. For details see C.H. Stem, J.H. Makin and D.E. Logue, *Eurocurrencies and the International Monetary System* (Washington, DC, American Enterprise Institute, 1976),pp. 311–19.
8. See OECD Regulations Affecting International Banking Operations, 1982, pp.86–87 for references.
9. Federal Reserve Regulatory Service 2-415 (Washington, DC, Board of Governors of the Federal Reserve System).
10. Federal Reserve Press Release, 14 May 1981, p.3.
11. Letter dated 11 April 1980.
12. See *International Herald Tribune*, 6 May 1980.
13. See Thomas D. Simpson, 'The Redefined Monetary Aggregates', Federal Reserve Bulletin, February 1980.
14. Press Communiqué of the Ministerial Meeting of the Group of Ten and the European Economic Community, 16 March 1973.
15. See 'A Discussion Paper Concerning Reserve Requirements on Euro-Currency Deposits', 25 April 1979, reproduced in 'Hearings before the Subcommittee on Domestic Monetary Policy and the Subcommittee on International Trade, Investment and Monetary Policy of the Committee on Banking, Finance and Urban Affairs', House of Representatives, 96th Congress, First Session, July 1979, pp.206–22.
16. 'Discussion Paper Concerning Reserve Requirements', p.212.
17. 'Discussion Paper Concerning Reserve Requirements', p.217.
18. 'Discussion Paper Concerning Reserve Requirements', pp.3-10.
19. See *International Herald Tribune* survey, 'The Euromarket – 1979',Part Two, November 1979, p.14S.
20. *International Herald Tribune*, 6 May 1980.
21. See Hermann-Josef Dudler, 'Euromarket Growth, Risks in International Bank Lending and Domestic Monetary Management' in D. E. Fair and R. Bertrand, eds, *International Lending in a Fragile World Economy*' (The Hague, Nijhoff, 1983), p.132.
22. BIS Communiqué, 15 April 1980.
23. Federal Reserve Press Release, 15 August 1980, p.6.

24. Cynthia Lichtenstein, 'US Banks and the Eurocurrency Market', *Banking Law Journal*, Volume 99, June/July 1982.
25. See Allen B. Frankel, *Some Consequences of US Taxation of Foreign Banks*, International Finance Discussion Papers, No. 179 (Washington, DC, Board of Governors of the Federal Reserve System, 1981).
26. Federal Reserve Press Release, 15 August 1980, p.4.
27. See Federal Reserve Press Release, 25 August 1982, Docket No. R-0417, p.2.
28. 'Discussion Paper Concerning Reserve Requirements', p.188.
29. See 'International Banking Facilities in the United States', The New York Clearing House Association, 14 July 1978 and 'Memorandum Responding to Federal Reserve Board's Questions on International Banking Facilities', The New York Clearing House Association, 15 March 1979.
30. Staff Studies dated 14 December 1978 and 31 October 1980 (Washington, DC, Board of Governors of the Federal Reserve System).
31. October 1980 Staff Study, p.10.
32. October 1980 Staff Study, p.8.
33. Letter to Paul Volcker, Chairman of the Board of Governors of the Federal Reserve System, dated 7 November 1980.
34. On the legal aspects of IBFs see, for instance, Beth M. Farber, 'International Banking Facilities: Defining a Greater US Presence in the Eurodollar Market', *Law and Policy in International Business*, Volume 13, No.4, 1981; Note, 'Legal Prerequisites of International Banking Facilities in the United States', *Journal of International Law and Economics*, Volume 13, 1979.
35. See William Hall, 'IBFs: the First Two Years', *The Banker*, August 1983.
36. Dudler, 'Euromarket Growth', p.135.
37. See Herbert Grubel, 'The New International Banking', *Banca Nazionale del Lavoro Quarterly Review*, September 1983, pp.263–84.
38. This section is based partly on special surveys on Luxembourg published annually in the *International Herald Tribune* and the *Financial Times*.
39. Deutsche Bundesbank Annual Report, 1979, p.49.
40. Decree Law of 19 July 1983.
41. Most Scandinavian countries had regulations in the 1970s which prohibited domestic banks from making foreign currency loans to domestic companies. Such business was therefore booked through Luxembourg subsidiaries which were also subject to differentially low capital ratios (3 per cent against, e.g., 8 per cent for domestic Swedish banks).
42. Quoted in *International Herald Tribune* survey, 'Banking and Finance in Luxembourg', June 1981, p.125.
43. See OECD Regulations Affecting International Banking Operations, 1981-1, pp.64–65.
44. See *The Underwriting Business in Switzerland* (Zurich, Union Bank of Switzerland, 1979) and *Bank Taxation in Europe* (Frankfurt, Peat, Marwick, Mitchell & Co, 1979).
45. Implementing Ordinance for the Federal Law Relating to Banks and Savings Banks, 17 May 1972, Appendix 11(c).
46. This power is conferred by Article 10 of the Federal Law Relating to Banks and Savings Banks.
47. See generally Kelley, *Bankers and Borders*, Chapter 4.
48. See Thomas Horst, 'Taxation of International Income', p.355.
49. See Allen Frankel, *Some Consequences of US Taxation*, pp.12–13.
50. *Bank of England Quarterly Bulletin*, March 1982, p.51.
51. 'Controlling the Euromarkets', *Bank of England Quarterly Bulletin*, March 1976, p.76.
52. 'Controlling the Euromarkets', p.76.
53. 'Offshore Financial Centres', *Bank of England Quarterly Bulletin*, June 1982, p.267.
54. See OECD Regulations Affecting International Banking Operations, 1981-1, p.47.
55. OECD Regulations Affecting International Banking Operations, 1981-1, p.51.
56. OECD Regulations Affecting International Banking Operations, 1981-1, p.51.
57. Proposed amendments to the West German banking law approved by the Cabinet in February 1984 will, however, require domestic banks to present their accounts on a consolidated basis.
58. Deutsche Bundesbank, Annual Report, 1979, p.49.
59. See Dudler, 'Euromarket Growth', p.132.

60. 'Central Banks and the New Dimensions of International Banking', paper prepared for the 34th International Banking Summer School, Timmendorfer Strand, 1981, pp.24–25.

61. See remarks by Dr Helmut Schlesinger, Vice President of the Bundesbank, on the need for monetary controls over the Euromarkets, cited in *Financial Times*, 13 June 1984, p.3.

62. See, for instance, 'Tendencies in International Banking in the Far-East', paper presented by Koei Narusawa, 34th International Banking Summer School, September 1981.

63. For a description of Japan's financial system see Eric Hayden, 'Internationalising Japan's Financial System', mimeograph, Stanford University, December 1980; OECD Regulations Affecting International Banking Operations, 1981–1, pp.41–49; 'The Japanese Financial System' (Tokyo, Bank of Japan, 1978).

64. See *Japan Economic Journal*, 17 January 1984, p.3.

65. See 'Banking and Finance in Asia', *International Herald Tribune*, 22 November 1983, pp.7–8 for the background to this decision; also 'Finance Ministry and Bank of Japan conflict in offshore banking market', *Japan Economic Journal*, 24 August 1982, p.3.

66. See 'Gradual deregulation of interest rates is recommended by Council', *Japan Economic Journal*, 26 April 1983, p.1.

67. *Financial Times*, 27 May 1983.

68. See *Japan Economic Journal*, 5 June 1984, p.1.

69. In January 1984 Bank of Tokyo became lead manager in the first foreign currency loan syndication to be managed in Tokyo. However, because of Japan's withholding tax on interest payments the loan was 'booked' outside Japan. See 'Bank of Tokyo Brings Management of Foreign-Currency Loan to Japan', *Wall Street Journal* (Europe) 6 January 1984, p.9.

70. See Aninda Bhattacharaya, *The Asian Dollar Market: International Offshore Financing*, (New York, 1977); Zoran Hodjera, *The Asian Currency Market: Singapore as a Regional Financial Centre*, IMF Staff Papers, June 1978, pp.221–47; and Robert Effros, ed., *Emerging Financial Centres: Legal and Institutional Framework* (Washington, DC, IMF, 1982), pp.913–1150.

71. For the chronology of deregulation see *The Financial Structure of Singapore*, Monetary Authority of Singapore, 1980, Appendix C.

72. See Monetary Authority of Singapore, Annual Reports, 1979/80 and 1980/81.

73. See 'Banking in Hong Kong' (Hong Kong, Peat, Marwick, Mitchell & Co, 1981).

74. *The Asian Wall Street Journal Weekly*, 1 March 1982.

75. To be tax-exempt the income must be derived from loans in which half the lead managers are Singapore-based institutions; there must be at least three lenders; and the majority of the loan arrangements must be made in Singapore.

76. See 'Offshore Banking for Sydney?', *The Banker*, March 1984, p.13.

77. See *Bahrain – an International Financial Centre* (Bahrain Monetary Agency, 1982); 'Onshore and Offshore Banking In Bahrain' in *Arab Financial Markets* (London, Euromoney, 1981); Peter Field, *The Currency Draught that Threatens Bahrain*' (London, Euromoney, April 1979); and Peter Field, 'Stepping on the Toes of Local Banks', *Gulf Banking Survey* (London, Euromoney, August 1978).

78. *Arab Financial Markets*, p.90.

79. In February 1983 the Saudi Arabian Monetary Agency took further steps to discourage Saudi banks from participating in offshore riyal business. See *Financial Times*, 10 February 1983.

80. For a full description of Panama's financial system see Effros, *Emerging Financial Centres*, pp.799–908.

81. See Andrew Brimmer and Frederick Dahl, 'Growth of American International Banking: Implications for Public Policy', *Journal of Finance*, Volume 30, No.2, May 1975, p.347.

82. From the end of 1981 to September 1983 the assets of US branches in the Bahamas and Caymans fell by 2 per cent, having increased by 20 per cent in 1981 and 14 per cent in 1980.

83. Dudler, 'Euromarket Growth', p.131.

84. Governor Wallich has put it as follows: 'Reserve requirements are not the only means

of improving competitive equality between the domestic and the EuroMarkets. Prudential restraints of various sorts present at least a conceptual alternative.' See 'Why the Euromarket Needs Restraint', p.22. For a broader consideration of these two sides of the regulatory problem see Edward Frydl, 'The Eurodollar Conundrum', *Federal Reserve Bank of New York Quarterly Review*, Volume 7, No.1, Spring 1982, pp.11–19.

3 The Case for Bank Regulation

In virtually all developed market economies the banking industry[1] is more heavily regulated than any other commercial or industrial sector. There are various reasons for this.[2] To begin with, bank deposit liabilities are 'money', the quantity of which national authorities seek to control through minimum reserve requirements and other forms of monetary regulation. Secondly, because banks play a key role in channelling financial resources to the rest of the economy, governments may seek to control the direction of their lending or even place them under public ownership. Thirdly, the banks' role as a repository for the public's savings makes them a prime target for consumer protection legislation. And finally, because they are considered to be vulnerable to financial collapse, banks are subject to extensive 'prudential' regulation designed both to minimise the risks and to reduce the costs of failure.

The prudential rationale for bank regulation, which is the main focus of this chapter, is closely related to the monetary rationale. That is to say, official concern for the stability of banks reflects the danger that multiple bank failures might lead to a sudden contraction of the money supply and a correspondingly severe dislocation of the real economy, as occurred during the 1930s depression. There is also overlap between the prudential and consumer protection grounds for regulation, since the stability of banks is crucially dependent on depositors' confidence. The case for prudential regulation therefore rests both on the uniquely damaging consequences of bank failures and on the special susceptibility of banks to individual and multiple collapse.

Why are banks and banking systems inherently unstable? In the first place, the intermediary function of banks necessarily implies a relatively high degree of financial gearing, or ratio of debt to equity capital. In the very early stages of the development of banking the lending and depositary functions were largely separated; the great early banking houses such as the Fugger lent out not other people's money but their own capital, while other institutions accepted money for safe keeping only. However, following the fusion of these two functions banks were, by the early nineteenth century, operating on capital ratios of around 40 per cent in Europe and 70 per cent in North America, ratios that have since declined, gradually but, in a cumulative sense, dramatically, to the point where today major multinational banks typically command equity capital resources equivalent to $3\frac{1}{2}$–$4\frac{1}{2}$ per cent of their total assets.[3] No doubt the regulatory climate has itself contributed to the more recent decline in capital ratios, but if banks are to continue to fulfil an intermediary rather than a mere lending function they are bound to operate on a relatively modest capital base.

Because of their high financial leverage banks can best be described as 'conditionally' solvent, the condition being that depositors do not collectively exercise their contractual right of withdrawal and thereby force the bank into distress sales of its assets. Since the value of a bank loan can be determined only after a careful appraisal of the borrower's credit standing (itself a costly process), such loans are not readily marketable assets and can be disposed of promptly (if at all) only at a significant discount on their book value. In short, a loan portfolio is likely to be worth considerably more to the original lending bank than to any subsequent purchaser of that portfolio. Accordingly, a severe liquidity squeeze resulting from sudden deposit withdrawals can very quickly be transformed into a solvency problem, as the victim bank tries to unload essentially unmarketable assets. The implication is that even the soundest of banks is viable only so long as it continues to enjoy the confidence of financial markets, the business of banking being in this literal sense a large-scale confidence trick.

The vulnerability of banks to sudden deposit withdrawals also increases the likelihood of such withdrawals. This is because depositors will be alert to the need to withdraw their own funds ahead of others in the event of any disturbance that could adversely affect confidence. In this context it is often said that a widely dispersed deposit base protects banks from sudden deposit shifts because of the law of large numbers. However, this is a dangerous oversimplification. Given the close connection between liquidity and solvency, individual depositors cannot afford to confine their assessment of a bank's creditworthiness to objective criteria of soundness, but must also consider the possibility that a bank may be threatened by false rumours and similar developments affecting the behaviour of other depositors. Where banking is concerned it matters little whether crises of confidence are ill-founded, since they are liable in any case to be self-fulfilling.

There is another reason why banks are prone to sudden precautionary deposit withdrawals in an unregulated market setting. The financial condition of a bank is not readily determinable even by analysts with sophisticated techniques at their disposal, let alone ordinary depositors, since crucial risk parameters such as the quality of the loan portfolio (or the extent of maturity mismatching) cannot be assessed on the basis of published accounts or other publicly available information. Furthermore, even if the relevant information were obtainable it would be very quickly outdated, since banks can adjust their risk profile (for instance by taking foreign exchange positions) within a very short space of time. This lack of transparency means that on the one hand a bank's financial condition can deteriorate markedly before financial markets become aware of the fact, while on the other hand even the soundest of institutions can fall victim to ill-founded rumours that cannot easily be dispelled. For similar reasons, a bank experiencing deposit withdrawals cannot necessarily rely on the pricing mechanism – that is, an increase in the interest rate it is prepared to offer on deposits – to correct the situation. As others have noted, in the absence of reliable sources of information about the condition of a bank, the interest rate it is prepared to offer will be viewed as a risk indicator. Under these circumstances a unilateral increase in deposit rates will very likely be interpreted as a signal that the bank's condition has deteriorated, and will therefore be self-defeating.[4]

These three characteristic attributes of banks – high financial gearing, reliance on widely dispersed withdrawable funds and lack of transparency – create the potential for a vicious circle of precautionary deposit withdrawals leading to collapse and insolvency. Beyond this, there is the danger that the failure of one institution will lead to the failure of others through a process of contagion, as depositors act on the belief that the problems of the failed bank also affect other institutions, that other institutions have had direct dealings with the failed bank or, more simply, that in an atmosphere of heightened nervousness banks in general have become more prone to collective deposit withdrawals. The very same considerations that make individual banks susceptible to a loss of confidence also make the banking system as a whole vulnerable to a generalised crisis of confidence leading to widespread bank insolvencies.

Against the background of these inherent risks, and in the wake of the financial disorders of the 1930s, governments have imposed extensive prudential controls on their domestic banking systems. These controls fall into two broad categories: *preventive* regulation, designed to curb risk-taking by banks and thereby reduce the likelihood of liquidity and solvency problems; and *protective* regulation, designed to provide support to both banks and their depositors should problems in fact arise.

PREVENTIVE REGULATION

In examining the scope and rationale of preventive regulation it is important to distinguish three quite distinct motives for imposing curbs on the risks incurred by banks. Such restraints may be viewed, first, as a surrogate for market forces, compensating for the lack of information available to depositors by seeking to lay down the kind of conditions that depositors would themselves wish to make were they in a position to do so. A second objective may be to rule out the *additional* risk-taking that would otherwise be encouraged as a result of the liquidity and other support provided to banks and their depositors through protective regulation; in other words, the removal of normal market penalties for excessive risk-taking may necessitate offsetting official action to guard against such excessive risks. This is usually referred to as the 'moral hazard' problem. Finally, regulators may wish to take account of the social costs of bank failure by placing a ceiling on risk-taking lower than that which would prevail in a free market environment where depositors are fully informed about, and therefore able to control, the levels of risk incurred. Typically, national authorities do not differentiate among these three rationales for preventive regulation, but the connections between regulation, market discipline and moral hazard are widely recognised and should be borne in mind in the discussion that follows.

Anticompetitive Regulation

In general, preventive regulation is aimed at curbing the risks incurred by banks in order to reduce the incidence of bank failures and/or the need for official support. However, limits may also be placed on the competitive process itself with a view to both increasing the returns (and reducing the prospect of loss) associated with any given level of risk and restraining banks' own propensity for risk-taking. These limits are of two kinds: controls on market entry and restrictions on price competition. Market entry may be controlled through licensing conditions which include, in addition to the usual requirements of professional competence, a perceived 'need' for additional banking services of the kind proposed. Similar conditions may be applied to the opening of new branches or, alternatively, absolute constraints may be imposed on the geographical scope of branch networks. As one would expect, the evidence suggests that entry controls do indeed tend to increase banks' profitability, although the cost in terms of reduced efficiency is correspondingly high.[5]

Limitations on price competition may take the form of cartel-type interest rate agreements between banks themselves, officially administered ceilings on rates payable on bank deposits and/or the prohibition of interest payments on demand deposits. However, it is generally acknowledged that such restraints on pricing can create serious distortions in the financial system by promoting non-price competition in areas such as free chequing services, conferring a competitive advantage on unregulated non-bank financial institutions and encouraging financial 'disintermediation' – the channelling of funds directly to borrowers rather than through the banking system – during periods of tight money.

More generally, restraining the competitive process, although a common feature of much national banking legislation introduced in the 1930s, has been downgraded as a regulatory objective in many countries. Instead, the focus has shifted towards controlling the levels and kinds of risks incurred by banks within a regulatory framework that favours unfettered competition.

Capital Adequacy

Capital adequacy, which is usually assessed in terms of the ratio of capital to total assets, is the most important measure of a bank's soundness. Without sufficient capital even the most conservatively run institution cannot survive, while more aggressively managed banks can ride out the consequences of their risk-taking if they command sufficiently large capital resources. Curiously, some commentators have sought to deny the connection between capital adequacy and bank failures, despite the fact that a bank can be said to have failed only when it has exhausted its capital.[6] The confusion here is between the *concept* of capital as a cushion of 'own funds' available to absorb losses, and *published measurements* of capital which may give an entirely false reading because loan losses have not been taken into account or assets are otherwise overvalued.[7] The troublesome question of how capital should be defined and measured is discussed below, but the essential link between capital adequacy and bank failures cannot be disputed.

There are several reasons why regulatory authorities cannot safely allow the market itself to determine the level of bank capital. To begin with, even in an unregulated environment the market will fail to take account of the social costs of bank failures (as noted above). However, once a protective regulatory framework is imposed, market disciplines are removed and capital ratios will tend to be driven down still further. Most importantly, deposit protection in the form of flat-rate deposit insurance schemes such as exist in many countries encourages banks to substitute deposit insurance for capital, since they can lower their capital ratios without having to pay an additional risk premium in order to attract deposits. As one commentator has put it:

> 'Deposit insurance fees do not vary with a bank's capital structure, and the insurance enables highly leveraged banks to avoid having to pay more for deposits. Thus, the bank's private cost of a highly leveraged capital structure is below the social costs. The difference is paid for by the [insurance agency] in the form of a greater risk exposure.'[8]

More generally, the very presence of regulators responsible for ensuring the soundness of banks and preventing bank failures may induce both equity investors and depositors to rely on regulatory protection rather than on their own independent analysis of banking risks.[9] Furthermore, banks themselves may feel protected so long as their capital ratios are uniformly low on the assumption that the authorities would be obliged to provide support if the whole banking system were to be threatened with insolvency.

Given the need for regulatory action to correct the downward pull on banks' capital ratios, what criteria of capital adequacy should be applied? In the broadest terms the answer is that 'capital is "adequate" either when it reduces the chances of future insolvency to some predetermined level or, alternatively, when the premium paid by a bank to an insurer is "fair"'.[10] However, any regulatory authority trying to approach the matter in this way is immediately faced with a number of intractable difficulties. First, there is the problem of determining what kind of economic conditions (recession, high interest rates, etc.) a bank should be expected to guard against. Secondly, it is necessary to assess the impact of such an environment on a bank's profitability and balance sheet. This exercise immediately involves the regulator in a third area of difficulty. A bank's susceptibility to losses clearly depends on the riskiness of its activities as a whole, not merely on its financial leverage; therefore, an assessment of capital adequacy must take account of a bank's exposure to each and every category of risk.[11] Indeed, a narrow approach to regulation based solely on minimum capital requirements would invite the substitution of unregulated for regulated risk, possibly leaving a bank's overall risk profile unchanged.

In addition to the conceptual difficulties encountered in assessing capital adequacy, there is also the problem of defining and measuring capital. Most importantly, should a bank's capital be appraised on a going concern or a liquidation basis? If the former, then equity capital alone should be included, whereas if the latter, subordinated debt may be allowed as a form of protection for depositors. The most appropriate basis will presumably depend on whether the regulatory objective is to prevent failures or to protect depositors, and this in turn is influenced by the arrangements for deposit insurance. If deposit insurance is 100 per cent and universal there need be little concern that one bank's failure will have adverse effects on others and the avoidance of failure, as distinct from protection of the insurance fund in the event of failure, ceases to be an appropriate policy goal. However, if, as is generally the case, deposit insurance is something less than 100 per cent, regulators will be concerned both to protect the insurance fund against the consequences of individual bank failures and to prevent such failures for fear that a contagious effect on other, sounder institutions could lead to wider losses for the fund. Under these circumstances regulators will wish to choose the worst of both worlds when defining and measuring capital: subordinated debt should then be excluded (or strictly limited) while assets should be valued on a liquidation basis.[12]

More generally, regulators will wish to ensure that the valuation of a bank's assets reflects the likelihood of losses. The overstating of available capital can, after all, pose dangers just as great as the prevalence of excessively low published capital ratios. The propensity to overstate capital is, furthermore, suggested both by the absence, noted above, of any observable connection between recorded capital ratios and bank failure, and also by the fact that, at least in the US context, bank stocks have tended, in recent years, to trade at prices far below book values.[13] The implication is that regulators need to pay particular attention to stated asset values and provisioning for loan losses, a point which will be taken up again in connection with international loan portfolios.

Assuming that capital can be satisfactorily defined and measured, how might national authorities go about assessing and regulating capital adequacy? To begin with, a judgement must be reached as to the degree of economic adversity with which, in general, banks should be expected to contend and beyond which financial stability would become the responsibility of government. It would, for instance, be perverse to expect banks to be so well capitalised as to be able to ride out another depression as severe as that of the 1930s, given that one of the primary objectives of bank regulation is to prevent any repetition of such an event. In the words of one leading analyst, 'in environments which bring the financial system close to collapse, the only recourse of all institutions – including banks – is to the capability of the authorities to manage the economy out of crisis'.[14]

Having determined the kind of shocks to the system that banks should be in a position to absorb, there are a variety of possible approaches to regulating capital adequacy. First, authorities may lay down uniform minimum capital ratios while seeking, as a separate exercise, to place regulatory limits on the levels of risk-taking incurred by banks. Alternatively, these two aspects of regulation may be dealt with simultaneously by imposing standardised minimum capital requirements that are then adjusted for risk. Here, different categories of asset are accorded specified risk weightings which are then incorporated into the overall capital requirement calculation. A third approach would be to look at each bank separately and to apply a capital adequacy test related to the institution's own historic loan loss and earnings record.[15] Finally, regulators may form an essentially subjective judgement as to each bank's capital needs, based on contacts with management, prudential returns and/or on-site examinations.

Any of these approaches may be adopted; but there is no objective answer to the question of what constitutes capital adequacy. Financial theory has very little to offer in the way of practical guidance, as indicated by a recent authoritative study of this issue which was unable to determine whether the post-war decline in US banks' capital ratios is the result of benign market forces (reflecting, for instance, improved financial techniques) or of weaknesses in the regulatory system.[16] On the other hand, there are several indications that the secular decline in capital ratios world-wide has reached the point where banks' equity resources are well below the minimum levels that would be tolerated in an unregulated market environment. In the first place, there appears to have been a growing tendency to overstate capital, as suggested by shifts in the valuation of bank stocks: for instance, in 1968–70 US bank stock prices averaged 140 per cent of book values; in recent years the figure has fallen to around 65 per cent.[17] Secondly, the external risks facing banks, in the form of interest rate volatility and cyclical instability, have been increasing. Thirdly, internal risks that fall within bank management's own discretion have also been rising, as reflected, for instance, in growing dependence on non-captive or purchased funds and the increasing proportion of assets represented by advances. Finally, bank failures in the United States and elsewhere have been more frequent than in the past, while some major institutions have been prevented from failing only because of official intervention in the form of large-scale support operations.[18]

Liquidity

Liquidity is a term of art used loosely to describe a bank's ability to meet its future cash needs. An assessment of liquidity therefore involves consideration of prospective net cash requirements, as determined by the maturity distribution of assets and liabilities, and of the capacity to meet those requirements from existing cash holdings, the sale of realisable assets and/or new borrowings. Liquidity cannot be measured, since the ease with which assets can be realised depends on the time available to dispose of them; also, and more importantly, a bank's capacity to borrow is necessarily uncertain. This uncertainty applies both to the stability of a bank's existing deposit base and to its ability to 'purchase' fresh funds from the market should the need arise.

Conceptually, liquidity is distinct from solvency. Indeed, the essence of liquidity is the ability to raise cash to meet all maturing obligations in ways that do not impair net worth. Such impairment may occur either where assets have to be sold quickly at a discount on their book value or where borrowing must be undertaken at penal or above-market rates that result in funding losses. In addition, there is the risk that market-wide interest rates may move up, thereby exposing a bank to losses to the extent that it has borrowed short and lent long at a fixed interest rate. However, this last possibility of losses arising from maturity mis-matching or 'gapping' is best treated separately as an interest rate risk rather than as an aspect of liquidity, and is so discussed below.

Although liquidity and solvency are conceptually distinct, it may be asked whether in practice a bank can have a liquidity problem indepen-dent of a solvency problem.[19] That is to say, should not a solvent bank be able to borrow freely at market interest rates given that lenders can be assured of repayment? The answer to this is that, for reasons already explained, a bank's solvency can *never* be undoubted. In the first place, a bank's financial condition is always a matter of uncertainty to outsiders, and secondly, markets are alert to the fact that an otherwise sound institution can be pushed into insolvency through being forced into distress sales of its assets. A bank known to be experiencing liquidity problems therefore becomes a prime suspect and will either have to pay a risk premium on its borrowings or, more probably (since a risk premium may further frighten off potential lenders) be subject to credit rationing. Market fears that liquidity difficulties may be linked to solvency problems, even if initially groundless, can soon become self-fulfilling. The corollary is that a bank that would otherwise fail may be kept solvent through a temporary injection of liquidity – this being the underlying rationale for the lender of last resort function.[20]

Because lack of liquidity is separable from but can nevertheless lead to insolvency, bank regulators generally seek to impose liquidity as well as capital adequacy controls. However, the practical difficulties involved in formulating such controls are even more formidable than in the case of capital adequacy requirements.[21] To begin with, the extent of maturity mismatching, as a measure of funding risk (as distinct from interest rate risk), should take account of the fact that a retail deposit base is to some degree captive and therefore stable, whereas funds 'purchased' in the wholesale market through the issuance of certificates of deposit or interbank borrowings are highly interest rate sensitive and correspondingly volatile. Similarly, when assessing a bank's capacity to borrow as a potential source of liquidity it must be recognised that new funds will be most difficult to obtain under the conditions where they are most urgently needed, namely in the context of large-scale deposit withdrawals. The main emphasis should therefore be placed on a bank's holdings of cash and realisable assets as the only unconditional source of liquidity, although the classification of assets for liquidity purposes may itself present serious practical difficulties.

Of particular concern to many regulators is the growing role of the interbank market in banks' liquidity management. For instance, it is sometimes objected[22] that banks' claims on each other do not represent true liquidity since the liquidity position of the banking sector as a whole is unaffected. However, there is a danger of confusion here since, by the same token, deposit withdrawals cannot reduce the liquidity of a closed banking system, and yet it is against the prospect of such withdrawals that banks hold liquidity. The essence of liquidity, from a regulatory point of view, is the ability of the system to *redistribute* funds to those most in need: the collective liquidity of the banking system as a whole is more a matter for macro-economic policy than for prudential regulation.

Reciprocal deposit claims or 'back-to-back' loans of the kind undertaken by Citibank (see Appendix 2) are in a different category. Here one deposit is dependent on the other, so that a bank cannot realise its claim without having to redeem the counterparty's own claim against itself.

Under such circumstances neither bank's individual liquidity position is improved by the existence of the reciprocal arrangement.

Two general points should be made about the regulation of liquidity. First, a liquidity shortfall, unlike capital impairment, can in principle be remedied by the authorities through the exercise of their lender of last resort function. Furthermore, the moral hazard problem that would otherwise accompany such action can be eliminated by charging a penal interest rate that is calculated to deter banks from running down their liquidity positions in the expectation of being able to borrow through the official discount window.[23] Given the scope for such discretionary assistance, it is not clear that regulators need concern themselves with formal liquidity controls, particularly in view of the intractable difficulties involved. The second general point is that in a world of 100 per cent deposit insurance the liquidity issue becomes irrelevant. Under these conditions, an illiquid but solvent institution can presumably borrow freely on normal (or nearly normal) market terms without the risk of being subject to credit rationing. The link between illiquidity and insolvency is therefore broken and banks can be allowed to form their own judgements about their liquidity needs.

Interest Rate Risk

Maturity mismatching, as indicated above, carries with it two kinds of danger. First, if a bank is funding long-term loans with short-term borrowing it is open to the risk that it will have difficulty refunding itself when borrowings fall due; it may find that it is able to borrow only at above-market rates or, worse still, that it is shut out of the money markets altogether because of credit rationing. This funding risk is one aspect of the problem of liquidity management.

Secondly, even where a bank has unrestricted access to credit markets it may suffer a loss on its fixed interest rate loans if its short-term borrowing costs rise in response to a general market-wide increase in interest rates. This interest rate risk is quite separate from the funding risk: for instance, maturity mismatching must always involve a funding risk but need not give rise to an interest rate risk if the interest rate charged on loans 'floats' (i.e., is recalculated on the basis of market rates at specified intervals) and the rollover dates on loans coincide with the bank's borrowing maturities.

The interest rate or 'gapping' risk, unlike a liquidity shortfall, threatens an immediate impairment of net worth. This follows from the fact that a sudden rise in interest rates may erode lending margins while also reducing the capital value of a bank's fixed interest rate loan portfolio. In a world of volatile interest rates such losses can be dramatic; one recent study of bank risks concludes that the interest rate risk is the greatest danger facing financial institutions today.[24] On the other hand, individual banks' sensitivity to interest rate movements can be objectively measured, which suggests that this is an area amenable to regulatory control as well as market discipline.

Permissible Business Activities

Regulators frequently limit banks to banking and closely related areas of business activity. The reasons for such constraints on product diversification include political objections to concentrations of economic power in the form of financial conglomerates and a belief that the mixing of banking and non-banking business creates unacceptable conflicts of interest. In addition, there are a number of prudential concerns, centring on the possibility that banks may increase the overall riskiness of their operations by engaging in non-bank business. This could occur either because such non-bank business is inherently more risky or because banks might be tempted to engage in imprudent financial transactions, such as over-concentration of lending, in support of their non-bank activities. Finally, the involvement of banks in other business activities enormously complicates the task of the authorities in so far as the bank's operations in their entirety must be monitored and regulated.

Controversy over the separation of banking and non-banking business has focused on three separate issues. First, it can be argued that diversification into businesses whose risks are not co-variant with banking may actually reduce the overall degree of risk.[25] Secondly, it has been suggested that the danger of imprudent intra-group financial dealings can be avoided by appropriate regulation without any need for a blanket prohibition on diversification.[26] Thirdly, the view is sometimes advanced that banks can safely be permitted to engage in riskier non-bank activities if they conduct such business through legally distinct subsidiaries or affiliates.[27] Others, however, believe that it is not possible to 'build a wall' between banks and their non-bank business interests, if only because financial markets (and particularly depositors) are liable to link any difficulties experienced by a bank's subsidiary/ affiliate with the parent institution.[28]

Loan Limits

Since risk diversification is one of the key precepts of prudent banking, regulators typically impose a limit on the amount which banks can lend to a single borrower. This limit can be expressed as a percentage of the lending bank's capital, although the precise figure (which may vary according to whether or not the loan is backed by collateral) is necessarily arbitrary. Prudent diversification also demands that banks spread their lending among different sectors of the economy and avoid loan concentrations to businesses whose risks are co-variant. Smaller regional banks may be particularly vulnerable in this respect and it has been suggested that for this reason alone such institutions should be subject to a separate regulatory regime. Another problem for regulators is the need to determine what constitutes a separate borrowing entity for risk diversifi-cation purposes, an exercise that acquires special significance in the international context.

Bank Examination

Bank examinations serve a variety of purposes, among which are the evaluation of management, the assessment of interest rate control pro-cedures, the determination of asset quality and the enforcement of national laws and regulations. One of the broader objectives of the examination process is to identify problem banks with a view to ensuring that corrective action is taken before it is too late. Some commentators believe that remote computer-based early warning systems can also serve this purpose, thereby reducing the need for on-site inspections.[29] There is also controversy as to the extent to which examiners' findings and other prudential data should be disclosed to the public as a way of improving the operation of market disciplines on the banking system. The disclosure issue is closely related to the scope of deposit insurance and is considered further under that heading.

PROTECTIVE REGULATION

Deposit Insurance

National regulatory arrangements usually include some form of deposit insurance or provision to safeguard depositors in the event that a bank should fail. Such insurance may be provided as a form of consumer protection in recognition of the fact that the average depositor is unable to monitor or assess the riskiness of banks. More importantly, the exist-ence of deposit insurance helps to underpin the banking system as a whole by reducing or even eliminating the potential for large-scale precautionary deposit withdrawals that may lead to multiple bank failures. This stabilising effect has two separate elements: first, at any given level of risk-taking, an individual bank is less likely to fail because depositors will have less incentive to withdraw their funds when it experiences financial difficulties; and secondly, the failure of any one bank is much less likely to result in contagious failures elsewhere to the extent that depositors are assured of repayment. In their seminal monetary history of the United States, Milton Friedman and Anna Schwartz comment that 'deposit insurance is . . . a form of insurance that tends to reduce the contingency insured against'[30] and conclude that 'federal insurance of bank deposits was the most important structural change in the banking system to result from the 1933 panic, and indeed, in our view, the structural change most conducive to monetary stability since state bank note issues were taxed out of existence immediately after the Civil War'.[31] According to this view, which is now widely accepted, deposit insurance (or protection) is one of the key ingredients of any regulatory framework designed to safeguard the banking system.

But deposit insurance is not without its costs. If depositors know they are going to be repaid whatever risks may be taken with their money, they have no need to ensure that banks behave prudently. Banks will in turn have an incentive both to increase the riskiness of their assets and to reduce their capital, since a high-risk bank will pay no more for its deposits than a low-risk bank. Indeed, one study of the secular decline in US bank capital ratios that followed the inception of deposit insurance concludes that 'virtually all of the decline in the capital–deposit-ratio since the 1920s can be accounted for by the substitution of deposit insurance for capital'.[32]

While deposit insurance necessitates other forms of regulation, the nature and scope of that regulation will depend on the precise terms of the insurance scheme. In particular, the regulatory implications will vary according to the coverage offered and the way in which insurance premiums are calculated. The main alternatives are considered below.

One Hundred Per Cent Coverage with Flat Rate Contributions One hundred per cent deposit insurance, where provided as a legally enforceable right, eliminates the danger of contagious deposit withdrawals leading to multiple bank failures. In such a regime the appropriate regulatory objective is to protect the insurance fund rather than to prevent individual bank failures. Furthermore, liquidity regulation becomes redundant because it can be assumed that banks will always be able to fund themselves by borrowing at market interest rates. On the other hand, since high-risk banks will pay no more for their deposits or for the insurance of those deposits than low-risk banks, market restraints on excessive risk-taking will be severely eroded. Under these circumstances regulators must themselves formulate and impose capital adequacy norms as well as controls on banks' lending activities.

In the absence of formal 100 per cent insurance, regulatory authorities may nevertheless follow a policy of protecting depositors in full. *De facto* protection may be preferred to *de jure* insurance on the grounds that it will strengthen market discipline by creating uncertainty, but the danger is that it will also fail to prevent large-scale destabilising deposit withdrawals, particularly in times of crisis.

Partial Coverage Partial deposit insurance, which requires the depositor to bear some proportion of any loss, cannot be expected to reduce bank failures or serve any other prudential purpose. Since the transaction cost of shifting a deposit from one bank to another is close to zero, the prospect of any loss will presumably be enough to induce depositors to withdraw their funds from a suspect bank. Partial deposit insurance must therefore be viewed as a form of consumer protection rather than as a mechanism for safeguarding the banking system.

Full Coverage Subject to a Fixed Ceiling Many deposit insurance schemes provide 100 per cent coverage up to a specified maximum deposit size, beyond which there is no reimbursement. There may be a consumer protection rationale for this approach to the extent that small depositors are considered in some sense to be more deserving of protection than large or corporate depositors. However, there is also a prudential rationale based on the view that large depositors are in a better position than small depositors to monitor the financial condition of banks with which they place their funds. The reasoning here is that such sophisticated depositors will impose a needed market discipline, thereby encouraging a degree of self-regulation in the market place.

There are two difficulties with this line of argument. First, even with the benefit of extensive financial disclosure requirements, it is not clear that sophisticated depositors have the capacity effectively to assess the riskiness of banks.[33] Particularly in times of uncertainty, it is more likely that such depositors will favour large banks in the belief that these will not be permitted to fail.[34] Indeed, one reason for the prevalence of deposit insurance ceilings is that large banks tend to object strongly to universal 100 per cent coverage, knowing as they do that this would undercut their natural advantage as perceived safe haven institutions.[35]

Even if large depositors were able and willing to make a realistic assessment of bank risks, the way in which they acted on their assessment would very probably increase financial instability. As noted above, the pricing mechanism does not operate efficiently in financial markets, depositors often being more inclined to withdraw their funds from a suspect institution than to charge a risk premium. The danger of contagious precautionary deposit withdrawals would therefore remain. There is also an element of contradiction in a situation where 'captive' retail deposits are further stabilised through deposit insurance while potentially volatile wholesale deposits are viewed as a stabilising force.

Variable Rate Deposit Insurance The economists' ideal is a system of variable rate deposit insurance with 100 per cent coverage, where the premium payable by each bank is related either to its own particular risk characteristics or to its risk class.[36] The great advantage of such a system is not that the regulator's task would be eliminated or even lightened, but that the regulatory objective would switch from risk prevention to risk assessment. Each bank would be able to determine its own risk/return trade-off, although since risks undertaken would have to be paid for the moral hazard problem would disappear. The practical obstacle to any such scheme is, of course, the difficulties involved in developing a realistic and equitable system of risk appraisal, for which reason a number of variants have been suggested that would rely partly on market risk assessment.[37]

Lender of Last Resort

The term 'lender of last resort' covers a variety of official support operations. It may refer to injections of liquidity into the banking system as a whole as a means of alleviating generalised financial tensions; more loosely, it may be applied to a bank's access to the official discount window for routine liquidity purposes such as the need to meet a seasonal funding shortfall. Or again, the lender of last resort function may be viewed as emergency financial assistance provided to an individual bank experiencing severe funding difficulties.

The first and last of these roles may be linked in so far as some commentators believe that sound institutions can always be protected by having the central bank step in to provide general liquidity support rather than case-by-case assistance.[38] However, the focus here is on official support for particular banks on the assumption that, for reasons outlined above, otherwise sound institutions can experience liquidity problems that may threaten their survival. Considered in this way, the lender of last resort function may be characterised as the authorities' response to imperfections in financial markets, since in a perfect market no solvent bank would be denied credit.[39] In the real world, suspicions (whether or not justified) regarding a particular bank's solvency will typically result in the rationing of credit to that institution and the role of the lender of last resort is then one of compensating for this market failure. Such official assistance provided on market terms to a solvent but illiquid bank can be justified in its own right, quite apart from any additional costs in the form of damage to market confidence that might be associated with a forced closure. It is sufficient that a sound bank is 'wrongly' denied credit by the market and that the lender of last resort has a better view of the bank's true financial condition than outsiders.[40]

In practice, the distinction between solvency and liquidity is not straightforward. For one thing, as we have already seen, the net worth of a bank calculated on a going concern basis may be quite different from its value in liquidation. Where a bank is insolvent in the liquidation sense but solvent as a going concern it may make sense for the authorities to provide support on concessionary terms if heavy liquidation costs can thereby be avoided.[41] Indeed, even where a bank is clearly insolvent as a going concern it may still 'pay' the authorities to sustain it by means of a capital infusion if the alternative is a collapse leading to widespread loss of confidence and further bank failures. This loss minimisation rationale is, for instance, the basis on which the US Federal Deposit Insurance Corporation has on occasion exercised its authority to provide capital assistance to potentially insolvent institutions.[42] The implication is that the lender of last resort function cannot properly be confined to temporary liquidity assistance if the wider costs of bank failure are to be taken into account.

Official assistance provided to a solvent bank on market terms need not in itself involve moral hazard if in such circumstances it is the market that has malfunctioned, not the bank. More generally, however, a bank is likely to require liquidity support because the market has for some good reason lost confidence in its management and here the availability of official help does give rise to moral hazard. The view currently favoured by central bankers is that this hazard can be minimised by keeping the market guessing as to when and on what terms assistance might be given. For instance, Governor Wallich of the Federal Reserve Board has stated that 'there are dangers in trying to define and publicize specific rules for emergency assistance to troubled banks, notably the possibility of causing undue reliance on such facilities and possible relaxation of needed caution on the part of all market participants'.[43] On the other hand, some commentators have challenged this approach on the grounds that if banks are uncertain about what behaviour would disqualify them from support, they will not know what activities they should avoid.[44]

It should be stressed that moral hazard may operate to undermine both the *self*-discipline of individual banks and the disciplining of *others* by the market place. So far as self-discipline is concerned, the problem can in principle be handled by having the authorities provide liquidity assistance at a penal rate of interest and capital assistance on terms which penalise shareholders.[45] It is more difficult to counteract moral hazard as it affects general market discipline (even variable rate deposit insurance fails to do this) although since the penalties imposed by financial markets on excessive risk-taking are at best highly inefficient and at worst self-destructive it is not clear that this is a hazard that should be guarded against. After all, it is the deficiencies of the market as a disciplining mechanism that create the need for deposit insurance and a lender of last resort in the first place.

Some central bankers have broken their traditional silence on the subject of lender of last resort by indicating that support will not be forthcoming in cases of fraud.[46] However, from a moral hazard point of view this appears to be a perverse philosophy since financial markets can hardly be expected to detect wrong-doing in situations where a bank's management has succeeded in duping its auditors as well as its supervisory authority. On the contrary, if depositors are to lose money because of the fraud of others, they will be even less inclined to assess banks on the basis of published prudential data, and more inclined to place their funds with larger banks which are unlikely to be allowed to fail in any circumstances and which are also less vulnerable to fraud.[47]

CONCLUSIONS ON DOMESTIC BANK REGULATION

The case for some form of prudential regulation of banking is not seriously in dispute. Yet once protective measures are taken with a view to reducing both the incidence and the costs of bank failure, moral hazard problems arise which can only be corrected through extensive regulation of the preventive kind. In other words, removal of the more extreme market penalties on excessive risk-taking – itself widely viewed as a necessary measure in the interests of stable banking – demands offsetting action to control the levels of risk incurred. One possible corrective mechanism would be to impose special penalties on banks that fail in much the same way that unlimited liability used to be viewed as a safeguard against imprudent banking practices.[48] Indeed, there is much to be said for the argument that the management, if not the shareholders, of a failed bank should be subject to some form of financial levy.[49]

The only alternative to comprehensive preventive regulation is variable rate deposit insurance – an approach which, if practical difficulties could be surmounted, would reintroduce market-type financial disciplines without endangering the stability of the system. As matters now stand, however, most regulatory authorities try to have their cake and eat it: they safeguard the system through deposit insurance and lender of last resort facilities, but at the same time leave a window of uncertainty by placing a ceiling on insured deposits and refusing to disclose the circumstances under which lender of last resort assistance might be provided. Yet if the assumption behind protective regulation is that market disciplines do not work towards stabilising the system, it is difficult to see why a residual market uncertainty should be expected to do just that.

It may, however, be possible to harness market forces in such a way as to discipline excessive risk-taking by banks while avoiding destabilising side-effects. This might be achieved by requiring banks to maintain two types of deposit, category A and category B, one of which would be uninsured and the other fully insured. The proportion of uninsured deposits would be set at, say, 10 per cent of the total, that is, low enough to prevent precautionary withdrawals of uninsured funds from threatening insolvency but large enough to create a market in uninsured deposits. In order to attract the required volume of uninsured deposits each bank would have to pay a risk premium that reflected its credit standing in the market place. This premium could then be used by the regulatory authorities as a basis for calculating a (variable) insurance premium to be paid by each bank in respect of its insured deposits. The advantages, as well as the possible drawbacks, of this dual deposit scheme are outlined below.

Advantages

1. The risk premium on uninsured deposits would penalise risk-taking by banks.
2. The limited volume of uninsured deposits would prevent destabilisation of the system through large-scale movements of funds.

3. The role of the lender of last resort would no longer be open-ended, but kept within limits determined by the volume of uninsured deposits.
4. Because of reduced knock-on effects, large banks could more easily be allowed to fail.

Disadvantages

1. Smaller banks might have to pay a higher premium to attract uninsured funds because of economies of scale in the provision of information.
2. Because of the transparency problem, risk premiums might not differentiate efficiently between banks. This underlines the need for stringent disclosure requirements.
3. The system would have to be policed. For instance, it would be necessary to prevent reciprocal deposits between banks designed to lower the cost of deposit insurance.

   On balance, the dual deposit scheme offers most of the advantages, while avoiding some of the dangers, of other proposals aimed at shifting the regulatory burden from regulatory agencies to the market place. In particular, such a scheme, if properly designed, would eliminate the possibility of major financial disturbances arising from large-scale precautionary movements of funds.

NOTES

1. Defining 'the banking industry' is itself fraught with difficulties. Some would argue that banks are differentiated from non-bank financial institutions *because* of their unique regulatory treatment rather than vice versa.
2. For a comprehensive analysis of the various rationales for bank regulation see Robert Clark, 'The Soundness of Financial Intermediaries', *The Yale Law Journal*, Volume 86, No. 1, November 1976.
3. See George Vojta, *Bank Capital Adequacy* (New York, First National Citibank, 1973), p.8 and references cited therein.
4. See Norman Blackwell, 'An Investigation of the Theory of Credit Rationing', PhD thesis, University of Pennsylvania, 1976.
5. For a survey of the literature on this issue see 'An Economic Overview of Bank Solvency Regulation,' Report by the Comptroller General of the United States, February 1981, pp.11–15.
6. See, for instance, Vojta, *Bank Capital Adequacy*, p.8: 'The consensus of scholarly research is that the level of bank capital has not been causally related to the incidence of bank failure.'
7. It should also be noted that the decline in deposits (and assets) that typically precedes a bank failure will itself tend to *raise* reported capital/asset ratios.
8. Sam Peltzman, 'Capital Investment in Commercial Banking and its Relationship to Portfolio Regulation', *Journal of Political Economy*, Volume 78, January/February 1970, p.5.
9. On this point see Benjamin Wolkowitz, 'Bank Capital: The Regulator Versus the Market' in Lawrence Goldberg and Lawrence White, eds, *The Deregulation of the Banking and Securities Industries* (Lexington, Mass., Lexington Books, 1979), pp.243–56.
10. Sherman J. Maisel, ed., *Risk and Capital Adequacy in Commercial Banks* (Chicago, University of Chicago Press, 1981), p.20.

11. These risks can be categorised into credit risks, investment risks, liquidity risks, operating risks, fraud risks and fiduciary risks. See Vojta, *Bank Capital Adequacy*, pp.15–29.
12. See Hugo H. Colje, 'Capital Adequacy from the Viewpoint of the Banking Supervisor: A Quantitative Approach', paper presented to the International Conference of Banking Supervisors, Washington, DC, 24–25 September 1981.
13. See *Bank Quarterly* (New York, Salomon Brothers), various issues.
14. Vojta, *Bank Capital Adequacy*, p.21.
15. Vojta, *Bank Capital Adequacy*, pp.17–20.
16. Maisel, *Risk and Capital Adequacy*, p.5.
17. For an analysis of this trend see Maisel, *Risk and Capital Adequacy*, p.108ff.
18. For a general discussion of these developments in the US context see 'Deposit Insurance in a Changing Environment' (Washington, DC, Federal Deposit Insurance Corporation), April 1983.
19. On this point see Jack Revell, *Solvency and Regulation of Banks* (Bangor, University of Wales Press, 1975), pp.12–25; and Brock Short, *Capital Requirements for Commercial Banks: A Survey of the Issues*, IMF Staff Papers, September 1978, pp.532–35.
20. See Jeffrey Shafer, 'The Theory of the Lender of Last Resort and the Eurocurrency Markets', paper presented at the Bank for International Settlements, Basle, 14–15 December 1981, pp.13–19.
21. The practical difficulties involved in assessing and regulating liquidity are covered in a Bank of England discussion paper: 'The Measurement of Liquidity', August 1981. It should be stressed that, as with capital adequacy, liquidity requirements should take the form of norms rather than absolute limits so that the cushion of liquidity (or capital) can be used if need be.
22. 'The Measurement of Liquidity', pp.7–8.
23. Shafer, 'The Theory of the Lender of Last Resort', p.36.
24. Maisel, *Risk and Capital Adequacy*, p.92.
25. See, for instance, Fischer Black, Merton Miller and Richard Posner, 'An Approach to the Regulation of Bank Holding Companies', *Journal of Business*, July 1978, Volume 51, No.3, p.393.
26. Franklin Edwards, 'Banks and Securities Activities: Legal and Economic Perspectives on the Glass-Steagall Act' in Goldberg and White, eds, *The Deregulation of the Banking and Securities Industries*, pp.273–91.
27. This approach has been advocated by the US Treasury. See remarks prepared for delivery by Robert McNamara, Deputy Secretary of the Treasury, to the California Bankers' Association, Santa Barbara, 8 January 1982.
28. The US Federal Reserve has had reservations about the affiliate/subsidiary route to diversification for this reason. See statement by Charles Partee, Member, Board of Governors of the Federal Reserve System, before the Subcommittee on Securities of the Committee on Banking, Housing and Urban Affairs, US Senate, 4 February 1982.
29. For a discussion of this approach, see, for instance, Joseph Sinkey, *Problems and Failed Institutions in the Commercial Bank Industry* (Greenwich, Ct, Jai Press, 1979).
30. Milton Friedman and Anna Schwartz, *A Monetary History of the United States, 1867–1960* (Princeton, NJ, Princeton University Press, 1963), p.440.
31. Friedman and Schwartz, *A Monetary History*, p.434.
32. Sam Peltzman, 'Capital Investment in Commercial Banking and its Relationship to Portfolio Regulation', p.17. More generally on this topic, see 'Deposit Insurance in a Changing Environment'.
33. Other considerations apart, the mere fact that fraud plays such an important part in bank failures reduces the value of published balance sheet data. See Thomas Mayer, 'Should Large Banks be Allowed to Fail?', *Journal of Financial and Quantitative Analysis*, Volume 10, No.4, November 1975, p.605.
34. One US regulator has commented as follows on this point: 'Although there is obviously some degree of discipline being exerted by the market as it discriminates among banks, such discrimination appears to be largely based on the size of the individual banks and the perception that very large banks are so vital to the national interest of their home countries that they would not be permitted to fail.' John Ryan, Director, Division of Banking Supervision and Regulation, Board of Governors of the Federal Reserve System, 'Capital Adequacy – a Soundness Consideration for All

Banks', speech before the International Conference of Banking Supervisors, Washington DC, 24–25 September 1981.

35. A former FDIC official has confirmed this interpretation: 'I would like to say something about why we did not have insurance before and why we do not have 100 per cent deposit insurance now. There has always been, and is now, a lot of opposition from people who have interests at stake. One hundred per cent deposit insurance, for example, changes the relative attractiveness of large banks versus small banks. With 100 per cent insurance those firms or depositors who now prefer to have their $1mn deposits in Citibank would be indifferent as to where they put their deposit – a small bank in Iowa would be just as good. So, it is probably in Citibank's interest not to have 100 per cent deposit insurance.' Comment by Paul Horvitz, Assistant to the Chairman, FDIC, in Franklin R. Edwards, ed., *Issues in Financial Regulation* (New York, McGraw-Hill, 1977), p.121.

36. See, for instance, Kenneth Scott and Thomas Mayer, 'Risk and Regulation in Banking: Some Proposals for Federal Deposit Insurance Reform', *Stanford Law Review*, Volume 23, May 1971; Franklin Edwards and James Scott, 'Regulating the Solvency of Depository Institutions: a Perspective for Deregulation' in Maisel, *Risk and Capital Adequacy*, pp. 98–105.

37. For a full consideration of the practical problems involved and possible approaches to risk-related insurance premiums, see 'Deposit Insurance in a Changing Environment', Chapter II.

38. See, for instance, Thomas M. Humphrey, 'The Classical Concept of the Lender of Last Resort', *Federal Reserve Bank of Richmond Economic Review*, January/February 1975.

39. See Jack Guttentag and Richard Herring, *The Lender of Last Resort Function in an International Context*, Princeton Studies in International Finance No.151, May 1983, p.5.

40. See Shafer, 'The Theory of the Lender of Last Resort', p.27.

41. For consideration of the solvency/insolvency issue see Bulow and Shoven, 'The Bankruptcy Decision', *Bell Journal of Economics*, Volume 9, No.2, Autumn 1978.

42. The possibility of adverse knock-on effects was, for instance, a factor in the FDIC's decision to provide financial assistance to First Pennsylvania Bank in 1980 under Section 13(c) of the Federal Deposit Insurance Act. See 'Statement on FDIC Procedures in Handling Failed or Failing Banks', presented to the Commerce, Consumer, and Monetary Affairs Subcommittee, House of Representatives Committee on Government Operations, by Irvin H. Sprague, Chairman, FDIC, 16 July 1981, p.19.

43. Henry C. Wallich, 'Central Banks as Regulators and Lenders of Last Resort in an International Context: a View from the United States', Key Issues in International Banking Series, No.18 (Federal Reserve Bank of Boston, October 1977), p.95.

44. Shafer, 'The Theory of the Lender of Last Resort', p.9.

45. Shafer, 'The Theory of the Lender of Last Resort', p.36.

46. See, for instance, speech given by Peter Cooke at the Institute of Chartered Accoutants Banking Conference in London on 4 November 1982, p.14. However, the Group of Ten central banks were reported to have agreed in September 1974 that 'banks that get into difficulties through fraud will not necessarily be bailed out, but all deposits will be protected' (London, Euromoney, October 1974), p.5.

47. This aspect of the moral hazard problem is discussed in Thomas Mayer, 'Should Large Banks be Allowed to Fail?'

48. See A.S.J. Baster, *The Imperial Banks* (London, P.S. King & Son, 1929), p.20.

49. Various commentators have made proposals along these lines. See, for instance, Mayer, 'Should Large Banks be Allowed to Fail?', pp.608–9.

4 *International Banking Risks*

The case for prudential regulation applies just as forcefully to banks' international activities as it does to their domestic operations. Indeed, international banking involves new and distinct risks, particularly in the area of country risk, which have no counterpart in domestic financial markets. Furthermore, regulators have to take account of the complex legal and commercial relationships between parent institutions and their foreign offshoots. Finally, because of this multinational aspect and the difficulties involved in trying to impose prudential controls on global financial markets, it is necessary for national authorities to co-ordinate their activities and allocate responsibilities. This Chapter is concerned with the risks particular to international banking. The problem of regulatory co-ordination is considered in Chapter 7.

FOREIGN EXCHANGE RISK

The possibility that banks may incur losses on their foreign exchange business can be broken down into three separate risks: the risk of dealing and taking a position; the risk of losses caused by delinquent employees acting in excess of their authority; and the risk of default by the counter-party in either spot or forward transactions. So far as the first is concerned, it was management-approved speculative activity that was largely responsible for both the failure of the West German Bankhaus Herstatt in 1974[1] and the US Franklin National Bank's downfall in the same year.[2] Foreign exchange speculation may be difficult to detect, particularly if (as in these cases) it is combined with fraud, which prevents the true facts from emerging until it is too late. Partly for this reason, foreign exchange offers a tempting high risk/high return opportunity for banks which are already in trouble of one kind or another and which have therefore decided to adopt a 'go for broke' strategy in a last-ditch attempt to restore their fortunes. The appropriate regulatory response to this danger is continuous monitoring of banks' foreign exchange positions on a fully consolidated basis, coupled with formal or informal limits on such exposure measured as a percentage of capital.

Losses caused by *unauthorised* foreign exchange dealing were particularly heavy in the early stages of the floating exchange rate regime which began in March 1973. Lloyds Bank International lost $77 million in this way, while Union Bank of Switzerland lost approximately $150 million and Banque de Bruxelles something less than $40 million.[3] More recently, it was reported that the largest Japanese bank, Dai-Ichi Kangyo, had lost some $40 million as a result of unauthorised speculation carried out between 1978 and 1982 by the chief foreign exchange dealer of its Singapore branch.[4] Official surveillance of banks' internal control procedures is the only real safeguard against this kind of risk, although automatic prosecution of the culprits (rather than discreet dismissal as banks generally prefer) may also provide a needed deterrent.

The risk of default by the counterparty in a spot foreign exchange transaction was highlighted for the first time by the Herstatt collapse. Mr Andrew Brimmer, then a Governor of the US Federal Reserve Board, has described the relevant events as follows:

> 'The way Herstatt was closed disrupted the bank clearing mechanism at the heart of this market – since it cut short the settlement of spot transactions. Normally, in a spot foreign exchange trade, the buyer and seller of a currency promise to settle with each other within two days. In the Herstatt case, German marks were sold to Herstatt on June 24, 1974, by at least a dozen banks. Settlement was due – in dollars – on June 26.
>
> On that date, the selling banks instructed their correspondent banks in Germany to debit their mark accounts and deposit their funds in the Landes-Central Bank – the clearing house operated by the Bundesbank. The funds were then credited to Herstatt. The selling banks expected to receive dollars on the same day through London or New York clearing houses.
>
> However, Bankhaus Herstatt was officially declared bankrupt around 4pm on June 26, 1974. This was after the market had closed in Germany – but while foreign exchange was still being traded in New York. In the meantime, the Landes-Central Bank had credited Herstatt with funds in Cologne, but the latter's doors were shut before Herstatt's dollars were credited to foreign banks.'[5]

By closing Herstatt before dollar settlements for the day had taken place in New York, the Bundesbank exposed a risk of whose existence banks were until then unaware – namely, the interbank credit risk involved in spot foreign exchange transactions (that risk had, of course, already been recognised in relation to forward contracts). Once alerted to the danger, banks responded by imposing settlement limits on their foreign exchange dealings with one another. The counterparty risk in foreign exchange transactions is therefore an aspect of interbank risk.

THE INTERBANK MARKET

The international or Eurocurrency interbank market differs from domestic interbank markets first of all because of its size, which at mid-1983 was estimated to be over $1,100 billion.[6] The proportion of the international banking market represented by interbank funds is around 70 per cent – six or seven times the comparable ratio for the US domestic banking market. Secondly, the international interbank market typically involves long chains of intermediaries, resulting in both maturity and risk transformation that are hidden from the original providers of funds. As one analyst has observed:

'The interbank market may conceal from an individual bank the degree of transformation being undertaken by banks in aggregate. In addition, most banks taking funds from the interbank pool will be unaware of either the original source or ultimate use of the funds they are handling. An active interbank market may therefore increase the scope for behaviour which seems prudent at the level of the individual bank, but seems less so when the whole picture is examined.'[7]

A third source of concern is that weaker banks, without a natural funding base, tend to rely most heavily on interbank deposits[8] and would therefore be least able to replenish funds from other sources should the need arise. This potential weakness is all the more dangerous because empirical studies suggest that 'credit-rationing, rather than price adjustment, serves as the primary mechanism of discrimination between sound and risky banks'.[9] In other words, a small bank, heavily dependent on interbank funding, could quickly find itself high and dry if any doubts should arise as to its financial standing.

It is sometimes suggested that long interbank chains also provide a direct transmission mechanism whereby credit or other shocks are promptly felt throughout the international banking system.[10] The line of reasoning here is not always clear – it might be argued that such chains disperse risk and cushion shocks – but given the sensitivity of short-term deposit markets to confidence factors, financial disturbances in one area of the interbank market may become generalised, as demonstrated in the ripple effects of the 1974 Herstatt crisis.

Finally, the interbank market is subject to special risks where banks headquartered in debtor countries use their foreign offices to attract short-term funds for on-lending to home country borrowers. In this way the interbank market may become a back-door source of balance of payments finance, with potentially dangerous consequences – as recent experience with Mexico, Brazil and the Philippines has shown. This aspect of the interbank market is subsumed under the more general heading of country risk.

COUNTRY RISK

Bank lending to developing countries, which in previous years had been increasing at an annual rate of 20 per cent, came to an abrupt halt in the third quarter of 1982 as confidence evaporated in the wake of Mexico's financial collapse. This sudden interruption in the flow of credit threatened to precipitate multiple country defaults,[11] since without new money the major borrowers could not be expected to pay the interest on, let alone to repay the principal of, their existing loans. In order to avert this danger, national authorities, in conjunction with the Bank for International Settlements and the International Monetary Fund, orchestrated a series of emergency credit programmes under which banks were required to commit additional funds to problem borrowers according to a quota allocation system which used as its benchmark each bank's exposure to the country concerned. For the major borrowers the annual increment was set at around 7 per cent of banks' outstanding loans, a figure that was intended to meet these countries' minimum external financing requirements while enabling the banks to achieve a slight reduction in their country exposure relative to capital.[12] The authorities' response to the banking crisis therefore amounted to a recognition of the fact that, for the time being at least, the market recycling mechanism had broken down. The economic background to these developments has been discussed elsewhere;[13] the significance of the crisis for present purposes is that it highlights the crucial importance of country risk in international lending.

Country risk has been defined as 'the possibility that sovereign borrowers of a particular country may be unable or unwilling, and other borrowers unable, to fulfill their foreign obligations for reasons beyond the usual risks which arise in relation to all lending'.[14] The idea behind this definition is that there may be no legal redress against a foreign borrower that chooses to renege on its external obligations, and that whereas private sector borrowers are subject to legal process, they may be prevented from obtaining the necessary foreign exchange to service their foreign debt. As sub-categories of country risk, 'sovereign risk' may be viewed as the special risk arising from a sovereign borrower's immunity from legal process,[15] while 'transfer risk' refers to the danger that otherwise solvent entities may become bad credits because of local foreign exchange restrictions, in other words, the possibility that ordinary credit risk may be switched into country risk.

Exposure to country risk may take a variety of forms but two kinds of distinction – local versus foreign currency claims and public sector versus private sector credits – deserve special consideration.

Local versus Foreign Currency Claims

Typically, national authorities do not regard local currency claims against foreign borrowers as giving rise to country risk, at least where such lending is matched by local currency liabilities.[16] The reasoning here is that, normal credit risks apart, the kind of circumstances which might place a bank's local currency claims in jeopardy (such as revolution or expropriation) would also extinguish its local currency liabilities. However, a recent US court case involving Chase Manhattan Bank[17] points in the other direction.

In this instance, Chase had suspended the operation of its Saigon branch in April 1975 because of the deteriorating military situation in Vietnam. On 1 May 1975, the new communist government nationalised the branch and expropriated all of its assets. Subsequently, certain Vietnamese who held piastre deposits and certificates of deposit stated to be payable at and only at Chase's Saigon branch sued Chase for repayment in New York. The District Court dismissed all claims against Chase but the Court of Appeals reversed the decision and held Chase liable in the United States for the deposits formerly owed to the respondents by the foreign branch, on the grounds that closure of this branch had shifted the situs of Chase's debt to New York, and that the obligation to repay was therefore unaffected by the Vietnamese government's subsequent nationalisation decree. In addition, it was held that by operating in Saigon through a branch rather than a subsidiary, Chase 'accepted the risk' that it would be liable in New York for the obligations of the branch. The Supreme Court having disallowed an appeal against this decision, it is clear that as matters now stand local currency claims against foreign borrowers can give rise to country risk.

Private versus Public Sector Credits

The definition of country risk given above would suggest that foreign public sector credits, being subject to the possibility that the borrower will be either unable or unwilling to repay, are more risky (in a country risk sense) than private sector credits where the only danger is the borrower's inability to repay. However, such a conclusion would be misleading, if only because recent experience with debt-servicing interruptions suggests that in situations where a country is unable to meet its external obligations as they fall due, the private sector will tend to be last in the queue for scarce foreign exchange or otherwise placed at a disadvantage *vis-à-vis* public sector borrowers. Thus, in Mexico, private companies (often US multinationals) with hard currency borrowings have had difficulty in obtaining foreign exchange on any terms, while in Argentina the authorities have unilaterally converted short-term corporate debt into medium-term public sector debt.[18]

More generally, exchange rate depreciation and other forms of adjustment that may ultimately ease the public sector's debt-servicing problems can impose intolerable strains on private sector borrowers with net hard currency liabilities. Here it is abrupt liberalisation of, rather than new restrictions on, the foreign exchange market that may pose a threat to the private sector's debt-servicing capacity. Equally, a sudden shift to higher local currency interest rates, such as may be prescribed as part of an adjustment programme, will further weaken the financial condition of corporate borrowers. Paradoxically, therefore, measures taken to alleviate a country's 'problem debtor' status may reduce the credit standing of that country's private borrowers.

The above distinctions apart, interbank lending may involve special country risk considerations regardless of whether the debtor bank is state or privately owned. Funds placed with the foreign branch of another bank are subject to transfer risk arising both within the country in which the branch is situated and also within the country of the branch's parent. In addition, foreign banks originating in debtor countries may be expected to have extensive foreign currency claims on the countries concerned. Finally, the parent bank's central bank may not be in a position to act as lender of last resort in foreign currency if it is faced with a national foreign exchange crisis. For all these reasons, banks headquartered in problem countries can very quickly succumb to funding difficulties in their international operations, as recent Latin American experience has shown. Therefore, while interbank claims, because of their short maturity, may appear to be in a different risk category than syndicated loans, they are also vulnerable to being locked in when a crisis breaks.

The Nature of Country Risk

It is a troublesome paradox that while countries cannot go bankrupt they may still fail to pay. In attempting to assess the risk of failure to pay, analysts have drawn on domestic analogues and in particular on the distinction in domestic corporate finance between solvency and liquidity problems. In addition, a sharp distinction is sometimes made between a country's capacity and its willingness to pay in an attempt to identify circumstances where it may be in a country's interest to repudiate. However, such neat distinctions can be misleading in the country risk context where the relevant considerations are as much political as economic.

Solvency and Liquidity Professor Aliber has approached the country risk question on the basis that 'the distinction between solvency and liquidity used in the analysis of domestic financial firms can be usefully applied to the analysis of the external debt of individual developing countries'.[19] According to Professor Aliber, a solvency problem arises where the real interest on (marginal) foreign borrowing exceeds the increase in national income made possible by such borrowing, whereas a liquidity problem means simply that the borrower is unable to obtain the foreign exchange to service its foreign debt on schedule – i.e., there is a breakdown in the refunding mechanism. One important conclusion of this analysis is that where a country has borrowed so much abroad that its domestic income is adversely affected (because marginal investment returns fall short of borrowing costs) the present value of external debt needs to be reduced, for instance by some form of debt relief.

However, from an operational banking point of view the usefulness of this kind of distinction between solvency and liquidity must be doubted. *Ex ante*, it is impossible for either borrower or lender to assess solvency in this sense, if only because floating rate foreign currency debt must have a highly variable and unpredictable real cost to the borrower. More importantly, if, *ex post*, it turns out that the funds borrowed have failed to augment the debtor country's national income, it seems highly unreasonable that the lender should be expected to forgo some portion of what is owed to him on the pretext that the country is now 'insolvent'. Finally, even if a country is 'solvent' it would be imprudent to assume that increases in national income generated by foreign borrowing will always be available to repay that borrowing.

The solvency/liquidity distinction is invoked in order to determine whether a country is in a position to service its external debt. However, this is essentially a political matter which will be determined by whether the government of the day has both the interest and the ability to manage the economy in a manner which generates sufficient foreign exchange. It is because country risk involves this political dimension that it is necessarily a concept which resists exact quantification.

Capacity and Willingness to Pay It is also tempting to simplify the country risk problem by drawing a distinction between a country's capacity to pay its debts and its willingness to do so. However, the only un-ambiguous indicator of a country's unwillingness to pay is outright debt repudiation. Between this boundary on the one hand and due debt repayment on the other lies a range of possible debt-servicing problems that may reflect varying degrees of incapacity and unwillingness to honour existing obligations. For instance, in the recent spate of debt reschedulings a commitment on the part of the bank creditors to provide a specified amount of new money was typically part of the rescheduling package. Since these funds were not obtainable from the market (see comments on page 76 regarding quota allocations among banks) it may be assumed that the lenders were actuated by the implicit (and in some cases explicit) threat of unilateral default on the part of the borrowers. Arguably, the governments of such countries as Mexico and Brazil *could* have cut back domestic demand sufficiently to permit rescheduling without the need for new borrowing. Yet by keeping alive the threat of default they were able to reach an agreement with their creditors which cushioned the burden of domestic adjustment. And, as the recent literature on default risk suggests, in such complex negotiating situations there is no clear line to be drawn between a borrower's capacity to meet its obligations and its willingness to do so.[20] The same line of reasoning suggests why formal debt repudiation is so rare: so long as a borrower can, through the threat of default, extract net new funds from the international banking system, it does not 'pay' to repudiate.[21] The conclusion, once again, is that country risk is a much less clear-cut concept than some commentators would have us believe.

Corporate versus Country Risk Given that the traditional distinctions between solvency and liquidity and between capacity and willingness to pay are not easily applied to country borrowers, it is necessary to consider in what other ways country risk differs from the risks incurred in lending to domestic corporate borrowers. The following appear to be particularly important:

1. Legal redress. Legal action against a defaulting government offers little protection.[22] A legal suit in the courts of the borrowing country may not be entertained or may not be successful or may not result in an enforceable judgement. Redress in the courts of the lender's country may not be available if sovereign immunity is involved, and cannot be effective if there are no assets to seize. More complex legal considerations apply where a private sector borrower is prevented through lack of access to foreign exchange from meeting its external obligations.

2. Sanctions. It follows from point 1 above that country borrowers and bank lenders are bound together not by enforceable contractual relations but by implicit threats: the lenders' collective threat to exclude a defaulting borrower permanently from international capital markets and the borrowers' threat to default if new funding should be denied. The disciplinary mechanism is therefore based on sanctions, not remedies.

3. Losses. Except in the rare event of formal repudiation, and because there is no equivalent of corporate bankruptcy proceedings, losses from country risk exposure are never crystallised. This gives rise to an 'all or nothing' risk situation in which loans, if in jeopardy, are in jeopardy to their full extent (assuming there is no collateral and that debt relief is not contemplated).

4. Equity. Countries have no equity capital to absorb external shocks. Consequently, bank creditors are fully exposed to such risks.

5. Conditionality. In the case of corporate borrowing, bond covenants are available to restrict the borrower from undertaking certain actions after the debt is incurred. These restrictions may relate to dividend payments, debt ceilings, maintenance of assets and disclosure requirements. Such provisions are, however, unenforceable against countries and are therefore not incorporated in international loan agreements. The most important consequence here is that lenders have no control over a country's prospective indebtedness.

6. Accountability. A private firm experiencing financial difficulties may improve its cash flow by closing plants and laying off employees. There is no conflict of interest because the firm is accountable not to its employees but to its stockholders, who share with the creditors an overriding interest in preventing insolvency. In contrast, a government experiencing debt-servicing difficulties,

whether democratically elected or not, is ultimately answerable to its own people, who must also bear the burden of adjustment.

7. Life expectation. It is often said that whereas a company may be extinguished by insolvency, a country goes on for ever. On the other hand, a government may be turned out of office at any time, giving rise to the possibility of politically motivated borrowing calculated to prolong its hold on power as well as to acts or threats of default that ignore the longer-term costs of exclusion from international financial markets.[23]

8. Number of creditors. Whereas a company is typically indebted to relatively few banks, a country may have foreign bank creditors numbered in hundreds (for instance, Mexico has 800 and Poland nearly 500). Banks can protect themselves against selective default by inclusion of a cross-default clause in loan agreements, but the existence of numerous unrelated lending institutions does offer a temptation for each creditor to try to 'get out' when debt-servicing problems arise (see below).

The Nature of Security

The differences noted above between corporate and country risk point to the greater dangers involved in international lending. It is therefore necessary to ask why banks are prepared to engage in large-scale lending to country borrowers without collateral, with no control over the use to which funds are put, without foreknowledge of or control over the debtor's subsequent borrowing and with no effective legal redress should default occur. The answer appears to be that banks rely on three kinds of safeguard: the self-interest of country borrowers in honouring their external obligations; the risk-spreading protection offered by geographical diversfication; and the interest of the banks' own national governments in maintaining the stability of the international financial system.

So far as the self-interest of borrowers is concerned, default carries with it heavy costs in terms of permanent exclusion from credit markets, possible seizure of assets and interference with trade. Even so, lenders will wish to ensure that, collectively, they do not commit so much to a particular country that it may 'pay' that country to default.[24] Yet given that there is at present no machinery for agreeing on or enforcing such an aggregate credit ceiling, lenders can never be sure that borrowers will not pass the threshold at which default becomes a serious option.

Formal default models generally fail to distinguish between the different time horizons of *governments* and *countries* and may therefore underestimate the possibility of default. Nor do they take into account the full range of potential outcomes in debt renegotiations. Nevertheless, the recent literature in this area does provide a useful insight into the much lower incidence of debt repudiation in modern times compared to the pre-1930 period when international lending took the form of bond rather than bank finance.[25]

Regarding the security offered by diversification, the conventional view has been that the economic performance of country borrowers is sufficiently uncorrelated to offer the opportunity for effective spreading of risks.[26] However, in the light of recent events it is evident that certain elements of systematic or non-diversifiable risk have been seriously underestimated. In the first place, the bulk of third world bank borrowing has been in the form of floating rate dollar debt with the result that the stability of the international debt structure is highly dependent on the course of real dollar interest rates (which may be higher for country borrowers than for US domestic borrowers). Secondly, prolonged recession in the industrialised countries has a leveraged impact on third world countries who have to contend with adverse movements not only in the volume but also in the terms of trade. Any, finally, there is a strong propensity for debt problems to spread from one country to another by a contagious process that reflects an erosion of confidence among bankers (see below).

Since the debt crisis erupted in 1982, banks have been forced to look to their ultimate source of security – namely, the common interest of all governments in ensuring the stability of the international financial system. To date official intervention has taken the form of bilateral government-to-government loans, multilateral lending under the auspices of the Bank for International Settlements and an expedited review of IMF quotas. However, even these initiatives have been insufficient to keep the international banking system intact. The result is an emergency regime of quota-based bank lending that cannot be expected to endure indefinitely. Looking further ahead, therefore, the question that needs to be addressed is: what kinds of regulatory or institutional changes may be necessary to reconstitute a sound market in international lending?

Regulatory Implications

Some would argue that improvement of the present international recycling mechanism is not necessary since lending to foreign governments is no riskier than lending to domestic governments.[27] Others believe, on the contrary, that financing of balance of payments deficits is much too risky a task for the private banking sector under any circumstances and should be left to governments or the international agencies.[28] A middle view is that there are certain defects in the present regulatory framework of international banking which, if corrected, could prevent any recurrence of the kind of global debt crisis that developed in 1982.

The key weakness in the present international recycling mechanism, which has been highlighted by recent events, is the 'feast or famine' characteristic of banks' lending behaviour. There are a number of explanations for this phenomenon, the first of which concerns the competitive process itself. Whereas most industrial firms compete for business on the basis of relative efficiency and production costs, in international banking the cost of funds for the major banks is, broadly speaking, equal and competition is based on the lowest perception of *risk* as reflected in quoted spreads on international loans. Where risks take time to build up and eventuate, as in the case of country risk exposure, the normal penalties for excessive risk-taking may not materialise until it is too late. Meanwhile, the more cautious banks will be under pressure as their share of the international loan market declines and banks which may have lent prudently to countries that appeared at the time to have tolerable debt burdens will see the credit standing of such country debtors undermined as a result of subsequent excessive lending by more aggressive banks. In short, risk-based competition propels the entire system towards excessive levels of indebtedness. Furthermore, once an individual bank's exposure to a single country reaches around 60 per cent of capital it has little or no incentive to refrain from further lending or, indeed, to charge a risk premium on such loans. This is because the incremental risk incurred is inconsequential. In other words, market discipline breaks down when a bank's exposure passes the threshold at which default by the borrower would threaten insolvency.

Nor can country borrowers be expected to impose a prudent limit on their own indebtedness. If a country is prepared ultimately to default, it will generally be in its interests to continue to make net drawings (that is, net of all debt-servicing payments) on the international banking system for as long as it is able to do so. When the resulting erosion in its credit standing eventually causes a drying-up of funds, it may then threaten to default. If at this point banks are persuaded under duress to provide new money as part of a rescheduling agreement the problem is again deferred. Furthermore, since *governments* have shorter time horizons than *countries*, they are more inclined to borrow to the limit regardless of any adverse impact on future access to credit markets.

The dangers of excessive country lending are compounded by the propensity of the international credit system to unravel when confidence is shaken. To begin with, as noted above, the fact that there are so many creditors gives each an incentive to withdraw if it can when a debtor country gets into difficulty. Secondly, there is the well-known phenomenon of 'contagion' in financial markets which may, via effects on confidence, transmit debt-servicing problems from one country to another. The explanation for contagion appears to be that the credit standing of a country, in the face of a large number of creditors, depends not so much on each creditor's objective view of the country's prospects as on each creditor's assessment of how others may react to adverse developments elsewhere. In these respects, country debtors have the same susceptibility to infectious collapse as do banks in an unregulated setting, the common characteristic being that both are dependent for their continued financial viability on the collective confidence of their creditors/depositors.

The international credit market's propensity to sudden collapse is also due to the tendency for the pricing mechanism to break down when confidence evaporates – also a feature of domestic financial markets in times of crisis. Once credit rationing sets in, countries can no longer attract new funds by accepting higher spreads on their loans and are therefore effectively shut out of the credit markets. It is interesting to note that the Task Force on Non-Concessional Flows, in a report to the IMF/World Bank Development Committee dated April 1982, seriously underestimated this danger when it commented that the behaviour of spreads in 1980/81 'does suggest that the pricing mechanism in international lending is functioning'.[29] On this basis the report concluded:

> 'Developing country borrowers with adequate policies and reasonable growth prospects are not likely to be denied continued market access solely because exogenous factors – such as a deterioration in their terms of trade or the adverse impact on debt service of high world interest rates – may have rendered their circumstances somewhat more problematic in the short run.'[30]

The lesson to be learned from recent events, however, is that the market cannot be relied upon to absorb severe shocks to the system any more than it can be relied upon in more normal times to impose a prudent ceiling on individual country indebtedness. It should by now be apparent that international lending has a strong tendency to boom or bust that must be restrained in both directions if stability is to be restored to world financial markets.[31] To date the international banking community, as well as bank regulators, have been focusing on ways of improving their assessment of individual country risks on the assumption that if only they can lay their hands on the right information a sound basis for prudent decision-making can be established. For instance, it is the perceived need for improvements in the gathering and analysis of information which lies behind the Ditchley Group's decision to set up the Institute of International Finance in Washington. However, the implication of the discussion above is that it is the framework within which international banking is conducted, and its impact on banks' behaviour, which creates instability and which therefore needs to be overhauled.

The first requirement is for a cap on the total indebtedness of each country. As indicated earlier, a free market cannot impose such a limit and the choice therefore must lie between a cartel-type agreement between *all* banks covering appropriate credit ceilings for each country, a commitment by borrowing countries to adhere to some self-imposed limit acceptable to lenders, or IMF guidelines on debt that would be indicated to country borrowers but also made known to financial markets, which would be expected to take their cue accordingly. The third route would appear to be the most practicable since the fund already specifies country debt ceilings as one of the conditions for its lending programmes. The important point, however, is that the limit should be continuously in place and constantly monitored – and not introduced after the event when debt servicing has been interrupted.[32]

In developing debt guidelines attention should be given not only to the debt-carrying capacity of individual countries[33] but also to an appropriate global pattern of payments surpluses and deficits.[34] For this purpose it is necessary to consider what is a manageable current account deficit, not so much from a welfare economics point of view (i.e., applying the usual marginality conditions) but from a banking standpoint. For instance, one commentator has suggested the following test:

> 'To be commercially creditworthy, a country should be in a position to balance its current account within the time frame of the loan, i.e., five to seven years for typical bank loan maturities. This is not to say that the current account *will* be balanced in that time frame, but the potential for eventual balance must be visible.'[35]

While it is necessary to impose some upper limit on lending to countries, it is equally important to eliminate the potential for a sudden credit contraction. To achieve this, several steps might be necessary. First, because of the parallel characteristics of the creditor bank/country debtor relationship and the ordinary depositor/bank relationship, a case can be made for an international lender of last resort to countries with a view to stabilising confidence and preventing bank 'runs' on country borrowers. Presumably such a lender of last resort should have some means of putting bank creditors on 'hold' so far as their existing commitments are concerned so that it does not end up simply refinancing bank loans (the BIS acted as such a lender of last resort in 1982/83 but on an *ad hoc* basis and without a clear mandate).

Secondly, something has to be done to control the maturity distribution of international credit, since a rapid build-up of short-term debt is a recipe for subsequent withdrawal and collapse. This has been the case in Latin America; more particularly, in Mexico, where, in the first half of 1982, banks lent $7.3 billion of which no less than 60 per cent was short-term (under one year),[36] apparently on the assumption that the funds could be withdrawn if economic conditions continued to deteriorate. One prominent banker has commented as follows on this phase of the Latin American debt crisis:

> 'It is this build-up of short-term debt . . . that explains the apparent suddenness with which the problems of Argentina and Mexico have burst upon the international financial market. Both borrowers and lenders were in effect attempting to buy time, in the hope that interest rates would come down, and export earnings revive . . . Unfortunately, the lenders did not tally what each one was doing, partly because of the delay in the expected improvement, and also because of the lagged availability of statistics, until it

became apparent that even more short-term lending would be required. At that point, sometime in mid-1982, a major retraction of lending took place.'[37]

The problem here is two-fold. There is an information gap that needs to be closed through the provision of more comprehensive and timely data on country indebtedness than currently exist. This suggests that a country's access to international credit markets should be conditional on the availability of continuously updated information on both private and public sector debt. More importantly, there is the additional problem that banks, sometimes unwittingly encouraged by their own regulatory authorities,[38] shift to short-term financing in times of uncertainty and then seek to 'get out' when debt-financing interruptions are anticipated. There is therefore a case for IMF guidance on the appropriate maturity distribution of a country's debt.

To conclude: within the present international banking framework long-term lending is unsafe because, in the absence of any debt ceiling, the borrower's financial condition can deteriorate rapidly during the term of the loan. On the other hand, short-term lending is unsafe because it can lead to a sudden credit contraction. The proposals outlined above would, by correcting excesses in both directions, make a major contribution to stabilising the system.

Other radical reforms have been suggested, which cannot be fully considered here, but may be briefly mentioned. For instance, the prevalence of floating rate debt, and associated unpredictable swings in real interest rates, have been identified as a further major source of instability which might be removed by imposing a limit on the quantity of such debt[39] or by developing new lending techniques which, by means of adjustable amortisation schedules, would stabilise borrowers' annual debt service payments.[40] Alternatively, it might be possible to incorporate provisions for partial debt relief in the loan agreement in the event that certain trigger clauses, relating to real interest rates and/or the borrower's terms of trade, were activated. Because such debt relief would be negotiated *ex ante* and relate to events outside the borrower's control, it need not lead to moral hazard problems.

It has also been suggested that arrangements should be made to introduce a secondary market in bank loans so that banks can 'get out' (at a price) without withdrawing credit from the borrower.[41] However, the existence of such a secondary market would presumably limit the possibilities for debt reschedulings and thereby encourage routine repudiations of the kind that occurred under the pre-1930 bond-financing regime.

A further radical proposal is based on the idea that national banking systems should be insulated from international credit markets. This could be done by requiring banks to conduct their international business through separate affiliates, which would not be able to look to the support of their parent institutions in the event of country defaults.[42] By segregating in this way the difficult-to-assess but potentially devastating risks of international lending, national authorities could ensure that their domestic financial systems were not threatened by external disturbances.

Major reforms apart, recent events have focused attention on a number of other regulatory issues, some of which are currently under review. In particular, provisioning and disclosure have become the subject of controversy, because at a time when banking authorities have been trying to override market forces in order to ensure a continuing flow of bank credit to country borrowers, others (notably the US Securities and Exchange Commission)[43] are working to strengthen market forces by requiring banks to disclose more fully the nature and extent of their country risk exposure. There is also a question as to whether a bank's exposure to individual countries, measured as a percentage of its capital, should be subject to a regulatory ceiling. Previous attempts to impose informal guidelines in this area appear to have been largely ineffective,[44] so that exposure to the major borrowers of 40–60 per cent is not uncommon among, for instance, US[45] and Japanese banks.[46]

Finally, bank regulators have been giving more attention to the evaluation of country risk. The difficulty here is that if the regulators' assessment is shared by the market then either this risk perception will already be reflected in lending spreads or else 'stronger' countries will over time attract new lending to the point where their credit standing is impaired. In other words, in a free market setting, individual country risks will tend to converge, thereby defeating regulatory initiatives designed to channel banks' lending to borrowers perceived as stronger. As indicated above, the need is not for more refined techniques to appraise financial prospects in individual countries, but rather for a deeper appreciation of the nature of country risk and of the inherent instability of an unregulated market in international lending.

NOTES

1. See Andrew Brimmer, 'International Finance and the Management of Bank Failures', paper presented to the American Economic Association and the American Finance Association, Atlantic City, 16 September 1976, pp.20–33.
2. See Joan Spero, *The Failure of Franklin National Bank* (New York, Columbia University Press, 1980), Chapter 3.
3. See James Dean and Ian Giddy, *Averting International Banking Crises*, Monograph Series in Economics and Finance, 1981–1 (New York University, Salomon Brothers Center) pp.4–8.
4. *Japan Economic Journal*, 28 September 1982, p.2.
5. Brimmer, 'International Finance', p.22.
6. Morgan Guaranty Trust, *World Financial Markets*, January 1984, p.9.
7. J. G. Ellis, 'Euro-banks and the Inter-Bank Market', *Bank of England Quarterly Review*, September 1981, p.359.
8. Ellis, 'Euro-banks', p.352.
9. Ian Giddy, 'Risk and Return in the Eurocurrency Interbank Market', unpublished paper, August 1981, p.2.

10. See, for instance, Jack Guttentag and Richard Herring, 'Uncertainty and Insolvency Exposure by International Banks' (The Wharton School, University of Pennsylvania, 1982), pp.20–25.

11. The term 'default' can apply to a variety of debt-servicing interruptions, ranging from formal repudiation to unilateral suspension of principal and/or interest payments. Default may be *de facto* or, where declared by the creditors, *de jure*. Suspension of interest payments has particularly serious consequences for banks because interest income can no longer be accrued and losses are therefore incurred.

12. See statement by Paul Volcker, Chairman of the Federal Reserve Board, before the Joint Economic Committee, 27 January 1983, p.13.

13. See, for instance, Bank for International Settlements, Annual Report, June 1983, pp.118–31.

14. Group of Thirty, *Risks in International Bank Lending* (New York, 1982), p.6.

15. The legal aspects of foreign risk are discussed in 'Symposium on Default by Foreign Government Debtors', *University of Illinois Law Review*, Volume 1982, No. 1.

16. The measurement of country risk typically covers banks' cross-border and non-local currency claims to foreign borrowers.

17. See *The Chase Manhattan Bank* NA v. *Vishipco Line* et al., motion of the Federal Reserve Bank of New York for leave to file a brief as *amicus curiae* in support of the petition, 26 March 1982.

18. In effect the Argentine central bank refused to honour its foreign currency swap agreements with local companies which had borrowed funds from abroad. See 'Argentine Bank Refuses to Pay Foreign Debt', *Washington Post*, 20 November 1982, p.D9.

19. Robert Z. Aliber, *A Conceptual Approach to the Analysis of External Debt of the Developing Countries*, World Bank Staff Working Paper No. 421, October 1980, p.5.

20. See, for instance, Jeffrey Sachs and Daniel Cohen, *LDC Borrowing with Default Risk*, National Bureau of Economic Research (Cambridge, Mass.), Working Paper No. 925, July 1982.

21. See also Jeffrey Sachs, *LDC Debt in the 1980s: Risk and Reforms*, National Bureau of Economic Research, Working Paper No. 861, February 1982.

22. For a discussion of available legal remedies, see Reade H. Ryan, Jr, 'Defaults and Remedies under International Bank Loan Agreements with Foreign Sovereign Borrowers – a New York Lawyer's Perspective' in 'Symposium on Default by Foreign Government Debtors', pp.89–132.

23. For the view that country borrowing may, in this sense, be politically motivated, see, for instance, Lawrence J. Brainard and Thomas J. Trebot, *The Role of Commercial Banks in Balance of Payments Crises: the Cases of Peru and Poland* (New York, Bankers Trust, March 1981).

24. A major conclusion of the debt repudiation literature is that lenders will seek to impose an aggregate debt ceiling on country borrowers such that the benefits of default do not exceed the costs of default. However, it is far from clear how this can be achieved. See Jonathan Eaton and Mark Gersovitz, *Poor-Country Borrowing in Private Financial Markets and the Repudiation Issue*, Princeton Studies in International Finance No. 47, June 1981.

25. Sachs, *LDC Debt in the 1980s*, pp.35–55.

26. See Laurie S. Goodman, 'Bank Lending to Non-OPEC LDCs: are the Risks Diversifiable?', *Federal Reserve Bank of New York Quarterly Review*, Summer 1981; Jonathan Eaton and Mark Gersovitz, 'LDC Participation in International Financial Markets', *Journal of Development Economics*, Volume 7, No. 1, 1980; Ingo Walter, 'Country Risk, Portfolio Decisions and Regulation in International Bank Lending', *Journal of Banking and Finance*, Volume 5, No. 1, 1981, p.77.

27. See, for instance, Walter B. Wriston, 'Banking Against Disaster', *New York Times*, 14 September 1982.

28. See, for instance Harold Lever, 'The World Banking Crisis', 1982 Churchill Lecture, London, 6 December 1982.

29. Task Force on Non-Concessional Flows, Final Report to the Development Committee, 5 April 1982, p.19.

30. Task Force on Non-Concessional Flows, Final Report, p.19.

31. The evidence suggests that bank lending to individual countries tends to fluctuate

sharply in conformity with their commodity price cycle. See *External Indebtedness of Developing Countries*, (Washington, DC, IMF, May 1981), p.31.

32. The President of the Federal Reserve Bank of New York has advocated an IMF-indicated debt ceiling for country borrowers. See Anthony Solomon, 'Remarks Before the Bicentennial Financial Symposium', New York, 7 October 1982, pp.10–14. The Fund announced in 1983 that it would monitor external debt management policies as part of its regular Article IV consultations, but it remains to be seen whether and, if so, how its conclusions will be transmitted to the marketplace. See IMF *Survey*, September 1983, p.287.

33. The literature on debt-carrying capacity is summarised in *External Indebtedness of Developing Countries*, pp.50–51.

34. Solomon, 'Remarks', pp.10–11.

35. David O. Beim, 'Rescuing the LDCs', *Foreign Affairs*, July 1977, p.720.

36. BIS Press Release, December 1982. However, banks appear to have ignored earlier warning signs of a build-up of Mexican short-term debt. See A. Lamfalussy, Assistant General Manager, BIS, letter to the *Financial Times*, 11 January 1983.

37. Pedro-Pablo Kuezynski, 'Latin American Debt', *Foreign Affairs*, Winter 1982/83, p.348.

38. For instance, the Japanese supervisory authorities until recently confined their monitoring of banks' country risk exposure to medium and long-term loans. See *Japan Economic Journal*, December 1982, p.1.

39. See Solomon, 'Remarks', p.11.

40. Laurie S. Goodman, 'An Alternative to Rescheduling LDC Debt in an Inflationary Environment', *Columbia Journal of World Business*, Spring 1982.

41. See Jack Guttentag and Richard Herring, *The Current Crisis in International Banking*, Brookings Discussion Papers (Washington, DC, Brookings Institution, December 1983), pp.19–26.

42. Beim, 'Rescuing the LDCs', p.719.

43. See SEC Regulation SAB 49.

44. See, for instance, comments on the limited effectiveness of the US regulatory authorities' country risk supervisory system in *Bank Examination for Country Risk and International Lending* (Washington, DC, US General Accounting Office, 2 September 1982).

45. *Country Exposure Lending Survey* (Washington, DC, Federal Financial Institutions Examination Council, 6 December 1982).

46. *Asian Wall Street Journal*, 27 September 1982, p.12.

5 Preventive Regulation: a Comparative Survey

National authorities use a variety of approaches and controls to foster bank safety and soundness, and to maintain confidence in the banking system as a whole. The techniques employed fall, briefly, into three main categories: preventive regulation, designed to limit risks incurred by banks; schemes which offer protection to depositors in the event of bank failure; and support provided by national monetary authorities to banks experiencing liquidity difficulties (the lender of last resort function). This Chapter focuses on preventive regulation in the major financial centre countries; Chapter 6 deals with deposit protection and lender of last resort arrangements.

OVERVIEW OF NATIONAL REGULATORY ARRANGEMENTS

Among measures aimed at controlling the levels of risk incurred by banks are those concerned with market entry, capital and liquidity adequacy, permissible business activities, foreign currency exposure, concentration of loans and country risk exposure, and bank examination. The first part of this Chapter provides a comparative overview of national practices under these headings; regulatory arrangements in individual countries are described in the second part.

Market Entry

In virtually all national banking systems, regulation begins at the market entry stage. Before they can be authorised, banks must satisfy various requirements. These, typically, include a reputable management and some minimum amount of subscribed capital, the capital requirement, where formalised, varying from the equivalent of just under $1 million (Belgium, Switzerland) to nearly $13 million (Hong Kong). For both competitive and prudential reasons branches of foreign banks must generally possess a specified amount of endowment capital, although the United Kingdom imposes no such requirement, while Hong Kong has introduced a minimum assets criterion for foreign banks seeking to establish local branches. Several countries apply an economic need criterion and in such cases market entry may be restricted or (as in Italy and Hong Kong) suspended from time to time with a view to curbing excessive and destabilising competition. In financial centres such as Singapore, where domestic and offshore banking operations are separated, entry controls may allow a greater degree of competition in the offshore market than is permitted in the domestic sector.

Entry of foreign-owned banks may be formally limited to subsidiaries (as in Canada) on the grounds that locally incorporated entities can be more effectively regulated by the host authority. In contrast, some other countries (including Japan, Hong Kong and Singapore) have preferred to confine full banking status to branches rather than subsidiaries of foreign banks, because a branch is considered to enjoy the full support of the group to which it belongs.

It is also the practice of a number of countries (Canada, the United Kingdom, Hong Kong and Singapore) to request letters of comfort from foreign banks wishing to establish local financial subsidiaries. Although not generally considered to be legally binding, these letters are in some instances being requested in a form which the banks concerned believe to have the force of law. A few countries (such as Hong Kong and Singapore) adjust their prudential requirements according to whether or not a letter of comfort has been obtained, while others (for example, France and Belgium) are prepared to waive certain solvency or liquidity requirements where a specific guarantee has been received from the foreign parent bank. German subsidiaries of foreign banks may have to provide binding letters of indemnification from their parent institutions in respect of any payments that may be made by the German Deposit Protection Fund to the subsidiary's depositors. Italy appears to be unique in requiring Italian branches of foreign banks to produce a formal declaration from their head office stating that, under its own law, the head office is liable to the full extent of its assets for the liabilities of its foreign branch.

Capital Adequacy

In addition to a stipulated minimum amount of capital, banks are generally required to maintain an appropriate relationship between capital on the one hand, and total assets, risk assets or liabilities on the other. However, some countries (including Hong Kong, Italy and Japan) do not formally regulate capital adequacy while others make an essentially judgemental assessment. Most European countries apply solvency ratios of varying complexity which incorporate different weightings for different categories of risk asset. In this last case, the weightings applied to similar categories of asset may vary. For instance, whereas Switzerland applies a premium weighting to all foreign assets, the Netherlands accords a preferentially low weighting to loans to foreign banks and governments (although the degree of preference has recently been reduced). Belgium applies a solvency ratio which discriminates in favour of larger banks on the grounds that small banks are more risky. The United Kingdom calculates both a gearing and a risk assets ratio but does not apply a general norm to all or any class of banks.

Definitions of capital differ, particularly in the treatment of subordinated debt. A few countries, such as Germany, exclude subordinated debt altogether, others include it up to a limit that varies between 10 per cent and 50 per cent of total capital while the US federal supervisory agencies are divided in their approach to this question. Because of the variety of methods used in capital adequacy assessment, it is not possible to make direct comparisons between requirements in different countries. Nevertheless, where capital adequacy guidelines are or can be expressed in terms of a gearing ratio (the precise definition of which may vary) this can range from $50\times$ for a foreign-owned merchant bank in Singapore with a letter of comfort from its parent, to $33\times$ for Luxembourg banks, $30\times$ for the larger Canadian domestic banks, $20\times$ for a foreign-owned Canadian bank and $15\times$ for a foreign-owned consortium bank in Singapore. The maximum gearing guideline for both regional and multinational US domestic banks supervised by the Comptroller of the Currency or the Federal Reserve is $20\times$, the comparable guideline for smaller US banks being $17.7\times$. Where, on the other hand, capital adequacy is assessed against risk assets rather than total assets the indicated norm ranges between 9 per cent (as in the Netherlands) and 5 per cent (France and Belgium). It should, however, be stressed that exemptions, special risk categories and different definitions of capital make direct comparisons hazardous.

Capital adequacy may or may not be assessed on a world-wide consolidated basis, although the general trend is towards consolidation and within the European Community consolidated supervision will become mandatory from 1 July 1985 as a result of the 1983 EEC Directive to this effect. Even so, the treatment for consolidation purposes of non-wholly-owned subsidiaries and minority interests may differ. In general, host countries monitor and regulate the capital adequacy of foreign banks' local subsidiaries; some host countries also treat branches of foreign banks as separate entities for capital adequacy purposes, although this may reflect competitive rather than prudential concerns.

Liquidity Control

Approaches to the measurement and control of liquidity also vary considerably. Some countries (including the United States and Canada) choose not to lay down formal prudential liquidity requirements, while others (notably the Netherlands, Germany and Switzerland) apply a number of ratios designed to limit the extent of maturity mismatching in banks' balance sheets. In a few cases (for instance, France and Italy) banks which accept short-term deposits are regulated separately from those engaging in longer-term banking business and special limits may be placed on their term lending. Where regulation is formalised, distinctions may or may not be drawn on the assets side between primary, secondary and other classes of liquidity and on the liabilities side between interest rate sensitive money market funds and retail deposits. Although most national schemes seek to classify liabilities by both maturity and volatility, with a view to determining the extent to which funds may prudently be used as a basis for maturity transformation, direct comparisons of permissible transformation are not possible because of the variety of assessment methods and other institutional differences. In general, liquidity regulation does not take account of undue deposit concentrations, although the Netherlands imposes extra liquidity requirements on 'large item' liabilities.

It is generally recognised that the management of foreign currency liquidity may present special problems in so far as banks lack direct access to the lender of last resort in that currency. However, there is no common approach to the treatment of foreign currency items for liquidity purposes. Some financial centres, such as Singapore, specifically exempt banks' foreign currency operations from the liquidity requirements that apply to local currency business. Others, such as Hong Kong, apply liquidity norms uniformly to local and foreign currency items. Japan pays particular attention to Japanese banks' Eurocurrency activities, which are subject to a special mismatch limit; France requires separate calculations to be made for local and foreign currency liquidity; and Germany applies limits to foreign exchange exposure which serve the additional purpose of limiting maturity mismatching in foreign currencies. More usually, however, foreign currency business is not subject to liquidity rules or guidelines.

Some countries (notably the United States) assess liquidity on a worldwide consolidated basis, some (such as Japan) include foreign branches but not subsidiaries in the assessment process, while others (for instance, France) confine their regular assessments to banks' domestic offices. Branches of foreign banks may or may not be assessed for liquidity by the host authority.

Permissible Business Activities

Typically, banks are limited as to the kinds of business in which they may engage. Such restrictions may in part reflect non-prudential concerns such as potential conflicts of interest or undue concentrations of economic power; there is no generally accepted view as to what is and what is not legitimate banking business. Some countries (notably the United States, Canada and Japan) formally separate commercial from investment banking and prohibit commercial banks from underwriting equities. Restrictions are more often imposed on banks' investments in property and also on equity holdings in non-bank companies. In the latter case limits may be expressed as a percentage of the lending bank's capital, the ceiling here varying between 100 per cent (France) and 25 per cent (Hong Kong), and/or as a percentage of the non-bank company's equity, with the maximum holding ranging from 2 per cent (Italy) to 20 per cent (France).

Several countries prohibit the mixing of banking and non-banking business within the bank entity, while permitting participation in at least some kinds of non-banking activity through bank holding companies, subsidiaries and/or minority interests. Other countries (such as the Netherlands) permit the bank entity itself to engage directly in non-banking business but limit the scope for investment in non-bank companies. A third approach (illustrated by France before enactment of the 1984 Banking Law) permits a wider range of activities to be undertaken by a special category of separately regulated 'universal' banks. Finally, some countries (such as the United Kingdom, Switzerland and Germany) impose few formal restrictions on the kinds of business in which banks may engage, whether directly or through affiliates, although these countries typically impose heavy risk weightings on certain kinds of business activity for the purpose of calculating solvency requirements.

In the case of international operations, restrictions may be relaxed so as to enable foreign offices of domestic banks to compete more equally with the local banks in their country of residence. Alternatively, where the home authority imposes no authorisation requirements or other controls on bank's foreign establishments, the host jurisdiction alone determines the extent of permissible activities.

Foreign Currency Exposure

In the area of foreign exchange risk, most countries monitor banks' exposure and seek to ensure adequate internal control procedures, but there are marked differences in regulatory procedures. Some countries (including the United States, Canada and France) prefer to avoid general limits or norms, others (such as the Netherlands and Switzerland) apply incremental capital requirements to uncovered positions, while a third group (including the United Kingdom and Germany) imposes guidelines or formal limits on aggregate and, in some cases, individual foreign currency positions.

Where exposure limits are indicated, they are generally stated as a percentage of capital, although Japan places limits on each bank based in part on the volume of foreign exchange transactions. The United Kingdom operates an exposure guideline for all currencies together equal to 15 per cent of capital. Since this is expressed as an aggregate net short position (rather than a combined net long and short position) it is equivalent for most purposes to Germany's 30 per cent of capital limit which relates to the difference between a bank's foreign currency assets and liabilities. However, because the UK guideline embraces sterling, whereas Germany's excludes Deutschmark items, German banks have twice the latitude of UK banks when taking long or short positions in their local currency.

Few countries (the United States being an exception) monitor or regulate foreign currency exposure on a consolidated basis. Most countries exclude foreign subsidiaries, some exclude foreign branches and the treatment of local branches of foreign banks also varies.

Loan Concentration and Country Risk

Most supervisory authorities seek to limit risk concentrations by imposing formal or informal limits on each bank's loans to any single borrower. Stated as a percentage of the lending bank's capital, the limits vary between 100 per cent (Italy) and 15 per cent (the United States), subject to varying definitions of capital for this purpose. These limits may or may not be applied on a consolidated basis and branches of foreign banks may or may not be separately assessed (several countries, for instance, look to group rather than branch capital in this context).

In general, lending limits to individual borrowers are not applied to country risk exposure involving several borrowing entities from the same country. The United States is, however, an exception in that its 15 per cent statutory lending limit has been interpreted to apply collectively to loans to foreign governments, their agencies and instrumentalities unless the borrower has an independent source of repayment and the loan is to be used for the borrower's business. The US approach to country risk is also distinctive in that federal regulators categorise countries into three risk classes for the purpose of determining prudent lending limits for each country beyond which a bank's loans may be 'listed' or subject to comment. Furthermore, US regulators now have a statutory obligation to identify high-risk countries for the purpose of imposing mandatory provisions on bank loans to such countries. Few other authorities claim to take an independent view of individual countries' financial prospects, although the United Kingdom does make such an assessment. The Swiss authorities have used surveys of banks' own provisioning policies and loan preference records to make an objective assessment of high-risk country borrowers. More generally, supervision of country risk is influenced by the fact that regulators are often reluctant to be seen to challenge the judgement of commercial bankers in an area which can also give rise to political difficulties.

Until recently only the United States and United Kingdom measured country risk on the basis of world-wide consolidated data, embracing cross-border and non-local-currency loans to foreign borrowers adjusted for third party guarantees. Since 1982, however, most industrial countries have taken steps to monitor country risk on a consolidated basis, although consolidation techniques may vary. In several countries (for instance Germany and Switzerland) it is the monetary rather than the supervisory authorities who will obtain this information from the banks and it is not clear to what extent the data may be used for prudential rather than BIS-reporting purposes.

Several countries (notably Germany, Switzerland and Belgium) require banks to report their methods of country risk evaluation. On the other hand, not all authorities to whom such reports are made have developed a procedure for assessing the adequacy or otherwise of such evaluation techniques. There appears, too, to be a division between those regulators who feel they have a duty to screen banks' country risk evaluation methods and those who wish merely to alert banks to the need for country risk assessment.

While country risk is now among the foremost supervisory concerns, regulators have not attempted to impose an absolute limit on total country risk exposure, but focus instead on the need for diversification. Switzerland, however, applies a special premium capital requirement to banks' foreign assets, and the Belgian authorities have recommended that banks' exposure to countries outside the EEC's 'preferential zone' should not exceed 50 per cent of capital.

Few countries impose provisioning guidelines in respect of country risk. Among those that do are Switzerland, which requires a flat 20 per cent provision on loans to countries categorised as high risk, the United States, where legislation enacted in 1983 provides a statutory basis for country-specific provisioning, and Japan, which has also introduced country-specific provisioning guidelines. Several other countries attempt to ensure that there is reasonable consistency in banks' provisioning practices but leave the general level of provisioning to the judgement of banks and their auditors.

Bank Inspection

The role of bank inspections in the regulatory process varies considerably from country to country. At one end of the spectrum is the United States, where regular on-site examinations lie at the heart of the supervisory system and whose examiners are required to provide a composite rating of each bank on a standardised basis. At the other end of the spectrum is the United Kingdom, which eschews bank inspections in favour of a surveillance system based on interviews with management backed by extensive reported data. Routine on-site bank examinations, where they do occur, may be conducted by the supervisory authorities' own inspectorate (as in the United States, Canada, Italy, France and Japan), special auditors appointed and paid for by the authorities (Belgium), auditors licensed by the authorities and subject to special statutory duties (Switzerland) or general auditors (Germany). More generally, there is a tendency, exemplified by recent legislation in Hong

Kong and Singapore, to require bank auditors to report certain matters directly to the regulatory authorities. Official examinations may take place annually (as in Canada), every three to four years (Italy) or at intervals varying between one to two and ten years, depending on the size and standing of the institution concerned (France). Several countries confine on-site examinations to banks' head offices while others (such as Japan) make a random selection of branches for inspection purposes.

The principle of parental responsibility dictates that home country supervisors should have access to information about banks' foreign establishments. Few countries, however, conduct examinations of foreign branches or subsidiaries, although the United States aims to do so routinely (the Comptroller of the Currency has a permanent office in London for this purpose), while Japan and Germany also carry out periodic examinations of foreign branches. On the other hand, several countries, notably France, Luxembourg, Singapore and Switzerland, do not allow access to foreign inspectors; moreover, in all of these except France, bank secrecy laws limit the flow of information both between host and home authorities and between foreign-owned banks and their parent institutions. The principle of on-site examinations by foreign inspectors was not conceded in the 1983 EEC Directive on consolidated supervision, which instead provides for the appointment of auditors from the host country by the home country supervisory authorities.

POLICY IMPLICATIONS

Each national financial system has distinctive institutional characteristics which have a direct bearing on the authorities' approach to bank regulation. Some countries have a highly concentrated banking industry, favouring an informal regulatory regime based on direct contact with management, while others have a fragmented structure calling for more formal methods of control. Similarly, where supervisory responsibility is vested in a ministry of finance or central bank it is likely to be exercised with a wider degree of discretion than in those countries where a banking commission, operating within defined statutory limits, is the primary supervisory agency. In some countries, regulatory arrangements may vary according to whether a bank has a national or regional base, or is federally or state chartered. Finally, the concept and definition of a 'bank' varies from country to country and deposit-taking institutions may, for regulatory purposes, be differentiated according to whether or not they enjoy full banking status.

Despite these and other institutional differences among countries, certain common trends in regulatory practice have emerged in recent years, due in part to growing international co-operation in this area. In the first place, there has been a tendency towards a more formal regulatory framework even in those countries which have traditionally preferred a non-statutory approach to bank supervision. Secondly, several countries have in recent years extended their regulatory coverage to non-bank deposit-taking institutions. Thirdly, in the wake of the third world debt crisis greater attention is being given to the measurement and control of country risk as well as to undue concentrations of risk. Finally, there has been a general endorsement of the principle of consolidated supervision, for which purpose most national authorities are beginning to use consolidated data when applying solvency and other prudential criteria to domestic banks with foreign branches and/or subsidiaries (see Table 8).

Table 8 Supervision Based on Consolidated Accounts

Country	Solvency	Liquidity	Risk concentration	Currency exposure
Austria(**)	yes	yes	–	–
Belgium	yes	(b)	yes	(b)
Canada	yes	yes	yes	yes
Denmark	yes	yes (a)	yes	yes (a)
Finland	yes	yes	–	–
France	yes	–	yes	–
Germany(*)	(a)	–	(a)	(b)
Ireland	yes	yes	–	–
Italy	(b)	–	–	–
Japan	yes	yes	yes	–
Luxembourg(**)	yes	yes	yes	yes
Netherlands	yes	–	yes	yes
Portugal	–	–	–	–
Spain	(b)	(b)	(b)	(b)
Sweden	yes (a)	–	–	–
Switzerland	yes	–	–	–
United Kingdom	yes	–	yes	(***)
United States	yes	yes	yes	yes

Notes: (a)   Legal proposal.
         (b)   Under consideration.
         (*)   In Germany, foreign branches of German banks are supervised on a fully consolidated basis. With regard to foreign subsidiaries, supervision based on consolidated returns applies to a limited extent (solvency and risk concentration on the basis of the gentlemen's agreement).
        (**)   Branches only.
       (***)   Partial consolidation as supervision of currency exposure extends to foreign branches of United Kingdom-registered banks, but not to subsidiaries.
Source: R. M. Pecchioli, *The Internationalisation of Banking: the Policy Issues* (Paris, OECD, 1983), p.105.

Despite these signs of gradual convergence in national regulatory arrangements, both the comparative survey above and the country studies that follow give evidence of wide regulatory disparities in all the main areas of prudential control. With the emergence of global banking networks straddling numerous national jurisdictions, such unevenness in regulatory practice can endanger international financial stability in a number of ways. Banks headquartered in tightly regulated jurisdictions may be tempted to route their international (and even domestic) banking business through foreign establishments outside the reach of their home country regulatory authorities. Both Swiss and German banks have in the past used Luxembourg to bypass home country solvency regulations; Banco Ambrosiano employed a Luxembourg holding company to escape regulation of its overseas activities (as discussed in Chapter 6); and Schröder, Münchmeyer Hengst's downfall (also discussed in Chapter 6) was the result of excessive loan concentrations, mainly booked through Luxembourg. Taking this tendency to its ultimate conclusion, multinational banks may quite legitimately engage in 'regulatory arbitrage', routing business through a variety of financial centres to exploit regulatory loopholes or concessions in different jurisdictions. An illustration of such practice is given by the Citibank case study in Appendix 2.

At a more general level, disturbances originating in a weakly regulated jurisdiction can quickly spread to other parts of the international financial system. For instance, even tightly supervised jurisdictions may be destabilised by the presence of foreign banks originating from more permissive regimes. The interbank market also acts as a powerful transmission mechanicm through which any local breakdown in confidence may be rapidly generalised. The overall policy conclusion, therefore, is that in a truly global banking system, fragmented regulatory arrangements that give rise to wide variations in the quality and extent of prudential control tend to undermine international financial stability. More succinctly, the most permissive regimes can pose a serious threat to the system as a whole. Growing awareness of this fact has led to various official co-ordinating initiatives, which are described and assessed in Chapter 7.

COUNTRY STUDIES
Belgium

Under the 1935 Banking Law the Commission Bancaire (CB) is the body responsible for supervising the Belgian banking system. Although the CB has broad statutory powers to lay down prudential regulations, it has preferred to adopt a less formal approach. Accordingly, only banks' capital adequacy is governed by formal prudential ratios.[1] The CB also has authority to supervise banks' international operations on a consolidated basis, but has recently achieved this result on the basis of informal agreements. The CB's functions are confined largely to preventive regulation and supervision, emergency assistance and deposit protection being the province of a separately constituted public body, the Institut de Réescompte et de Garantie (IRG).

Entry Control Banks are required by Article 5 of the Banking Law to register with the CB before they can undertake operations. Registration is only effected when the CB is satisfied that the following criteria for authorisation have been satisfied: appropriate legal form (a bank must be a *société commerciale*, thereby excluding one-man firms); a minimum capital of BFr50 million; and a reputable and competent management. Branches of foreign banks are subject to the same authorisation requirements, the branch's capital endowment being for this purpose defined as capital funds permanently allocated to the branch for its activities in Belgium.

Capital Adequacy The solvency regulation stipulates that a bank's holdings of fixed assets should not exceed its capital and reserves. It also applies a test of the relationship of capital to risk assets, which (for prudential reasons) favours larger against smaller banks while requiring higher capital cover both for risky assets and for high concentrations of risk exposure to individual borrowers. The capital/risk assets test involves three steps. First, a bank's total risk quotient is calculated by aggregating the specified solvency requirements applicable to different categories of asset. For this purpose risk-bearing assets are in general subject to a 5 per cent capital requirement with an additional 2.5 per cent demanded where loans to individual borrowers exceed 20 per cent of capital; interbank loans attract a lower requirement of 1 per cent; and certain public sector loans (including those to member states of the EEC) are exempt. Secondly, the first and subsequent BFr10 million tranches of the total risk quotient are adjusted upwards by BFr10 million and BFr5 million respectively, the purpose and effect of this being to impose higher capital ratios on smaller banks. Finally, those assets (notably participations of over 10 per cent) requiring 100 per cent capital backing, having been excluded from the original risk quotient calculation, are added to the adjusted risk quotient to arrive at a bank's total capital requirement.

Capital is defined as the sum of equity capital, reserves (published and hidden), retained earnings and general provisions. In addition, the CB may, at its discretion and subject to certain restrictive conditions, include subordinated debt up to a limit of 50 per cent of total capital. As an exception to the general capital adequacy rules the CB may grant a concession to foreign banks' branches in Belgium and to their subsidiaries enjoying a parent bank guarantee whereby the ratios are applied to their Belgian business alone and not to their international business. The CB is now applying the solvency regulation on the basis of banks' consolidated accounts, covering subsidiaries that are majority owned or effectively controlled. Two circulars to this effect were issued in February and March 1982.

Liquidity Control In contrast to the detailed requirements relating to capital adequacy, the CB does not formally regulate liquidity, although it has the statutory authority to do so. Liquidity is monitored through the banks' normal statistical returns and through auditors' assessments. No precise definition of what constitutes sufficient liquidity has been formulated.

Permissible Business Activities The only statutory restrictions on the kinds of business banks may undertake relate to their equity investments. In general, banks are prohibited from holding shares in non-bank companies, but this so-called 'law against universal banks' has been relaxed in recent years. In particular, banks may now hold shares in connection with their underwriting business, while the CB is authorised to allow investments in bank-related businesses such as leasing, factoring and data processing.

Foreign Currency Exposure The CB is authorised to issue regulations establishing limits for foreign exchange exposure but has so far declined to do so. The solvency regulation imposes a 0.2 per cent capital requirement on total claims arising from forward foreign exchange transactions, but there is no requirement relating to uncovered positions, whether spot or forward. Nevertheless, banks are subject to extensive reporting requirements on their foreign exchange exposure and the CB, through bank auditors, seeks to ensure that each bank's internal controls are fully adequate.

Loan Concentrations and Country Risk Loans to individual customers exceeding 20 per cent of the lending bank's capital are required by the solvency regulation to be backed by additional capital (see section on capital adequacy above). The CB also has statutory authority to formulate and apply loan limits. To date it has not issued regulations in this area but it has as a matter of practice recommended certain banks to reduce their loans to single borrowers in cases where the loans exceeded 50 per cent of the bank's capital.

There are no formal limits on country risk exposure. However, the authorities collect and monitor data on country risk and, since November 1980, have required bank auditors to report on each bank's approach to country risk evaluation. The CB has also strongly recommended that loans to countries outside the EEC's 'preferential zone' should not exceed 50 per cent of the lending bank's capital. There are no provisioning guidelines for international loans, but banks must explain and justify the provisions they make.

Bank Examination Under Belgian law bank auditors play a special role in the supervisory process.[2] They are appointed and paid for by the CB, and their statutory functions go well beyond the verification of the annual accounts; for instance, they must satisfy themselves of each bank's compliance with the regulations and must also monitor the bank's solvency and liquidity position. While reliance is placed on bank auditors for routine supervision purposes, the CB maintains its own inspectorate which is used for on-the-spot checks, which usually only take place in special circumstances.

Canada

The Office of the Inspector General of Banks (OIB), as the agency responsible to the minister of finance for the administration of the Bank Act, is charged with supervision of the banking system. The OIB must report to the minister at least once a year on the financial soundness of each bank and advise the minister on applications for the incorporation of banks.

The OIB's traditional approach to supervision has been characterised by informality, bilateral discussions and an absence of regulations and directives. However, the latest decennial revision of the Bank Act, which came into force at the end of 1980,[3] in providing for the chartering of foreign banks increased the number of federally supervised banks from 12 to around 70. Accordingly, the new Act authorises the issuance of regulations on capital adequacy and liquidity, as well as directives to individual banks, should the need arise. It remains to be seen whether changed circumstances will oblige the authorities to resort to such formal controls in due course.

The 1980 Bank Act for the first time provides for the chartering of foreign bank subsidiaries, while continuing to prohibit the establishment of branches of foreign banks. Foreign-owned banks nevertheless face important constraints on their expansion: individually their domestic assets must not exceed 20 times their deemed authorised capital (changes in which can be made at the discretion of the authorities) and collectively their domestic assets must not exceed 16 per cent of the total domestic assets of all banks in Canada.[4]

The revised Act also provides for the incorporation of two classes of banks: Schedule A banks, whose shares are widely held, and Schedule B banks (including foreign bank subsidiaries) whose shares are closely held.

Entry Control No bank can commence business without the approval of the authorities, although only foreign bank subsidiaries are subject to formal licensing requirements. The criteria applied in considering approvals include capital adequacy (generally over and above the statutory minima for authorised capital set out in the Bank Act) and a reputable and experienced management. Foreign banks wishing to establish Canadian subsidiaries must meet additional statutory and non-statutory criteria, notably: (a) the potential to make a contribution to competitive banking in Canada; (b) reciprocity for Canadian banks in the home jurisdiction; (c) a certificate of good standing from the home jurisdiction; (d) a favourable earnings record over the last five years;

(e) adequate supervision by the home supervisory authority; and (f) a letter of comfort with regard to the proposed subsidiary.

There are no domestically imposed branching constraints on Canadian banks, either at home or abroad.

Capital Adequacy The 1980 Bank Act requires every bank to maintain adequate capital in relation to its operations and to comply with any regulations or directives that may be issued in this connection. In practice, the authorities have continued to avoid formal regulation and rely instead on broad guidelines which focus on banks' gearing ratios.

In 1983 the OIB developed a new basis for measuring capital adequacy, which distinguishes between primary and secondary capital. Primary capital consists of shareholders' equity, permanent preferred shares, long-term convertible preferred shares and permanent subordinated debentures; secondary capital comprises redeemable preferred shares and subordinated debentures with: (a) a minimum original maturity of five years; (b) straight line amortisation in the last five years of life; and (c) no restrictive covenants. Secondary capital counts towards total capital in so far as it does not exceed primary capital. The total capital gearing ratio (gross assets divided by total capital) should not exceed 30× for well diversified Canadian banks, 25× for other domestic banks and 20× for foreign bank subsidiaries, although this last norm may be relaxed for larger, well diversified institutions. As from November 1981 gearing ratios have been calculated on a consolidated basis.

Liquidity Control The Bank Act requires every bank to maintain adequate and appropriate forms of liquidity, with parallel provision for the issuance of regulations and directives. To date neither regulations nor informal guidelines have been utilised, although liquidity is reviewed regularly as part of the bank examination process.

Foreign bank subsidiaries have been advised that they should not fund more than 5 per cent of their Canadian assets with foreign currency liabilities. This is to ensure that foreign banks establish themselves in the local money markets and do not become over-dependent on offshore funding that could be interrupted.

Permissible Business Activities The revised Bank Act sets out the powers of banks while also specifying certain restrictions on their activities. Subject to certain limited exceptions, banks may not own more than 10 per cent of the voting shares of any Canadian company; they cannot undertake insurance business or fiduciary activities, or underwrite equities; and there are various restrictions on their dealings in securities and property holdings. However, the Act does permit banks to engage in factoring and leasing through wholly owned subsidiaries.

The limitations on Canadian banks' activities apply equally to their international operations.

Foreign Currency Exposure There are neither formal limits nor informal guidelines relating to banks' foreign exchange exposure. However, the authorities attach considerable importance to internal management controls (the OIB has carried out special inspections of control procedures in the big six Canadian banks); banks must submit their currency exposure limits as agreed by their respective boards; and *de facto* exposure amounting in aggregate to over, say, 10 per cent of capital would be a matter for official concern.

Loan Concentration and Country Risk In 1982 the OIB advised banks to limit loans to single names or connected names to 25 per cent of share-holders' equity, or 50 per cent in special circumstances. For foreign bank subsidiaries the indicated ceiling is 50 per cent, rising to 100 per cent in special circumstances, but these higher limits are to be adjusted down-wards in due course. Country exposures are not subject to a formal or informal ceiling although the authorities obtain consolidated exposure data each quarter and banks are expected to justify their country risk evaluation procedures.

In mid-1984 the OIB circulated new disclosure rules prohibiting the accrual of interest on loans more than 90 days in arrears, except where management is satisfied that there is no reasonable doubt about the collectability of principal and interest. At the same time the OIB issued provisioning guidelines covering loans to some 36 countries.

Bank Examination The OIB has a statutory duty to inspect banks annually to ensure that the provisions of the Act relating to the safety of the creditors and shareholders are being observed and that the banks are in a sound financial condition. Each on-site inspection typically involves three examiners for a period of two to four days, with particular attention being given to the quality of loans. Inspections are confined to the bank's head office where all relevant information relating to branches and subsidiaries is expected to be maintained. Accordingly, inspections do not extend to domestic banks' establishments abroad. Bank exami-nations, together with quarterly statistical returns, form the basis of the supervisory process.

France

Prior to July 1984 regulation of the French banking system was divided among the Treasury, the Bank of France, the Conseil National du Crédit (CNC) and the Commission de Controle des Banques (CCB), with the Association Française des Banques (AFB) also playing a formal role in the supervisory process. On 24 January 1984 a new Banking Act was approved which came into effect on 20 July of the same year.[5] Under this

Act the CNC retains a consultative role but general regulatory powers are exercised by a new committee, the Comité de la Réglementation (CR), while the granting of authorisations to individual institutions is the responsibility of the Comité des Établissements de Crédit (CEC). The Commission Bancaire (CB) replaces the CCB with expanded supervisory responsibilities over all credit institutions.

The commercial banks were legally categorised into deposit banks, investment banks and medium- and long-term credit banks. However, restrictions on the permissible activities of each type of institution (for instance the extent to which investment banks must rely on term rather than sight deposits) have been eased in recent years and the functional distinctions have become correspondingly less important. The new Banking Act weakens these distinctions further and for the first time brings all credit institutions within a single legal framework.

The CCB had been supervising the solvency of French banks on a consolidated basis *de facto* prior to 1984 but the new Banking Act makes consolidated supervision a legal requirement. The Act also empowers the CB to inspect the foreign branches and subsidiaries of French banks.

Entry Control Banks must obtain the approval of the CEC before commencing business. The new statutory requirements include: (a) a minimum capital to be determined by the CR; (b) corporate legal form; (c) management consisting of at least two people of integrity and adequate experience; and (d) that the applicant's objectives are attainable in conditions compatible with the healthy development of the banking system. These criteria apply equally to foreign banks seeking to establish branches or subsidiaries in France.

Capital Adequacy An experimental solvency regulation introduced by the CCB in 1979 remains in force.[6] The regulation establishes a risk assets/capital ratio target of 5 per cent which banks are expected to meet by June 1985. For this purpose assets are accorded different weightings depending on their risk category: for instance, ordinary advances, including loans to foreign governments, are accorded a weighting of 100 per cent, interbank loans are subject to a weighting of 5 per cent and loans to or guaranteed by the French government and certain public sector bodies are given a zero weighting.

Capital is defined to include share capital, reserves, general provisions and (to a theoretically unlimited extent) subordinated debt, with a deduction for investments in banking subsidiaries and affiliates. Under the 1984 Banking Act the solvency ratio must be applied on the basis of consolidated accounts. French branches of foreign banks may be exempted from the solvency ratio requirement on condition that solvency is adequately regulated in the country of origin and that the parent bank gives a formal guarantee to support its French branch.

Liquidity Control The CCB introduced two liquidity ratio requirements under its previous statutory authority to regulate banks.[7] The first relates liquid assets (defined to include cash, interbank deposits of under three months' maturity, rediscountable paper and various marketable securities) to short-term liabilities (liabilities at sight and due within three months) and specifies that, in the case of investment and deposit banks, liquid assets must at all times equal at least 60 per cent of short-term liabilities. The second requirement, which applies to all commercial banks, relates certain medium and long-term loans to capital plus savings accounts (essentially deposits with over three months to maturity) and specifies that if the former exceeds the latter by a factor of more than three, then an alternative liquidity rule must be met. This in turn specifies that 80 per cent of medium and long-term loans must be covered by capital plus savings accounts plus interbank borrowings with at least two years to maturity.

These rules are subject to special procedures where foreign currency assets or liabilities exceed 10 per cent of a bank's balance sheet. In such cases the 60 per cent liquidity ratio applies only to French franc items, the foreign currency business then being monitored rather than regulated, while the medium-term liquidity co-efficient must be calculated separately for both French franc and foreign currency transactions.

French subsidiaries of foreign banks are in principle subject to the above requirements and in order to ensure that the medium-term liquidity co-efficient is met in respect of foreign currency business the authorities may demand a guarantee or stand-by line of credit from the parent bank.

In addition to the above liquidity rules, banks have since 1967 been prohibited from paying interest on sight deposits. This restriction is designed to encourage reliance on longer-term deposits and thereby reduce the degree of maturity mismatching in banks' balance sheets.

Permissible Business Activities Banks are in general prohibited from engaging directly in activities which have no connection with banking. However, deposit banks may purchase holdings in non-bank companies up to a ceiling of 20 per cent of the share capital of any one company, so long as the total amount of such holdings does not exceed the investing bank's capital. Investment banks may hold 100 per cent of the share capital of a company but must not finance non-bank equity holdings with sight deposits and term deposits due in less than two years. Deposit banks are not permitted to invest their sight deposits, or term deposits due in less than two years, in property. The above rules will be replaced in due course by regulations issued by the CR.

Foreign Currency Exposure Although, for balance of payments reasons, French banks are prohibited from taking open positions against the

French franc, they are permitted to take positions in one foreign currency against another. Such exposure is nevertheless monitored closely by the authorities, who may intervene where risks are considered excessive.

Loan Concentrations and Country Risk Under a new standard introduced in 1979, no customer may account for a risk equal to more than 75 per cent of a bank's capital, although the rule does not apply where the risk amounts to 5 per cent or less of the bank's total risk exposure to all customers and to 50 per cent or less of the customer's bank debts.[8] In addition, the total of individual risks in excess of 25 per cent of capital must be less than ten times capital. Interbank lending is excluded for the purpose of these calculations. Under the 1984 Act these limits are to be applied on a consolidated basis.

The loan limits do not cover country risk exposure which is, however, monitored through reporting procedures which embrace French banks' world-wide operations.

Bank Examination Bank auditors do not have a special role to play in the supervisory process and the authorities therefore rely on on-site examinations by the Bank of France's inspectorate to verify prudential returns, assess internal control procedures and examine the quality of loans. Inspections may be *ad hoc* or routine (though the frequency may vary from every one or two years to every ten years), and under the 1984 Act may now extend to the foreign branches and subsidiaries of French banks.

Hong Kong

Prudential regulation of banks in Hong Kong is based on the Banking Ordinance of 1964 (as amended) which is administered by the Commissioner of Banking (CB).[9] For regulatory purposes there was until 1981 a two-tier banking structure comprising licensed banks and registered deposit-taking companies (DTCs). However, the rapid growth of DTCs raised concerns about the size and stability of the secondary banking sector and led to a new distinction between licensed and registered DTCs.[10] Registered DTCs were required to phase out their short-term retail borrowing by mid-1983 and thereafter to accept from the public only deposits of more than HK$50,000 with a maturity of more than three months. Licensed DTCs, on the other hand, can take deposits of over HK$500,000 for any maturity. Only the licensed banks can now accept short-term retail deposits.

At the beginning of 1983 the new banking structure comprised 125 licensed banks, an emergent group of 22 licensed DTCs or merchant banks and over 300 registered DTCs. Registered DTCs have become more reliant on interbank funding with the phasing out of their retail deposits and this has meant a steady decline in the number of 'independent' DTCs, i.e. those not owned by banks.

Reflecting the importance of local banks' overseas operations, the Banking Ordinance was amended in early 1982 with a view to strengthening the CB's supervision of these activities.[11] At the same time the CB's discretion to allow foreign supervisors to inspect banks in Hong Kong was formalised. Both these initiatives were designed to conform to the principle of parental responsibility in supervisory matters.

Entry Control Bank licences are issued by the Governor in Council on the advice of the CB. Although there are a number of criteria that must be met before a licence will be granted, the decision whether or not to grant remains discretionary and from time to time the authorities have declared moratoria on new licensing with a view to avoiding excessive competition within the banking industry. Licences are granted only in respect of branches, not subsidiaries, of foreign banks on the grounds that branches enjoy the full support of the group to which they belong. Such branches may be licensed only if: (a) the parent bank is effectively supervised in its country of origin and the parent's supervisors have no objection; (b) the parent bank has total assets of at least US$12 billion; and (c) some acceptable form of reciprocity exists. Locally incorporated banks, on the other hand, must have paid-up share capital of at least HK$100 million, deposits from the public of at least HK$1.75 billion and total assets of HK$2.5 billion, and they must have been in the deposit-taking business for at least ten years.

Capital Adequacy A licensed bank incorporated in Hong Kong is required to appropriate at least one-third of its published earnings each year to a published reserve until the paid-up capital and published reserve together amount to HK$200 million. In addition, banks are encouraged to maintain inner reserves which can be used to absorb unexpected losses. Beyond this the CB has recently been given statutory powers to obtain detailed information from locally incorporated banks relating to their overseas subsidiaries and affiliates. It is intended that such data should in due course permit the introduction of a capital ratio to be applied on a consolidated world-wide basis. The capital adequacy of banks incorporated outside Hong Kong is, however, viewed as a matter for the parent bank's supervisory authorities.

Liquidity Control Hong Kong's liquidity rules, which relate to monthly averages, have a prudential rather than a monetary function. The rules embrace foreign as well as local currency business and they apply also to local branches of foreign banks, which for this purpose are deemed to be separate entities. Banks must hold the equivalent of 25 per cent of their deposits in the form of liquid assets realisable within seven days and 15 per cent of their deposits (included in the 25 per cent) in the form of highly liquid assets realisable on demand. The amount of liquid assets is calculated after deducting short-term interbank borrowings from other banks in Hong Kong. Highly liquid assets include cash, gold and demand and call money at other banks, while the broader category of liquid assets includes money at short notice at other banks, certain export bills of exchange, various government or government-guaranteed securities which are deemed to be realisable within seven days, and such money market instruments as the Financial Secretary may specify. From April 1983 banks and licensed DTCs have been allowed to include marketable CDs as part of their liquid assets, up to a maximum of 2 per cent of their deposits.

Permissible Business Activities There is no formal separation of commercial and investment banking in Hong Kong. A bank must not engage in any wholesale or retail trade but can provide most financial services, including the underwriting of securities, so long as the book value of its non-bank shareholdings does not exceed 25 per cent of its capital and reserves. A similar 25 per cent limit applies to holdings of property (excluding bank premises) while unsecured lending to directors, their relatives and related companies is limited to 10 per cent of capital and reserves. All three classes of restricted asset are subject to an aggregate limit of 55 per cent of capital, or 80 per cent if account is also taken of property used as banking premises.

Foreign Currency Exposure Non-consolidated foreign currency exposure data is collected on a month-end basis but there are no guidelines in this area. Formal exposure limits might be expected to give rise to difficulties in that the Hong Kong Bank, which in effect holds the banking system's residual liquidity offshore, has a naturally long position in foreign currencies (windfall profits and losses from this exposure being taken into or absorbed by hidden reserves).

Loan Concentration and Country Risk For both banks and DTCs there is a maximum lending limit to any one customer of 25 per cent of capital and reserves. For an institution incorporated outside Hong Kong the limit is measured against the capital of the head office in the country of incorporation. Locally incorporated but foreign-owned DTCs are expected to provide letters of comfort from their parent shareholders and in such cases the 25 per cent limit may be waived, if the parent bank is under adequate supervision in its home country. These letters of comfort are not legally binding, although they must be the result of a board decision and be issued with the knowledge of the parent institution's supervisory authority.

Under a recently introduced regulation, where a bank or DTC has granted credit to a foreign bank and the CB believes this is not in the interests of the lending institution, he may prohibit further advances to the foreign bank or, where moneys are at call, instruct the bank or DTC to demand repayment.[12]

The loan concentration limit does not apply to country risk where several borrowing entities are involved. Country risk exposure is not at present regulated, although consolidated exposure data are provided for the purposes of reporting to the Bank for International Settlements.

Bank Examination The CB aims to examine locally incorporated banks and DTCs once every 12 months and branches of foreign banks once every 24 months. In March 1982 the CB was also given powers to inspect the foreign branches (but not subsidiaries) of locally incorporated banks. This legislation formalised the existing practice of allowing appropriate foreign supervisory authorities to inspect the Hong Kong branches or subsidiaries of banks incorporated in their jurisdiction. It also relaxed the domestic secrecy laws so as to permit the CB to provide information on local banks to appropriate foreign supervisory authorities.

An amendment to the Banking Ordinance that came into force at the end of 1983 places special statutory responsibilities on auditors, who may now be required to report any contravention of general banking regulations as well as matters adversely affecting the financial condition of a bank.[13]

Italy

The Bank of Italy is responsible for regulating the domestic banking system, subject to directives from the Inter-Ministerial Committee for Credit and Savings (ICCS) and within the framework of the Banking Law of 1936.[14] The Banking Law draws a distinction between short-term and longer-term banking business: banks entitled to accept short-term deposits (defined as up to 18 months) are not permitted to accept medium- or long-term deposits and their term lending beyond 18 months is also subject to restrictions.

The structure of the banking system is complex and, at the regional level, highly fragmented. There are some 900 rural, co-operative and savings banks, over 100 privately owned commercial banks and around 30 commercial banks (including the four largest) controlled either by the Treasury or the state industrial conglomerate, IRI.

In moving towards the principle of consolidated supervision, the Bank of Italy collects data on banks' individual majority-owned subsidiaries but does not require routine reporting of consolidated prudential data. Legislation now before parliament authorises the Bank of Italy to supervise banks on a consolidated basis in line with the EEC Directive on consolidation.

Entry Control Banks may not commence business or open new branches without prior authorisation, the main criteria being minimum capital, a reputable management and economic justification. The Bank of Italy has not laid down a uniform minimum capital requirement, although branches of foreign banks must possess dotation capital of at least $12 million. Since 1966 the economic need criterion has been invoked to withhold all new bank authorisations, other than those for branches of foreign banks. In addition, the Bank of Italy has confined the smaller banks' domestic branching activities to prescribed geographical regions, with a view to avoiding excessive competition which might threaten the stability of the banking system.

Italian banks seeking to establish foreign branches or subsidiaries must obtain the approval of the Bank of Italy, which is in practice granted only to the larger institutions. In 1981 the Bank of Italy introduced the stipulation that shareholdings by Italian banks in foreign banks should not be held through intermediate non-bank or holding companies. Any bank wishing to acquire a shareholding in a foreign bank must also give an undertaking that information necessary for proper supervision will be supplied to the Italian authorities. These principles were implemented after the Banco Ambrosiano collapse in respect of Italian banks' Luxembourg holding companies. Current legislative proposals would also give the Bank of Italy powers over the ownership of banks so that if, for instance, the owners were not identifiable the voting rights attached to the shares could be suspended.

Capital Adequacy The Bank of Italy has statutory powers to lay down minimum capital ratios, subject to the approval of the ICCS. However, no formal ratios have been established, the official view being that standardised capital adequacy requirements are inappropriate to a heterogeneous banking system such as Italy's, that such requirements might prove to be an unacceptable burden given the various constraints imposed on banks' balance sheets for monetary policy purposes, and that the loan concentration and liquidity ratios (among others) already provide banks with an incentive to maintain their capital base.

The Bank of Italy monitors capital adequacy on the basis of both gearing and capital/risk asset ratios. Capital is defined to include reserves (undisclosed reserves are no longer allowed) and general provisions, but not loan capital. One of the main objectives of the monitoring process is to identify those banks whose capital ratios are significantly below the average for their category.

Liquidity Control Although there is no formal prudential liquidity requirement, the Bank of Italy does monitor banks' liquidity on the basis of seven separate ratios. For this purpose foreign currency and local currency items are considered both separately and in the aggregate while a distinction is also made between primary and secondary liquidity.

Banks entitled to accept short-term deposits may now make medium-term loans, with maturities ranging from 18 months to five years, but only up to a total of between 10 and 15 per cent of their deposit liabilities. The precise limit is calculated according to a scale based on the lending banks' capital ratio. Foreign offices (including branches) of Italian banks are subject to specific ceilings on medium-term lending, determined on a case-by-case basis.

Permissible Business Activities In practice the Bank of Italy does not permit banks to engage in business other than banking and equity participations in non-bank companies are generally limited to complementary activities such as data processing. Beyond this, banks are entitled to make share purchases of up to 2 per cent of a company's share capital without prior authorisation, but fixed assets plus equity holdings must not in total exceed 100 per cent of the acquiring bank's capital. Banks are not normally permitted to invest in property other than their own premises.

Foreign Currency Exposure No formal prudential limits are applied although net positions in individual currencies must be reported at least monthly and foreign exchange activity is strictly regulated for exchange control purposes. In particular, banks may not take net positions against the lira and must maintain balanced positions in US dollars, in EEC currencies taken together and in other currencies taken together.

Loan Concentration and Country Risk Loans to a single customer may not exceed the lending bank's capital without special authorisation from the Bank of Italy. Furthermore, 'large' loans (defined as those exceeding 20 per cent of capital) may not in total exceed a ceiling varying between 25 and 40 per cent of non-bank deposits, the precise limit depending on the bank's capital ratio. These loan limits are not, however, directly applicable to country risk exposure involving several borrowing entities from the same country.

With effect from the beginning of 1983 a new quarterly reporting system has been introduced covering the country risk exposure of Italian banks. This quantifies exposure for the parent bank, its foreign branches and foreign subsidiaries (taken separately), and provides a maturity breakdown of foreign claims as well as details of risk transfers via guarantees.

Bank Examination On-site bank inspections, aimed *inter alia* at verifying prudential returns and assessing the quality of loans, are carried out by the Bank of Italy on both an *ad hoc* and a routine basis, the broad objective being to examine each bank's head office every three to four years. Foreign offices of Italian banks are not normally inspected, although under a recently concluded bilateral agreement the US and

Italian supervisory authorities may inspect branches of their respective domestic banks on each other's territory.

Japan

At the end of 1981 Japan had 76 domestic commercial banks, comprising 13 city banks and 63 regional banks. In addition there were 70 foreign banks, 10 long-term lending banks, 71 *sogo* or mutual banks and some 1,000 credit associations and co-operatives.[15] The foreign banks' operations are in effect confined to branch rather than subsidiary form, reflecting in part the authorities' preference for branches on prudential grounds.

The relatively small number of commercial banks has enabled the authorities to adopt a highly informal approach to bank supervision based on administrative guidance. For this purpose the Banking Bureau and the International Finance Bureau of the Ministry of Finance (MoF) are the main supervisory agencies, although the Bank of Japan (BoJ) also has a role in this area which it fulfils in close consultation with the MoF. The new Banking Law, which came into effect on 1 April 1982,[16] is intended, among other things, to shift the emphasis away from administrative guidance towards a more formal regulatory regime. However, the new law does not have a great deal to say on the subject of prudential regulation and the MoF retains considerable discretionary powers regarding those matters which are covered. Furthermore, informal guidance continues to be given outside the new legal framework.

The Japanese authorities have accepted the desirability of supervising banks on a consolidated basis and are in the process of implementing this principle.

Entry Control All banks must be licensed by the MoF. The statutory licensing requirements are: (a) adequate resources (a minimum capital of 1 billion yen is currently specified but this may be raised by Cabinet Order); (b) a reputable and competent management; and (c) fulfilment of an economic need criterion. The MoF may impose additional conditions in the public interest while foreign banks are subject to a reciprocity test as well as to any other special conditions that may be determined by Cabinet Order.

Capital Adequacy The MoF does not impose formal capital ratios but it can and does influence banks' capital accumulation by offering guidance on maximum dividend pay-outs. The recently introduced ceilings on loans to single borrowers (see section on 'Loan concentration' below) have also induced banks to increase their capital. For the purposes of capital adequacy assessment capital is defined as equity capital plus reserves. Until 1982 the issuance of subordinated debt was allowed only to the long-term credit banks but in February 1983 the MoF began to allow city banks to issue bonds in overseas markets through their foreign sub-sidiaries.[17]

Liquidity Control As with capital adequacy, the MoF has declined to impose general liquidity norms, although it has encouraged banks to raise the ratio of current assets to total deposits to at least 30 per cent. Following the disturbed financial conditions of 1974/75 the Japanese authorities have also sought to limit maturity mismatching in banks' Eurocurrency operations, the original guidance here being that 40 per cent of term lending for one year or more should be funded by term deposits or other debt of over one year's maturity. In February 1983 this ratio was raised to 45 per cent and for loans longer than three years the proportion of borrowings with matching term was set at 15 per cent. These guidelines have been applied to the foreign branches but not subsidiaries of Japanese banks, although foreign subsidiaries have recently been authorised to issue long-term debt (as noted above). Finally, the concentration of domestic long-term lending in the long-term credit banks and trust banks is calculated to reduce maturity mismatching in the banking system as a whole.

Permissible Business Activities Following the American pattern, the Securities and Exchange Act of 1948 prohibits banks from underwriting securities other than public sector bonds. However, the separation of commercial and investment banking is regarded as an historical accident rather than a prudential necessity and is currently under review. Already the distinction is becoming blurred in overseas markets, where sub-sidiaries of Japanese banks underwrite Eurobonds and the European offices of Japanese security houses have, with MoF approval, applied for local banking status. This issue apart, the 1982 Banking Law prohibits banks from engaging in activities other than banking, as defined, while the Anti-Monopoly Law restricts banks' equity investments in bank-related businesses.

Foreign Currency Exposure Monitoring of foreign currency exposure embraces the foreign branches but not the subsidiaries of Japanese banks. Each bank is given an absolute net (spot and forward combined) exposure limit based on both the volume of its foreign exchange trans-actions and its capital base. A general norm, measured in terms of percentage of capital exposed, is not applied, although as a matter of practice exposure is generally kept below 10 per cent of capital.

Loan Concentration and Country Risk The Banking Law provides for maximum lending limits to individual borrowers to be determined by Cabinet Order, subject to certain exemptions in respect of loans to or guaranteed by the public sector. The present ruling is that loans to a single borrower should not exceed 20 per cent of capital in the case of commercial banks, 30 per cent for long-term credit and trust banks and 40 per cent for the one specialised foreign exchange bank (Bank of Tokyo). This differentiation reflects the traditional business roles of the institutions concerned – for instance, the Bank of Tokyo has large exposures to the Japanese trading houses – rather than special prudential considerations. The loan limits applicable to Japanese branches of foreign banks are calculated on the basis of each bank's group capital.

Since 1979 Japanese banks have been subject to a 20 per cent of capital limit on medium- and long-term loans to individual countries. Prior to 1982, the MoF had not monitored banks' short-term country risk exposure but in September of that year it proposed the imposition of a new 30 per cent of capital limit on loans of all maturities to single countries.[18] However, in order to accommodate new lending under IMF programmes this proposal, as well as the original 20 per cent limit, was suspended in favour of a more flexible policy towards international lending.[19] Under guidelines introduced in February 1983 banks are expected to restrict their foreign currency assets to 15 times equity capital while limiting interbank transactions to less than 60 per cent of foreign currency assets.[20] Also, beginning with the half year to March 1983 the MoF has advised banks to maintain loan loss reserves against loans to specified financially troubled countries.[21] Under these guidelines total loan loss reserves (which were made tax deductible in early 1984) should not exceed 5 per cent of a bank's loan portfolio, but for loans to individual countries the guideline figure may be as high as 50 per cent. The categories of countries subject to such reserves are: (a) countries whose payments of principal or interest are more than one year overdue; (b) countries which have signed refinancing or rescheduling agreements within the last five years; and (c) countries that have requested a rescheduling of loans.

The MoF has given extensive guidance on the overall volume of Japanese banks' new international lending (generally expressed as a percentage of the total syndicated loan market), the proportion of such lending to be directed to developing countries, the maximum participation of Japanese banks in individual syndications (recently raised from 20 per cent to 50 per cent), the desirability of Japanese banks exercising independent judgement by acting as lead managers and agents, and the size of spreads. Guidance in these areas reflects a number of concerns, notably the MoF's view that, because of their domestic business experience based on a rigid interest rate structure, Japanese banks are inclined to compete for volume in international markets without sufficient regard for price and quality.

In March 1983 the Japan Centre for International Finance was established by the domestic banking industry with the backing of the Japanese authorities. The purpose of this research unit is to provide information on country risk to its sponsors.

Bank Examination On-site bank examinations are of three kinds. The MoF's International Finance Bureau carries out inspections mainly in the area of foreign exchange dealings; the Banking Bureau undertakes a broader prudential examination; and the Bank of Japan (which has a separate inspectorate) makes a mainly qualitative assessment of loan portfolios and bank management. The Banking Bureau aims to examine the head office and randomly selected branches (including foreign branches) of domestic banks every two to three years. Japanese branches of foreign banks are examined every five to six years, although foreign supervisors may be permitted to carry out their own inspections.

Luxembourg

Since June 1983 the newly established Luxembourg Monetary Institute (MIL) has been responsible for supervising and regulating the banking system, having taken over this function from the former Commissariat au Controle des Banques.[22] In exercising its regulatory responsibilities the MIL is advised by a Consultative Committee which includes representatives from the banking industry but not from the government.

Because Luxembourg has no central bank or lender of last resort the authorities look to foreign parent institutions (and their central banks) for support of their Luxembourg operations.

Entry Control The authorisation requirements for banks wishing to establish themselves in Luxembourg include a reputable and competent management and a minimum capital which is currently set at LFr350 million, of which LFr250 million must be paid up. The relatively high minimum paid-up capital requirement applies equally to branches of foreign banks, and is designed to limit market entry to banks of substance.

Each bank must also show that it is of good credit standing, which may be demonstrated by securing irrevocable stand-by credit lines from other banks. The adequacy of such credit lines is treated on a case-by-case basis. No letters of comfort are required from the parents of foreign bank subsidiaries.

Capital Adequacy In addition to the minimum capital requirement, the MIL is authorised, with the approval of the Ministry of Finance, to set a mandatory solvency ratio (ratio of capital to liabilities) within a statutory range of 3–10 per cent. Since its inception this ratio has been held at the minimum level of 3 per cent. The ratio is applied to the combined assets and liabilities of Luxembourg banks and their foreign branches and also to the branches of foreign banks.

In early 1984 the MIL requested banks to provide consolidated accounts so that capital adequacy and other requirements could be applied on a consolidated basis, in conformity with the EEC Directive on this subject. It is intended that legislation will formalise these arrangements in due course.

Capital is defined to include share capital, reserves, retained earnings and general provisions while subordinated debt due in over one year may, at the MIL's discretion, be included up to 50 per cent of the amount of paid-up capital and reserves. In the case of branches of foreign banks, liabilities exclude short-term liabilities to the bank's head office. As a separate requirement, fixed assets plus participations must not exceed capital (excluding subordinated debt).

Since mid-1983 fiduciary deposits have been excluded from both sides of banks' balance sheets and are not therefore included in the assessment of capital adequacy.[23] This reflects the new legal position whereby fiduciary depositors have a direct claim on the assets in which their deposits are invested, instead of being creditors of the deposit-taking bank.

Liquidity Control The MIL does not enforce any prudential liquidity ratios, although it has recommended that banks should hold liquid assets (as defined) equal to 30 per cent of their liabilities.

Permissible Business Activities There are no statutory restrictions on the type of business that a bank may undertake. Nor are there any restrictions on shareholdings in non-bank companies, although such participations are included in fixed assets and must therefore be covered by equity capital.

Foreign Currency Exposure Banks' operations in the official market are subject to foreign exchange controls. There is no formal prudential regulation of foreign currency exposure in the free market (chiefly used for capital transactions) although banks' open positions, both spot and forward, are regularly reported and any position in excess of 30 per cent of capital is monitored closely.

Loan Concentration and Country Risk There are no formal limits on loans to single borrowers although loans of more than LFr50 million (or, in the case of banks with capital below LFr500 million, loans equivalent to 10 per cent or more of capital) must be reported to the MIL. Country risk exposure is not formally regulated. The whole question of lending limits is under review following the failure in 1983 of Schröder, Münchmeyer Hengst, whose Luxembourg subsidiary (as well as the German parent) had lent a large multiple of its capital to a single group of companies.

Bank Examination Routine examinations by the MIL take place annually and an independent audit of banks is also now mandatory. Foreign supervisory authorities are not permitted to inspect banks in Luxembourg but the Luxembourg secrecy laws have been relaxed to enable Luxembourg subsidiaries of foreign banks to make more information on their lending available to their parent institutions. In addition, the Luxembourg authorities now have a broad discretion to disclose information about locally based banks to foreign supervisors.[24] The MIL considers that with these relaxations all relevant information for the purposes of consolidated supervision can be made available to the home country supervisory authorities of foreign banks.

The Netherlands

The Nederlandsche Bank is responsible for enforcing the Act on the Supervision of the Credit System which was substantially revised in 1978.[25] The central bank's prudential responsibilities cover the universal banks, co-operative banks, savings banks and mortgage institutions, although in the case of the savings banks and certain co-operative banks supervision has been delegated to the appropriate association. The supervisory system is in one sense highly formal, involving, for instance, detailed regulations on solvency and liquidity requirements,[26] but the central bank also attaches considerable importance to its informal contacts with management.

The solvency requirements were revised with effect from 1 June 1983 in order to reflect the risks of lending to foreign governments, foreign banks and semi-public domestic entities, all of which had been exempt from such requirements.[27] In order to avoid any general increase in capital needs, however, the solvency requirements in respect of other loan categories were relaxed somewhat.

Branches of foreign banks are, for prudential purposes, treated in the same way as domestic banks. The revised Act also confers on the creditors of such branches preferential rights to branch assets in the Netherlands, thereby offering some possibility of the recovery of their claims in the event that the parent institution should fail.

Entry Control In order to be licensed by the Nederlandsche Bank, commercial banks must have a minimum capital of DFl5 million and a managing board consisting of at least two persons of proven expertise and trustworthiness. Branches of foreign banks must meet the same licensing criteria as domestic banks and for this and other purposes are required to maintain separate branch accounts, identifying the amount of dotation capital subscribed by their parent institutions.

Capital Adequacy The solvency regulation requires that a bank's capital must at least equal the total value of its fixed assets. More importantly, assets are broken down into different risk categories against which capital must be held in proportions varying between nil and 100 per cent, with a norm for risk-bearing assets of 9 per cent. Under this scheme loans to foreign entities are treated relatively favourably: for instance, loans guaranteed by foreign public authorities or foreign banks are subject to a 5 per cent capital requirement while loans to foreign governments and banks are subject to a 1 per cent requirement. In addition to risk assets, certain contingent liabilities as well as uncovered foreign exchange positions are included in the ratio calculations. Large credits, as defined, attract a premium solvency requirement (see section on 'Liquidity Control' below).

Solvency ratios are calculated on a consolidated basis, with consolidation of majority holdings and minority holdings of over 25 per cent effected *pro rata*. Capital is defined, for the purpose of the regulation, to include paid-up capital plus reserves (published and hidden) plus subordinated debt but only in so far as (a) it does not exceed 100 per cent of capital and reserves, and (b) annual redemptions do not exceed 5 per cent of capital and reserves (the latter constraint means that subordinated debt is in practice generally no greater than one-third of capital and reserves). For branches of foreign banks, capital is calculated after deducting funds channelled back to the head office.

Liquidity Control The liquidity regulation distinguishes between non-liquid, broadly liquid and highly liquid assets, although the requirements relating to the last category are not yet in operation. Highly liquid assets include balances at the central bank and giro institutions, call money, Treasury bills and notes due in 90 days or less, advances against such bills or notes, bank deposits due within one month and certain public sector loans due within three months. Broadly liquid assets consist of highly liquid assets plus rediscountable bills and notes, securities and advances against securities.

The precise regulations are complex but in essence liabilities are classified by both category and maturity band; certain non-liquid assets are then deducted from liabilities within the same maturity band; and the resulting net liability positions attract a liquidity requirement that varies according to both maturity band and category of liability. In general, net liabilities due within two years require a 20 per cent backing of broadly liquid assets, and a 4 per cent backing of highly liquid assets, but there is an exception, for instance, in the case of interbank liabilities due within one month where the requirement for broadly liquid assets is 100 per cent.

The liquidity regulation is designed not merely to limit the extent of maturity mismatching but also to guard against excessive reliance by banks on money market financing. In addition, it is intended to discourage undue deposit concentrations by imposing extra liquidity requirements on 'large item' liabilities which individually amount to between 1 per cent and 2 per cent and together to 15 per cent or more of total liabilities, or which individually amount to over 2 per cent of total liabilities.

Permissible Business Activities There are no direct restrictions on the types of banking business that may be undertaken and in practice banks engage in a wide range of activities including securities business and underwriting. On the other hand, equity participations of 5 per cent or more are subject to the approval of the minister of finance, which has been automatically withheld in the case of investments in non-financial companies. However, this policy was relaxed in 1980 and limited equity stakes in non-financial companies are now permitted if certain specified conditions are met. A bank's total investments in fixed assets (including property and non-financial companies) must not exceed its capital.

Foreign Currency Exposure There is no specific limit on banks' open foreign exchange positions but the central bank may require such exposure to be reduced where it exceeds the level considered appropriate for normal banking activities. In addition, the solvency regulation imposes a 2.5 per cent capital requirement on uncovered foreign exchange positions. Banks report monthly on their forward and spot positions in all convertible currencies and copies of certain forward contracts must also be submitted.

Loan Concentration and Country Risk Under the solvency regulations, a bank is subject to an additional solvency requirement if its loans to one borrower exceed 15 per cent of capital, while loans to one borrower exceeding 25 per cent of capital are not, in general, permissible without the prior approval of the central bank. For this purpose only, the branch of a foreign bank is assessed on the basis of group not branch capital.

Since 1 June 1983 the loan concentration limits have applied to claims on foreign governments as well as to claims on domestic and foreign banks. In such cases the threshold concentrations are twice the normal limits (i.e. 30 per cent and 50 per cent of capital rather than 15 per cent and 25 per cent), except for claims on foreign banks with share capital of DFl2 billion or more, where the upper lending limit is 100 per cent and the threshold for extra solvency requirements is 60 per cent. In calculating these limits due account is taken of guarantees from foreign parent institutions.

The rules on loan concentration do not apply directly to country risk. The central bank monitors country risk on the basis of half-yearly consolidated country exposure reports which banks have been required to submit since 30 June 1981. Primary responsibility for risk assessment rests with the banks themselves, but the authorities do seek to ensure that provisioning against country risks meets reasonable minimum standards.

Bank Examination The central bank has broad powers to inspect banks with a view to verifying returns received and, as a matter of practice, on-site inspection forms an integral part of the supervisory process. In addition, annual accounts must be drawn up according to a specified model by registered accountants who can be required by the central bank to supply any information that may reasonably be considered necessary for the central bank to carry out its duties. In the case of foreign banks, on-the-spot inspections are freely allowed to supervisors from the parent country.

Singapore

The Singapore banking system separates local banking business from international and offshore operations.[28] This dual structure enables the authorities to promote Singapore's role as an international financial centre while avoiding excessive competition in the domestic market. Accordingly, within the commercial banking sector foreign-owned banks are in general prevented from engaging freely in local currency business, the precise limitations depending on whether the bank has a full, restricted or offshore licence. On the other hand any commercial bank can apply for an Asian Currency Unit (ACU) licence enabling it to set up a separate book-keeping unit authorised to participate in the Asian dollar market.

Foreign-owned commercial banks are confined to branch form on the grounds that a branch enjoys the full support of the group to which is belongs. There is, however, a separate category of locally incorporated merchant banks which are not permitted to accept deposits from the public but which can (and typically do) set up their own ACUs.

Under the Monetary Authority of Singapore Act 1970 the Authority (MAS) fulfils all the functions of a central bank, other than the issue of currency, and is also responsible for supervising the banking system within the framework of the 1970 Banking Act. In carrying out its supervisory function the MAS has recently adopted a policy of deregulation in the sense that detailed supervision of individual institutions is being replaced by generally applicable guidelines, and greater reliance is being placed on external auditors in lieu of extensive prudential returns. At the same time responsibility for the supervision of foreign-owned banks is being shifted more to the parent institutions and their home supervisory authorities.

Entry Control All banks are licensed by the MAS and for this purpose have to meet certain statutory capital requirements. Locally incorporated banks must possess paid-up capital of at least S$3 million while branches of foreign banks are subject to a S$6 million group capital requirement, S$3 million of which must be held in the form of approved assets in Singapore. In practice, however, the MAS may insist on capital requirements more stringent than the statutory minima. In addition, foreign banks wishing to establish an office in Singapore must be substantial and internationally reputable institutions. Finally, foreign-owned banks are expected to provide letters of comfort from their parent institutions undertaking to make good any local or foreign currency liquidity short-fall in their Singapore establishments. Reflecting the authorities' increased emphasis on the principle of parental responsibility, the form of these undertakings has recently been hardened (a main Board reso-lution is, for instance, required) to the point where they are considered to be legally binding by some of the banks concerned.

Capital Adequacy The MAS is authorised to impose mandatory capital ratios but has so far refrained from imposing any general norms for commercial banks. However, commercial banks must maintain a reserve fund to which they are required to transfer at least 50 per cent of annual net profits. If the reserve fund is between 50 per cent and 100 per cent of paid-up capital, the transfer need only be 25 per cent of net profits and if the fund exceeds paid-up capital, the transfer may be reduced to 5 per cent of net profits. Foreign-incorporated banks may apply for exemption from these requirements.

Foreign-owned merchant banks are subject to a maximum gearing ratio, which is set at 15×, 30× or 50× depending on whether a letter of comfort has been obtained from the parent institution and whether the bank itself is an affiliate or a wholly-owned subsidiary. It is expected that some form of capital ratio requirement will in due course be applied to commercial banks.

Liquidity Control Each bank is required to maintain a minimum cash balance with the MAS, which is currently set at 6 per cent of the bank's liability base. This ratio is used by the MAS as an instrument of monetary policy for the regulation of bank liquidity. Banks are also required to hold a minimum amount of liquid assets equivalent to 20 per cent of their liability base, half of which must be in the form of primary liquidity (excess cash balances with the MAS, notes and coins, money at call with the discount houses, Treasury bills and other government securities with less than 12 months to maturity). Secondary liquidity includes com-mercial bills (up to 5 per cent of the liabilities base) and government securities of over 12 months to maturity. The liquidity ratio serves both prudential and monetary purposes. ACUs and merchant banks are exempt from the cash and liquidity requirements.

Permissible Business Activities There is no separation of commercial and investment banking in Singapore, but banks are prohibited from engaging in wholesale or retail trade and may not hold equity interests in non-bank undertakings exceeding in the aggregate 40 per cent of the investing bank's capital funds. A bank's property investments (excluding its own business premises) are limited to 40 per cent of its capital funds, while lending for the purpose of property development and/or financing must not exceed 30 per cent of a bank's deposits in Singapore (or 60 per cent with the approval of the MAS). A bank may not acquire more than 20 per cent of the share capital of a company without approval of the MAS.

Foreign Currency Exposure The MAS monitors the volume of banks' foreign currency trading and in January 1984 banks were instructed to report daily on their foreign exchange transactions instead of monthly, as previously. However, there are no exposure limits on foreign exchange transactions.

Loan Concentration and Country Risk Under the Banking (Amendment) Act 1983 loans to a single customer must not in total exceed 30 per cent (or 100 per cent with MAS approval) of the lending bank's capital. In addition, a bank shall not grant 'substantial' loans which in the aggregate exceed 50 per cent of its total credit facilities or such other percentage as the MAS may determine. A 'substantial' loan is defined as one which exceeds 15 per cent of a bank's capital funds. These lending limits are subject to a number of exceptions – notably an exemption applying to all interbank transactions – which may be extended at the discretion of the MAS.

The above loan limits do not apply to country risk exposure involving several borrowers from the same country, although the MAS does monitor the country exposure of local banks on a consolidated basis.

Bank Examination On-site bank examinations by the MAS inspectorate are undertaken on an occasional rather than a regular basis. The foreign establishments of local banks are not at present inspected and foreign supervisors are not permitted to inspect foreign-owned banks in Singapore. Bank secrecy laws prevent the communication to foreign supervisors of information relating to foreign-owned banks in Singapore, but the Banking (Amendment) Act 1983 permits the head office of a bank outside Singapore to obtain information regarding credit facilities granted by its Singapore branch. The 1983 statute also imposes special reporting duties on bank auditors, who must now advise the MAS immediately of, *inter alia*, any serious breaches of the Banking Act or any situation where the position of creditors is jeopardised.

Switzerland

The Federal Banking Commission (FBC) which is independent of both the National Bank and the Federal Council, is charged with the supervision of the Swiss banking system. The National Bank's statutory functions are of a non-prudential nature, although as a matter of practice it has maintained an active interest in this area. The FBC's supervisory activities are governed first by the Federal Law Relating to Banks and Savings Banks, which dates back to 1934, and secondly by an Implementing Ordinance of 1972 that has been periodically updated.[29] In a referendum vote taken in May 1984 the Social Democratic Party's proposals for overhauling Swiss banking laws were decisively rejected. Subsequently Switzerland's Federal Council drafted a more modest programme of reform which was expected to be presented to the legislature in 1986.

All banks resident in Switzerland are subject to the Banking Law, whether or not their business is conducted there. The law applies equally to institutions conducting a banking business in Switzerland, wherever their residence may be.

Entry Control In order to receive a licence from the FBC, banks must meet certain statutory conditions. These include an organisational structure that ensures effective supervision of the management, a minimum capital of SF2 million and a management of sound reputation. Foreign-controlled banks are subject to supplementary requirements, including reciprocal treatment of Swiss-controlled banks in their country of origin. Any institution has a right to obtain a licence once the statutory conditions have been satisfied.

Capital Adequacy The regulations affecting capital adequacy were amended in 1980.[30] The new guidelines (a) shift the basis for calculating required capital ratios from outstanding liabilities to various categories of asset; (b) allow banks limited use of subordinated loans to meet capital requirements; (c) introduce new rules for banks' investments in non-banking assets; and (d) direct that consolidated accounts be used to assess capital needs. The capital adequacy requirements apply equally to Swiss branches of foreign banks, although such branches are expected to be given an exemption in 1985 as a result of the new emphasis on parental responsibility.

Under the new scheme, required capital ratios are graduated according to the presumed riskiness of different types of asset, as illustrated by specifications of 6–8 per cent for domestic advances, an additional 1.5 percentage point premium for foreign assets, 30 per cent for property investment (but 20 per cent for bank premises) and 40 per cent for non-bank affiliates. Certain contingent liabilities are also subject to capital requirements, as are forward transactions in currencies, precious metals and securities (0.3 per cent) and open positions in foreign currency (10 per cent) and precious metals (20 per cent). The ratios are guidelines rather than strict limits and may be varied by the FBC in special cases. They do not apply to fiduciary deposits (invested at the customer's risk but in the name of the Swiss bank receiving the deposit) although the National Bank has drawn attention to the fact that such deposits may involve risks both for the customer *vis-à-vis* the Swiss bank and for the Swiss bank *vis-à-vis* the ultimate borrower.[31]

Capital is defined to include paid-up capital, published and un-disclosed reserves and (a new addition) subordinated loans with at least seven years to maturity, up to a maximum of 10 per cent of total capital. As from January 1982, Swiss banks can no longer cover losses from unpublished reserves without revealing this in their profit and loss accounts.

Liquidity Control Banks must maintain an adequate balance of liquid and marketable assets in relation to short-term liabilities.[32] Liquid assets are defined as cash holdings and balances on giro and postal cheque accounts; marketable assets include bonds and bills that can be pledged or discounted at the National Bank, overdrafts secured by such assets, interbank deposits maturing within one month, gold, bonds issued by sovereign borrowers and prime bankers' acceptances maturing within three months. Short-term liabilities comprise all liabilities maturing within one month, sight deposits and 15 per cent of savings deposits.

Short-term liabilities must be backed in some measure by liquid assets and in a greater measure by liquid plus marketable assets. The extent of this required backing increases as the proportion of short-term liabilities in the balance sheet rises so that, for instance, the marginal liquid asset backing jumps from 6 per cent to 36 per cent as short-term liabilities rise from nil–15 per cent to over 35 per cent of total liabilities. Liquid and marketable assets together must in any event amount to at least 6 per cent of total liabilities. This approach to liquidity assessment is designed to place some formal limit on banks' maturity mismatching, while also ensuring a minimum cushion of realisable assets.

Permissible Business Activities There are no formal restrictions on the kinds of business that banks may undertake, and in practice Swiss banks are universal rather than specialised. The public sector, represented by 30 cantonal banks and 45 banks belonging to districts and communities, has nevertheless tended in the past to attract the bulk of savings deposits.

Foreign Exchange Exposure There are no specific limits on foreign exchange exposure other than the 10 per cent incremental capital require-ment for open foreign currency positions (see section on 'Capital Adequacy' above). However, strong emphasis is placed by the FBC on the sufficiency of internal control procedures. From the end of 1984 the National Bank will require banks to report their spot and forward foreign exchange positions each month.

Loan Concentration and Country Risk Loans to individual borrowers, measured as a proportion of the lending bank's capital, are subject to guidelines of 20 per cent for unsecured loans and 40 per cent for secured loans, with additional variations for interbank lending and loans to Swiss public bodies.[33] The limits are now calculated on a consolidated basis and cases of excess must be reported to the FBC, which may demand that the loans be reduced. However, these restrictions do not apply directly to country risk where several borrowing entities from the same country may be involved.

The new solvency requirements (see under 'Capital Adequacy' above) take some account of country risk by imposing an additional 1.5 percentage point premium on foreign assets. Also, the FBC has recently issued a circular requiring auditors to include in their reports to the Commission a description of each bank's approach to country risk evaluation. On the basis of a survey of banks' problem loans, the FBC in 1983 classified a number of countries as problem debtors and established a standardised rather than country-specific provisioning guideline of 20 per cent. This figure may be varied from year to year in line with world financial developments.

In order to improve its reporting coverage for the BIS, as well as to assess potential demands for liquidity, the National Bank will from the end of 1984 collect consolidated country exposure data from the banks. It is not yet clear, however, whether this information will be passed on to the FBC for prudential purposes.

Bank Examination The FBC does not undertake on-site examinations of banks in the normal course of its supervisory duties. Instead, reliance is placed on independent bank auditors, who have a special status under Swiss law.[34] Such auditors are appointed and paid for by the banks but are licensed by the FBC, for whom in effect they are required to act as agents. Auditors must ensure that all violations of law are either promptly corrected or reported to the FBC, which must also be immediately informed of irregularities or losses that might jeopardise the security of depositors. The auditors' reports to the FBC (in contrast to shareholders' reports) must also reveal banks' true profits before adjustments to the inner reserves. Parent supervisors are not permitted to inspect foreign banks in Switzerland; their access to information is also limited by the Swiss bank secrecy laws.

The United Kingdom

The Banking Act of 1979, which for the first time provides a statutory basis for banking supervision within the United Kingdom, was drafted in response to the secondary banking crisis of 1973–75 (see Chapter 6) and the harmonisation requirements of the 1977 EEC Directive on banking.[35] The Act imposes on the Bank of England primary responsibility for regulating and supervising deposit-taking business and for this purpose established two categories of institution: recognised banks and licensed deposit-takers. This two-tier system (which is not required by the EEC Directive) enables the Bank to maintain its traditional approach to the supervision of recognised banks based on direct contacts with management, while adopting more formal regulatory procedures in relation to licensed deposit-takers.

Entry Control The statutory requirements for recognition as a bank by the Bank of England are more stringent than those for obtaining a deposit-taking licence (section 3(1)–(6) and Schedule 2 to the Act). The main criteria are: (a) adequacy of financial resources (including a minimum capital requirement which is normally £5 million); (b) high reputation and standing in the financial community; (c) provision of a specified range of financial services; and (d) a management of integrity and prudence commanding appropriate professional skills. UK subsidiaries of foreign banks apply for recognition (or a licence) in their own right, although the reputation criterion attaches to their parent institutions. In contrast, a UK branch of a foreign bank must apply in its parent bank's name, and for this purpose the Bank of England has statutory power to delegate assessment of the bank's management and financial soundness (though not reputation) to the parent supervisory authority. Furthermore, whereas the capital and other solvency criteria apply in the normal way to UK subsidiaries of foreign banks, they are applied to the whole parent organisation in the case of branches, there being no formal requirement as to branch capital.

Capital Adequacy The Bank of England does not seek to apply a capital adequacy norm to all or any class of banks. However, in 1980 it devised two capital ratios which, after taking into account the particular circumstances of each institution, are used as a basis for assessing capital adequacy.[36] The Bank's approach is to take account of a banking group's consolidated world-wide operations in assessing capital needs, although UK subsidiaries of foreign banks are expected to be adequately capitalised in their own right.

The gearing ratio relates the capital base (with a deduction for premises) to all non-capital liabilities apart from contingent liabilities. The purpose of this ratio is to ensure that a bank's capital position is regarded as acceptable by its depositors and other creditors. The second and more important calculation is the risk asset ratio which tests the adequacy of capital in relation to the risk of losses that may be sustained. For this purpose various classes of asset are weighted according to their supposed susceptibility to credit, investment and forced sale risk, commercial advances being taken as a benchmark and therefore accorded a uniform weighting of one. The risk asset ratio is calculated by multiplying each balance sheet asset by its weighting to produce an adjusted total of risk assets which is then related to the capital base. The capital base is defined to include share capital and reserves, subordinated debt with a minimum five years to maturity, up to a maximum of one-third of total capital, and general bad debt provisions.

Liquidity Control In 1982 the Bank of England introduced guidelines for the assessment of liquidity although, as with capital adequacy, it does not seek to impose across-the-board norms or ratios.[37] The Bank's approach takes account not only of funding risk, that is, the risk of not having available sufficient cash to meet obligations falling due on a particular day, but also the interest rate mismatch risk, whereby a bank engaging in maturity transformation may suffer losses as a result of movements in interest rates. The measure is based on a cash flow approach, normally taking liabilities and assets in all currencies together. Liabilities and assets are inserted in a 'maturity ladder', with the net positions in each time period being accumulated. Marketable assets are placed at the start of the maturity ladder, subject to a discount where there is a credit, investment or forced sale risk. The result is a series of accumulating net mismatch positions in different time bands, which provides the basis for a qualitative assessment of liquidity.

Foreign branches and subsidiaries of UK banks may not be monitored for liquidity purposes on a consolidated basis where, because of local conditions, the liquidity needs of the parent and the operation abroad are very different. Until 1982 the Bank did not monitor the liquidity of UK branches of foreign banks, but it now proposes to do so, placing particular emphasis on sterling liquidity.

Permissible Business Activities There are no specific controls on the types of business in which banks may engage. However, the Bank of England would wish to ensure that any development of a bank's business could be accommodated comfortably within its managerial and financial resources.

Foreign Exchange Exposure The Bank of England's monitoring of foreign exchange risk is based on a distinction between 'structural' and 'dealing' positions in foreign currency.[38] Structural exposure arising from a bank's fixed and long-term assets and liabilities is not subject to guidelines, although it is included in the aggregate foreign currency position for purposes of capital adequacy assessment. In contrast, dealing positions reflecting day-to-day operations are subject to specific guidelines agreed individually with each institution. These guidelines are adapted to the particular circumstances and expertise of each bank, but for those experienced in foreign exchange the limits would generally be 10 per cent of capital base for net dealing positions in any one currency, and 15 per cent of capital base for the aggregate net dealing position in all currencies taken together.

The Bank does not apply separate guidelines to UK branches of foreign banks where the branch's own internal controls (those exercised by its head office) and the monitoring arrangements of its own supervisory authority are considered satisfactory. On the other hand, foreign branches (though not foreign subsidiaries) of UK banks are included in the Bank's guideline arrangements.

Loan Concentration and Country Risk The Bank of England has advised banks that exposures (loans, acceptances, guarantees, etc.) to one customer or group of customers should not normally exceed 10 per cent of the lending bank's capital base.[39] Where loan concentrations exceed this threshold the lending bank is normally requested to maintain a correspondingly higher level of capital. The guideline does not apply to country risk exposure which is, however, monitored on the basis of half-yearly returns detailing banks' consolidated claims on non-residents of the United Kingdom by borrower, country of borrower and maturity. The Bank of England takes a view on the prudential implications of exposures to particular countries as well as on the adequacy of provisioning against country risk,[40] but makes its assessment on the basis of each bank's particular circumstances.

Bank Examination There is no system of direct on-site examination of banks by the Bank of England and no regular assessment of the quality of a bank's loan portfolio (though details of large loans must be provided). The starting point for supervision is analysis of the relevant statistics, which then provides the basis for interviews with senior management. These interviews are the cornerstone of the Bank's supervisory system, the prime aim being to build up over time an intimate picture of each institution and to assess the capabilities of management to control the business and fulfil its objectives. Branches of overseas banks undergo less comprehensive supervision because of the reliance placed on the parent bank's supervisory authority.

The United States

The structure of the US banking system reflects various statutory limitations on geographical and functional diversification. The 1933 Glass–Steagall Act separates investment banking business from commercial banking; the 1927 McFadden Act restricts interstate banking and the 1956 Bank Holding Company Act limits the scope of a banking company's activities to those that are closely related to banking.[41] The effective prohibition of interstate banking has led to a highly fragmented financial system comprising some 14,000 banks, while limitations on the kinds of business banks may undertake has resulted in financial specialisation among commercial, savings and investment banks. However, changes in financial technology, more permissive regulatory policies and statutory deregulation (notably the Garn–St Germain Depository Institutions Act of 1982) have tended in recent years to blur the traditional distinction between banks and other financial businesses. Under legislative reforms proposed by Congress in 1984, the deregulatory process would be given further impetus, although political opposition to further moves in this direction began to build up in the wake of Continental Illinois' near collapse in the spring of that year (see page 164).

The supervisory process has been considerably complicated by a dual banking structure dividing regulatory responsibilities between state and federal authorities, as well as by the co-existence of three federal agencies concerned with the supervision of commercial banks. In essence the Office of the Comptroller of the Currency (OCC) supervises banks with national charters (including federally licensed branches of foreign banks); the Federal Reserve Board (FRB) and the states supervise state-chartered, Federal Reserve member banks; the Federal Deposit Insurance Corporation (FDIC) and the states supervise state-chartered, insured, non-member banks (including insured state branches of foreign banks); and the states alone supervise state-chartered, non-member, uninsured banks.

In early 1984 a Presidential Task Force formulated proposals for streamlining the regulatory process.[42] Under these arrangements a new federal banking agency would be set up in place of the OCC to regulate all but the 50 largest holding companies of federally chartered banks (these would continue to be regulated by the FRB). The new agency would determine the extent of permissible business diversification by bank holding companies, subject to the FRB's power of veto. The FRB would take over the FDIC's supervision of state banks while the FDIC would have expanded powers to set variable insurance premiums.

US offices of foreign banks are subject to 'national treatment' under the 1978 International Banking Act, that is, they enjoy the same rights and are subject to the same restrictions as US domestic banks.

Entry Control National banks are chartered by the OCC, state banks by the various state authorities. In considering charter applications, state and federal authorities apply similar criteria, including: (a) the bank's future earnings prospects; (b) the general character of the proposed management; (c) the adequacy of its proposed capital structure; and (d) the convenience to and needs of the community to be served.

Foreign banks seeking to establish branches, agencies or subsidiaries under state or federal licence are subject to the same chartering criteria and procedures as domestic banks. The establishment of foreign branches and subsidiaries of domestic banks is subject to approval by the FRB (or the FDIC in the case of state non-member banks).

Capital Adequacy In addition to being considered at the chartering stage, capital adequacy is also monitored regularly as part of the bank examination process. For this purpose federal agencies rate capital in relation to the volume of risk assets, the volume of inferior quality assets, bank growth experience, plans and prospects, and the strength of management. Furthermore, earnings trends and dividend pay-out ratios are examined in order to assess the prospective contribution of retained earnings to capital growth.

The OCC and FRB have recently introduced common guidelines[43] to be used in assessing capital adequacy which distinguish between primary and secondary capital. Primary capital consists of common and perpetual preferred stock, surplus and undivided profits, contingency and other capital reserves, mandatory convertible instruments and 100 per cent of the allowances for possible loan losses. Secondary capital consists of limited-life preferred stock and subordinated notes and debentures; it can amount to no more than 50 per cent of primary capital; and the secondary instruments must be phased out of the bank's capital beginning in the fifth year prior to maturity. Under the original guidelines regional and smaller banks were subject to specified capital norms whereas multinational banks were to be assessed on an individual basis with a view to raising their capital ratios, in due course, closer to those of the smaller banks. In June 1983, however, the OCC and FRB introduced a 5 per cent minimum guideline for the ratio of primary capital to total assets – the same ratio as for regional banks – for the 17 multinational banks.[44] The agencies have also established guidelines for the ratio of total capital to total assets and for this purpose specify three broad capital ratio zones which determine the degree of official monitoring of the institutions concerned. In July 1984 the three federal regulatory agencies proposed standardised capital ratio norms for all US banks based on a 5.5 per cent ratio of primary capital to total assets and a 6 per cent ratio of total capital to total assets.

The FDIC has issued its own separate statement of policy on capital which excludes all subordinated debt from the evaluation process.[45] This difference of approach reflects in part the FDIC's concern to protect depositors by ensuring the viability of banks as going concerns rather than by paying off depositors with banks which have failed.

Capital is evaluated by federal agencies on a world-wide consolidated basis. In the case of foreign joint ventures, account is taken of the possibility that financial support going beyond the initial investment by the US bank might be needed, while consideration is also given to the fact that foreign branches and subsidiaries of US banks may be permitted to engage in riskier activities than their parent institutions. US subsidiaries of foreign banks are assessed for capital in the normal way, while federally licensed branches of foreign banks are required to hold at a member bank deposits or investment securities equal in value to 5 per cent of their liabilities. These branch 'capital equivalent deposits' (which may also be required by state authorities for state licensed branches) are intended to ensure competitive equality by substituting for the capital required of national banks.

Liquidity Control Liquidity is considered during the bank examination process, although no attempt is made to impose liquidity norms by means of published ratios. The federal agencies rate liquidity with respect to: (a) the volatility of deposits; (b) reliance on interest sensitive funds and frequency and level of borrowings; (c) technical competence relative to structure of liabilities; (d) availability of assets readily convertible into cash; and (e) access to money markets or other ready sources of cash. The liquidity position is considered on a world-wide consolidated basis, although certain bank functions may be analysed separately.

Permissible Business Activities In general, commercial banks in the United States are confined to the business of commercial banking. They may not underwrite securities or engage in other securities-related activities or in commercial activities unrelated to banking, and they are subject to a variety of statutory restrictions on, for instance, real estate lending, permissible investment securities and the holding of corporate stocks. Since 1978, US branches and agencies (as well as subsidiaries) of foreign banks have been subject to parallel restrictions on their activities in the United States.

In recent years the strict separation of banking and non-banking activities in the United States has been eroded, a fact which may be given legislative recognition if the proposals now before Congress, permitting banks to engage in specified non-bank activities through legally distinct affiliates, gain acceptance.

Foreign Exchange Exposure The regulatory authorities do not lay down any specific limits or guidelines for foreign exchange exposure. However, they do monitor individual bank positions through a reporting system requiring weekly exposure returns in nine currencies and monthly breakdowns of foreign currency positions by maturity. The main focus of regulation is on banks' procedures for limiting foreign exchange risk and for this purpose the Uniform Guideline on Internal Control of Foreign Exchange in Commercial Banks sets out minimum standards for policy documentation, internal accounting controls and audit documentation.

Country Risk In order to co-ordinate their approach to country risk, the federal regulatory agencies have established an Inter-agency Country Exposure Review Committee (ICERC) which meets three times each year to categorise the credit standing of individual countries.[46] Countries may be designated strong, moderately strong or weak, the prudent exposure limit relative to capital, beyond which loans are 'listed' for the attention of directors, being respectively 25 per cent, 10 per cent and 5 per cent. Where debt servicing has been interrupted, loans may be classified as 'substandard', 'value impaired' (where a country has protracted arrears) or 'loss' (where there is little or no prospect of repayment). Classified loans are formally incorporated into the agencies' evaluation of a bank's asset quality and financial soundness. A new category of 'unclassified loan requiring attention' has recently been introduced to cover cases where debt-servicing interruptions are less severe or being remedied.[47]

Under the International Lending Supervision Act of 1983 the federal regulatory agencies must require banks to set aside special reserves on bank loans which are found to be 'impaired by a protracted inability of public or private borrowers in a foreign country to make payments on their external indebtedness' or where 'no definite prospects exist for the orderly restoration of debt service'. These special reserves are to be charged against current income and are not considered part of capital or allowances for possible loan losses.

Special reserves were imposed in February 1984 in the form of Allocated Transfer Risk Reserves or ATRRs.[48] Loans against which ATRRs must be held are those classified as 'value impaired' (see above). The first year's reserve will normally be 10 per cent, with annual increments of 15 per cent thereafter. If the agencies conclude that the reserves are no longer necessary, banks will be notified that they can be reduced. With a view to sustaining international credit flows, ATRRs are not required for *new* loans to countries carrying out an IMF or other economic adjustment programme when the new lending enhances the debt-servicing capacity of the borrowing country – even if existing loans to that country are subject to special reserves.

Bank Examination Regular bank examinations by the authorities' own examiners lie at the heart of the US supervisory process. Federal on-site examinations focus on capital adequacy, asset quality, management quality, earnings and profitability, and liquidity. This uniform rating system (known as 'CAMEL') is used to arrive at an overall composite rating which identifies, on a scale of one to five, those banks which are in sound condition and those with weaknesses requiring closer supervisory attention. The examination process is buttressed by remote computer-based systems designed to monitor the condition of banks between examinations and to serve as an early warning system to detect potential weaknesses. The present emphasis is on strengthening these systems in order to reduce the need for frequent, on-site examinations.

Federal examiners also conduct on-site examinations of foreign branches and, local laws permitting, foreign subsidiaries of US banks. US branches and subsidiaries of foreign banks are examined in the normal way, although in these cases the Federal Reserve imposes extensive reporting requirements relating to the parent banks' structure and condition on the grounds that a parent bank's activities may affect the soundness of its foreign branches and subsidiaries.

West Germany

Under the Banking Act of 1961, as amended, the Federal Banking Supervisory Office (SO) is charged with the supervision of banks, although it exercises its functions in close co-operation with the Bundesbank.[49] Thus, while the banks' financial reports are collected and evaluated by the Bundesbank, they are passed on to the SO whose responsibility it is to take appropriate steps in the light of such reports. Similarly, it is the SO's responsibility to issue detailed regulations on liquidity and capital adequacy, but only after reaching agreement with the Bundesbank.

Present supervisory arrangements reflect a number of reforms introduced in 1976, two years after the Herstatt crisis, including rules on risk-spreading and foreign exchange exposure, the establishment of a 'lifeboat' fund for banks experiencing liquidity difficulties, and an extended deposit protection scheme. More recently these arrangements have been supplemented by a series of 'gentlemen's agreements' aimed at extending the supervisory function to domestic banks' foreign subsidiaries.

In February 1984 the German Cabinet approved a draft amendment to the Banking Act requiring banks to produce consolidated accounts covering domestic and foreign subsidiaries in which they have holdings of 40 per cent or more. Under this proposal supervisory and regulatory requirements would be applied on a consolidated basis after a transition period of five years.

German branches of foreign banks are supervised and regulated as if they were domestic banks, and must comply with prudential ratios in the normal way.[50] Under German law, too, such branches are subject to separate liquidation proceedings and head office claims subordinated to those of branch depositors.

Entry Control Any person wishing to conduct banking business requires a licence from the SO. The SO can refuse a licence only if one or more of the following criteria are not fulfilled: (a) adequate capital (a minimum of DM6 million is currently applied); (b) a trustworthy and professionally qualified management; and (c) at least two managers actively involved in running the business. Although the SO does not have a discretionary authority to reject licence applications, it may subject any licence to conditions, which in the case of private commercial banks will normally include membership of the Deposit Protection Fund. German branches of foreign banks are subject to the same licensing criteria as domestic banks, for which purpose the head office must supply its branch with the appropriate amount of dotation capital. In addition, a licence may be (but seldom is) refused to a branch of a foreign bank incorporated outside the EEC if it is felt to be not justified in view of the overall needs of the German economy.

Capital Adequacy The basic capital adequacy rule is that loans and participations should not together exceed 18 times equity capital plus reserves (subordinated debt is not included).[51] However, certain secured and guaranteed loans as well as loans to foreign banks are assessed for this purpose at only half their value, while loans to domestic banks (including domestic branches of foreign banks) are assessed at only 20 per cent of their value. Furthermore, loans to the public sector are exempt from any capital requirement. After allowing for such adjustment capital ratios may in practice fall significantly below the implied basic minimum of 5.6 per cent. Failure to comply with the requirements creates a rebuttable presumption that the equity capital of the bank is insufficient and must be corrected.

German branches of foreign banks are, for reasons of competitive equity, subject to the same capital requirements as domestic banks. Branch capital is defined as the working capital made available to the branch by its foreign parent, plus operating surpluses retained by the branch, less any net claims by the branch on intercompany account.

Until now the capital adequacy criteria have not been applied on a consolidated basis, nor does the SO have the statutory authority to do so. Pending legislative reforms, however, the commercial banks have voluntarily undertaken to provide consolidated financial data in respect of wholly or almost wholly owned subsidiaries.

Liquidity Control There are two basic liquidity rules which together limit the extent of maturity transformation in a bank's balance sheet while also recognising that some proportion of shorter-term liabilities may be viewed as a stable funding base. The first rule states that specified long-term assets should not exceed the sum of long-term financial resources, as defined, and the second requires that certain other non-liquid assets be backed by appropriate financial resources, comprising specified proportions of different liability categories. A central feature of this formula is that bank liabilities are classified by both maturity and velocity of turnover with a view to determining the extent to which they may prudently be used as a basis for maturity transformation. As with capital adequacy, failure to conform to the liquidity guidelines carries a presumption that corrective action is needed. Liquidity is not assessed on a consolidated basis.

Permissible Business Activities Universal or multi-purpose banking is an established feature of the West German financial system. The Gessler Commission[52] recently examined the desirability of imposing constraints on the kinds of business (particularly securities business) that banks could undertake, but fundamental legislative reforms were not recommended and are not to be expected in this area.

Foreign Exchange Exposure A bank's net open position in foreign currencies and precious metals, irrespective of the maturity of individual commitments, should not in aggregate exceed 30 per cent of capital. Furthermore, in order to minimise the fulfilment risk arising from differing maturities of assets and liabilities, even where the positions are matched in amount, net foreign currency positions maturing in any calendar month or half year should not exceed 40 per cent of capital. Since net long as well as net short positions in individual foreign currencies are aggregated for the purpose of these calculations, the effective maximum long or short position in one foreign currency or group of foreign currencies against other foreign currencies is 15 per cent rather than 30 per cent of capital. In contrast, a bank's aggregate long or short position in foreign currencies against the Deutschmark may be as high as 30 per cent of capital.

Loan Concentration and Country Risk Article 13 of the Banking Act states that every 'large' loan, defined as a loan to one borrower exceeding 15 per cent of the lending bank's capital, must be reported immediately to the supervisory authorities. Furthermore, no single loan should exceed 75 per cent of a bank's capital while a bank's five largest loans and all 'large' loans together should not exceed, respectively, three times and eight times its capital. Under the proposed amendment to the Banking Act, a bank's loans to a single borrower would be limited to 50 per cent of capital, a 'single borrower' being defined to include all affiliates in which the borrowing concern has a 40 per cent or larger stake. German banks have informally agreed to keep within the 75 per cent loan limit in respect of their consolidated operations world-wide, but large exposures are not at present reported on a consolidated basis.

Country risk is monitored on the basis of data classified by various country groupings (EEC, other industrial, developing, OPEC and Comecon). Consolidated country exposure data (but not data on individual subsidiaries) are obtained by the SO under its gentleman's agreement with the banks.

In December 1983, the Bundesbank secured an agreement with the banks whereby they will, with effect from the end of 1984, provide monthly reports on each foreign subsidiary's balance sheet, with details of its lending to both German and foreign borrowers, including a breakdown by sector, country, currency and maturity (up to and over one year).[53] These reports will be made available to the SO, so that consolidated supervision of country risk exposure will be strengthened. At present the auditors' reports to the SO must refer to the methods used to evaluate country risk, but the authorities do not themselves take an independent view on individual countries' financial prospects. The SO does not apply provisioning guidelines but it does seek to ensure reasonable consistency between banks in the provisions they make against country risk.

Bank Examination Bank supervision is based on annual auditors' reports to the supervisory authorities rather than on-site examinations by the regulators themselves. Bank auditors are required by Article 29 of the Banking Act to report breaches of the law, facts which might endanger the existence of a bank and, at the request of the authorities, any other facts which suggest that the business of the bank has not been conducted properly. Under a recent amendment to the law the SO may itself carry out spot checks by conducting its own audits without any special reasons being given.

OBSERVATION RATIOS ADOPTED BY THE EEC ADVISORY BANKING COMMITTEE

The first EEC Banking Co-ordination Directive of 1977 provides, *inter alia*, for the establishment of 'ratios between the various assets and/or liabilities of credit institutions with a view to monitoring their solvency and liquidity' (Article 6(1)).[54] Initially such ratios are to be used for observation purposes only, although the Directive evidently envisages the possibility that harmonised prudential ratios might be applied in the longer term. In 1980 the EEC Advisory Banking Committee began to define a number of observation ratios which are now being calculated on a trial basis for a sample of banks within each member state.

The Advisory Committee currently employs two solvency ratios[55] (a risk assets ratio and a gearing ratio) as well as a profitability ratio[56] and a liquidity ratio.[57] The solvency ratios embrace the activities of banks' foreign (and domestic) branches, but because consolidated supervision has reached varying stages among different member states, there is no uniform approach to consolidation in the ratio calculations.

For the purposes of the solvency ratios capital is defined to include paid-up equity capital, reserves (hidden and published) and provisions with the character of reserves. However, because national practices with respect to subordinated debt vary, each solvency ratio is calculated twice, once including and once excluding subordinated debt as allowable capital. Investments amounting to 20 per cent or more of the share capital of bank affiliates are deducted so as to avoid double-counting capital that may be used as a basis for gearing both by the investing bank and the affiliate.

Risk Assets Ratio

The risk assets ratio is defined as the ratio of capital to risk assets. The

Advisory Committee has also devised rules for weighting risk assets according to both the nature and the country of origin of borrowers. Thus borrowers are classified as governments (central and local), banks and private non-bank entities, while countries of origin are divided into a preferential zone, comprising all EEC countries plus other industrial countries, and a residual non-preferential zone. Claims on banks are classified by country of operation in the case of subsidiaries and by country of incorporation of the head office in the case of branches. The following weightings are applied: (a) zero, on claims on or guaranteed by either preferential zone governments or specified international organisations; (b) 20 per cent, on claims on or guaranteed by preferential zone banks, and contingent liabilities incurred on behalf of such banks; (c) 50 per cent, on contingent liabilities incurred on behalf of non-preferential zone governments and banks and private non-bank entities; and (d) 100 per cent, on claims on non-preferential zone governments and banks and all claims on private non-bank borrowers. Fixed assets (comprising premises, other property, equipment and investments in non-bank affiliates) also come within this weighting category.

Gearing Ratio

This is defined as the ratio of capital to other liabilities, where 'other liabilities' consist of all non-capital liabilities including acceptances and other contingent liabilities. Fiduciary accounts are excluded from the calculation.

Profitability Ratio

This ratio, which is also used in assessing solvency, has been calculated both as the ratio of gross profit to total assets and as the ratio of net profit to total assets.

Liquidity Ratio

The first experimental liquidity ratio has been defined as the ratio of liquid assets to short-term liabilities. For this purpose liquid assets comprise notes and coin, gold, balances with the central bank, postal cheque accounts, interbank balances at call or notice of up to three months, assets rediscountable or eligible as collateral at the central bank, other money market instruments whose negotiability is considered by the supervisory authorities to be beyond doubt, and quoted debt securities. Short-term liabilities comprise all domestic and foreign currency liabilities of up to three months maturity, including all sight, term and savings deposits. Although the Advisory Committee favours the use of remaining rather than original maturity in calculating the maturities of assets and liabilities, it has not proved possible to standardise this practice. This ratio is not calculated on a consolidated basis and the assets and liabilities of foreign branches should also be excluded.

NOTES

1. The relevant regulation is CB Regulation of 13 June 1972, confirmed by Ministerial Decree of 7 August 1972.
2. Law of 30 June 1975 and Law of 8 August 1980.
3. Banks and Banking Law Revision Act, 1980.
4. In October 1983 Canada's then House of Commons Finance Committee recommended that Parliament remove the 8 per cent ceiling on foreign bank operations in Canada (by the end of August 1983 foreign banks accounted for 7.3 per cent of total domestic assets).
5. The 1984 Banking Act replaces the Banking Acts of June 1941 and December 1945.
6. Decree No. 79–561 of 5 July 1979 and CNC General Decision No. 79–561 of 24 April 1979.
7. CCB Instruction No. 77–02–A of 16 December 1977 and CCB Instruction No. 77–03–A of 16 December 1977.
8. Decree No. 79–561 of 5 July 1979 and CNC General Decision No. 79–07 of 6 July 1979.
9. See Laws of Hong Kong, Banking Ordinance, Chapter 155, October 1981.
10. See Laws of Hong Kong, Deposit-Taking Companies Ordinance, Chapter 328, October 1981.
11. Banking (Amendment) Ordinance No. 8, 11 March 1982.
12. Banking (Amendment) Act 1983, clause 7 amending section 23 of the Banking Ordinance.
13. Banking (Amendment) Act 1983, clause 13 amending section 57 of the Banking Ordinance.
14. For a full description of Italy's banking regulations see Jane Welch, ed., *The Regulation of Banks in the Member States of the EEC*, 2nd edn (London, Graham and Trotman, 1981), pp.161–80.
15. For a general description of the Japanese financial system see *The Japanese Financial System in Comparative Perspective*, a study prepared for the Joint Economic Committee of the US Congress (Washington, DC, US Government Printing Office), March 1982.
16. The new Banking Law replaces the Banking Law of 1927 and is based on recommendations made in 1979 by the Financial System Research Council. References to the Banking Law in this section are based on an unofficial English version made available by the Japanese Ministry of Finance.
17. *Japan Economic Journal*, 8 February 1983, p.1.
18. *Japan Economic Journal*, 21 September 1982, p.1.
19. *Japan Economic Journal*, 15 February 1983, p.1.
20. *Japan Economic Journal*, 15 February 1983, p.1.
21. See *Japan Economic Journal*, 21 June 1983, p.3.
22. See Law of 20 May 1983 concerning the creation of the Luxembourg Monetary Institute.
23. Decree of 19 July 1983.
24. See Articles 14–16 of Law of 23 April 1981.
25. See 'The Revised Act on the Supervision of the Credit System', Nederlandsche Bank, March 1979.
26. See 'Solvency and Liquidity Directives', Nederlandsche Bank, March 1977.
27. See Nederlandsche Bank, Annual Report, 1982, pp.110–11.
28. For references to financial regulation in Singapore see note 68, Chapter 2. See also 'The Financial Structure of Singapore', Monetary Authority of Singapore, June 1980.
29. See 'Swiss Federal Banking Law' (Zurich, Union Bank of Switzerland, November 1972) and Bernhard Müller, Director of the Secretariat of the Federal Banking Commission, 'The Supervision of Banks in Switzerland' (Berne, May 1981).
30. See Implementing Ordinance Amendment, 1 December 1980.
31. See M. F. Leutweiler, President of the Swiss National Bank, 'Considerations sur les Operations Etrangères des Banques Suisses', paper delivered to the Association of Foreign Banks in Switzerland, Berne, June 1981, pp.6–11.
32. Articles 15–20 of the Implementing Ordinance.
33. Article 21 of the Implementing Ordinance.
34. Article 21 of the Federal Law Relating to Banks and Savings Banks.

35.   See generally Ian Morison, Paul Tillet and Janet Welch, *Banking Act 1979* (London, Butterworths, 1979).

36.   Bank of England, 'The Measurement of Capital', September 1980.

37.   Bank of England, 'The Measurement of Liquidity', July 1982.

38.   Bank of England, 'Foreign Currency Exposure', April 1981.

39.   Bank of England, Notice to Institutions Authorised Under the Banking Act of 1979, April 1983.

40.   See Peter Cooke, speech given at the Institute of Chartered Accountants Banking Conference, London, 4 November 1982, pp.16–18.

41.   For a general description of the US regulatory framework see Carter Golembe and David Holland, *Federal Regulation of Banking* (Washington, DC, Golembe Associates, 1981).

42.   *Wall Street Journal* (Europe), 2 February 1984, p.9.

43.   OCC and FRB Joint Press Release, 26 May 1982.

44.   OCC and FRB Joint Press Release, 13 June 1982.

45.   'FDIC Statement of Policy on Capital Adequacy', 17 December 1981.

46.   For a full review of this system see Robert Bench, 'A Framework and New Techniques for International Bank Supervision' (Office of Comptroller of the Currency, 1982) and 'Bank Examination for Country Risk and International Lending', Report by the US General Accounting Office, September 1982.

47.   See 'Interagency Statement on Examination Treatment of International Loans', Joint News Release, 15 December 1983.

48.   See US Federal Reserve Press Release, 9 February 1984.

49.   For a general description and analysis of the Banking Act see Schneider, Hellwig and Kingsman, *The German Banking System* (Frankfurt, Fritz Knapp Verlag, 1978).

50.   See 'The Branches of Foreign Banks in the Federal Republic of Germany', Deutsche Bundesbank, Monthly Report, April 1972.

51.   The capital and liquidity requirements of German banks are governed by three principles drawn up by the Federal Banking Supervisory Office in January 1969, with subsequent amendments. Principle I covers capital requirements, principles II and III liquidity requirements while principle Ia, introduced as a direct result of the collapse of Herstatt Bank, covers foreign exchange dealings.

52.   See Summary, 'Basic Banking Questions', Report of the Commission of Enquiry (Bonn, May 1979).

53.   See *International Herald Tribune*, 24 November 1983.

54.   *Official Journal*, No. L322 of 17 December 1977; Doc. No. 77/780/EEC.

55.   Commission Doc. No. XV/195/80 Rev. 5.

56.   Commission Doc. No. XV/291/80–EN Rev. 3.

57.   Commission Doc. No. XV/100/82–EN.

6 Protective Regulation: Deposit Insurance and the Lender of Last Resort

Whatever constraints national authorities impose on banks in order to prevent socially costly failures, some banks will inevitably get into difficulties from time to time and certain of these, in the absence of official capital infusions, are bound to fail. Because the failure of individual institutions can threaten more widespread financial instability (as explained in Chapter 3) national authorities have adopted various techniques both to support troubled banks and to protect depositors in the event of insolvency. The first two parts of this Chapter describe the protective measures employed in major financial centre countries. The third part examines the handling of a number of recent bank failures in order to highlight some of the public policy issues that arise where the business of the failing bank has an international dimension.

OVERVIEW OF PROTECTIVE FACILITIES

Deposit Insurance

Most countries either already operate, or are in the process of introducing, deposit protection schemes. These may be official (as in Canada, the United Kingdom and the United States), organised by the banking industry itself with the encouragement of the authorities (as in France, West Germany and the Netherlands) or jointly administered by the authorities and the banks (as in Belgium and Japan). In general, participation is mandatory, although not every German bank is a member of the country's scheme and foreign banks having equivalent coverage from home-based schemes may be exempted. Countries which do not have any formal deposit protection arrangements include Hong Kong, Italy, Luxembourg and Singapore.

Typically, the protection offered is territorial in scope, thereby embracing branches and subsidiaries of foreign banks and excluding deposits with foreign offices of domestic banks. However, there are

141

exceptions: the German and Japanese schemes cover foreign branches of domestic banks while the Belgian and Japanese exclude local branches of foreign banks. All schemes cover both residents' and non-residents' deposits, but there is a split between those which protect foreign currency deposits (Belgium, Germany, the Netherlands and the United States) and those which do not (Canada, France, Japan and the United Kingdom). Most schemes exclude interbank deposits (Canada being an exception) while certain categories of term deposits as well as certificates of deposit may also be excluded.

In all cases there is a maximum amount per depositor per institution beyond which protection is not provided, the rationale here being that large depositors are in a better position to assess bank risk than small depositors. The deposit ceilings range from the equivalent of US$13,000 (Japan) to US$100,000 (United States), although Germany is unusual in imposing a limit equal to 30 per cent of the failed bank's stated equity capital while Belgium applies a discretionary deposit cut-off point (an approach that has recently been challenged in the Belgian courts). Also exceptional are the British and (proposed) Swiss schemes which require the depositor to bear some proportion of any loss, the purpose and effect here being to provide a limited form of consumer protection rather than to prevent precautionary deposit withdrawals.

The United States is unique in that its deposit protection agency has broad powers which can be used to assist or merge troubled banks and thereby avoid deposit pay-offs. Reflecting the agency's active use of these powers and its long-established aversion to deposit pay-offs, 99.8 per cent of all depositors with failed US banks recovered the full amount of their deposits in the period 1934–82. To this extent the $100,000 cut-off point for US deposit protection is largely redundant.

Most deposit protection arrangements are insurance schemes proper in the sense that depositors have a legal right to be paid off. However, the German and Belgian schemes are discretionary. Furthermore, there are wide differences in funding arrangements and in the capacity to make large-scale deposit pay-offs. Some schemes (as in France and the Netherlands) are unfunded and rely wholly or largely on *ad hoc* levies on participant banks to cover deposit losses as they occur. In the case of funded schemes the size of established funds varies between just under 1 per cent (United States) and 0.067 per cent (Japan) of insured deposits, although most funds can be supplemented by official borrowing. Contributions to funded and unfunded schemes are typically flat-rate and calculated on the basis of each bank's total deposits. France, however, provides for a graduated scale of contributions which discriminates in favour of larger banks on the grounds that they are less risky.

Lender of Last Resort and Emergency Measures
In general, national monetary authorities are prepared to provide

financial assistance to commercial banks experiencing temporary liquidity difficulties. A distinction can, however, usually be drawn between routine use of the official discount window, where conditions of access are often formalised, and longer-term support operations undertaken on a discretionary basis.

Although emergency assistance is typically extended directly by the central bank at a penal interest rate, there are alternative methods of support. In Belgium and Germany, for instance, funds are channelled through a special facility jointly established by the authorities and the commercial banks. More generally, support may be provided, with or without official encouragement, by one or more large domestic banks: the Hong Kong and Shanghai Bank has fulfilled this function in Hong Kong, as has the Bank of Tokyo in Japan (in respect of foreign currency liquidity), and the UK clearing banks were involved in large-scale emergency assistance during the UK secondary banking crisis of 1973–75. Similarly, the larger Italian banks formed a rescue consortium during the Banco Ambrosiano crisis in 1982.

Some financial centres, notably Luxembourg, Hong Kong and Singapore, have no indigenous central banks in the conventional sense. In Luxembourg there is no lender of last resort capacity; in Hong Kong the government's Exchange Fund is available for this purpose, while the Monetary Authority of Singapore has a statutory power to provide liquidity assistance to local banks.

Frequently, emergency support can be offered only on a secured basis to solvent institutions, although solvency in this context may not be easily determined. Some countries (for instance, Belgium and the United Kingdom) have broader powers of intervention where insolvency is threatened, while in other cases (as in Canada and the United States) the deposit insurance agency has lender of last resort powers which, at least in respect of potentially insolvent institutions, may exceed those of the central bank. Some central banks are disposed to act as the lender of last resort in domestic currency only, although such funds may in principle be converted if the recipient bank's need is for foreign currency liquidity. Elsewhere the capacity to provide foreign currency assistance is limited by the size of official reserves relative to the volume of locally placed foreign currency deposits.

As a matter of policy, and in order to discourage excessive risk-taking by banks, the precise scope of the lender of last resort function is not publicly stated. This calculated reticence applies both to the circumstances in which assistance may be given and to the allocation of support responsibilities between different national authorities. In several countries (for instance, Japan and the United States) foreign banks have a formalised right of access to the central bank's discount window, but this facility would not necessarily extend to emergency support. In general, national authorities expect foreign parent banks to provide all necessary assistance to their local subsidiaries, whether or not letters of comfort have been issued, although the threat of shareholders' actions could in theory place a limit on this commitment. So far as branches are concerned, the US authorities have in the past demonstrated a willingness to provide emergency support to the foreign branch of a US bank, using the head office as a conduit for such assistance.

Among other emergency measures that may be available to avert sudden bank failures are assisted mergers and the appointment of caretaker managers to troubled banks. Furthermore, as indicated above, financial centres frequently look to parent institutions to support foreign-owned banks to which they are host, for which purpose irrevocable lines of credit and/or letters of comfort may be required or encouraged. Letters of comfort may also serve the purpose of alerting foreign central banks to potential demands for liquidity assistance originating from abroad, particularly where (as for instance in Hong Kong) such letters are required to be issued with the full knowledge of the parent institution's supervisory authority.

Finally, where banks do fail, the ensuing liquidation proceedings may be specially designed to protect local depositors. For this purpose several countries treat branches of foreign banks as separate entities requiring their own liquidation. In such cases, too, branch creditors may enjoy a preferential claim to branch assets (as in the Netherlands and Singapore and also under New York State law), while offshore deposits may be subordinated to onshore deposits (Singapore being the major example of this).

COUNTRY STUDIES

Belgium

The Institut de Réescompte et de Garantie (IRG), a public body funded by the commercial banks and jointly administered by them and the government, offers both deposit protection and emergency liquidity assistance.[1] In its deposit protection role the IRG has a broad discretion (but no obligation) to pay off all creditors of a failed bank, the current practice being to impose a ceiling on the amount payable to each depositor which may vary from case to case. The IRG has not so far redeemed any foreign currency deposits, but is empowered to do so. Belgian subsidiaries, but not branches, of foreign banks participate in the scheme. The discretionary basis of the IRG's deposit protection was recently challenged in the courts[2] and there are now plans to introduce a formal deposit insurance scheme.

In its liquidity assistance role the IRG again has wide discretionary powers. In particular, support may be given to potentially insolvent institutions and funds advanced need not always be fully secured, the guiding principle being whether intervention is necessary in the public interest. Liquidity assistance may be given to foreign branches, but not subsidiaries, of Belgian banks. Participation in the scheme does not imply a right to intervention either in the bank's favour or in favour of its creditors/depositors.

The IRG's resources are based on the BFr1 billion of equity capital subscribed by the commercial banks, money market borrowings, borrowings from the National Bank of Belgium, and a special intervention reserve of BFr3 billion also subscribed by the banks. Bank subscriptions are proportionate to their balance sheet totals and their participation in the scheme is subject to renewal every five years. Following the failure of Banque Copine in 1982 some BFr1 billion was drawn from the intervention reserve to pay off depositors.

The National Bank of Belgium continues to provide routine liquidity assistance through its discount window and may also be viewed as the lender of last resort, although it has not been called upon to exercise this function since the Second World War.

Canada

Banks as well as federally incorporated trust and mortgage loan companies must become members of the Canada Deposit Insurance Corporation (CDIC).[3] Insurance is limited to C$60,000 per depositor per institution and the deposits must be made with an office located in Canada and denominated in Canadian dollars. Coverage extends to non-residents and to corporate and bank depositors. The CDIC is funded by an annual levy on member institutions although it has powers to borrow from the federal government. The fund currently amounts to approximately 0.2 per cent of insured deposits.

As part of its deposit protection function the CDIC may 'acquire assets from a member institution, make loans or advances to a member institution and take security therefor and guarantee loans to or deposits with a member institution, for the purpose of reducing a risk to the Corporation or reducing or arresting a threatened loss to the Corporation'.[4]

The Bank of Canada Act confers on the Bank of Canada broad powers as lender of last resort. All loans must be made on a secured basis although the revised Bank Act has substantially broadened the range of collateral eligible for this purpose. In 1981 the Bank of Canada formalised the terms on which it will lend as follows: lines of credit are extended by the central bank to each chartered bank and to each member of the Canadian Payments Association that participates directly in the daily clearing of payments items and maintains an account at the Bank of Canada for this purpose. The lines of credit for each institution are defined as the greatest of: (a) $2\frac{1}{2}$ per cent of its checkable deposits; (b) 10 per cent of its average primary reserve requirement; and (c) C$1 million.

'Ordinary' advances by the Bank of Canada shall not exceed the institution's line of credit; the advance is for one business day; there are restrictions on the frequency of drawings; the rate charged is Bank Rate; and collateral consists of securities issued or guaranteed by Canada or a province of Canada. 'Extraordinary' advances are advances that do not meet these conditions. In such cases the rate charged will normally be above the Bank Rate.

The CDIC also has a lender of last resort function (see above), which has been exercised in favour of a number of trust companies. Due partly to the high level of industry concentration there has been no bank failure since 1923.

Foreign banks are required to provide non-legally binding letters of comfort covering their Canadian bank subsidiaries. The Canadian authorities would accordingly look first to the parent institution for support in the event that a foreign bank subsidiary experienced liquidity difficulties going beyond unexpected clearing swings.

France

There is no official deposit insurance scheme covering French banks. However, the Association Française des Banques (AFB) set up its own deposit protection arrangements in 1979 when it became clear that the Treasury and the Conseil National du Crédit were considering the establishment of an official scheme. The AFB arrangements, which were formulated jointly with the authorities, are territorial in scope and therefore embrace all banks, including foreign banks, operating in France while excluding foreign branches of French banks.[5]

Deposits are protected up to a ceiling of FFr200,000 per depositor per institution subject to the exclusion of interbank deposits, certificates of deposit and foreign currency deposits. There is no deposit protection fund and participating banks are required to contribute directly to any deposit pay-offs according to a graduated scale, based on each bank's deposit total, which in effect favours the larger banks against the smaller. The scale of contributions, incorporating an absolute cut-off point beyond a specified deposit total, is designed to reflect the lower degree of risk attached to the large nationalised banks relative to the smaller private banks.

Under the French system of monetary control, which is based on quantitative credit ceilings, banks have automatic and unlimited access to official credit through the sale of eligible commercial paper to the Bank of France. In such a context it is difficult to distinguish the lender of last resort function from the normal functioning of credit markets. However, the Bank of France has on occasion lent to troubled institutions on the basis of purchase of non-eligible paper at a special rate and in other cases the central bank may, in principle, provide support through the intermediation of one or other of the larger banks.

Section 52 of the new Banking Act formalises previous practice with regard to troubled banks by enabling the Governor of the Bank of France either to call on shareholders to provide additional financial backing or to organise an industry-wide contribution to safeguard the interests of depositors and preserve the reputation of the banking system.

Hong Kong

Hong Kong has no formal deposit protection scheme. When the possibility of introducing such a scheme was raised after the financial disturbances of 1965–66, the larger banks objected and the matter was not pursued further. In one of the bank failures of 1965–66 depositors did lose approximately one-third of their money, but in a subsequent failure, when the authorities were particularly concerned about possible adverse confidence effects, means were found of protecting depositors in full. In March 1983, in the context of renewed domestic financial disturbances, the government again ruled out the introduction of a deposit insurance scheme.[6]

The day-to-day lender of last resort is the Hong Kong Bank which, in fulfilling its clearing function, may provide liquidity assistance on terms of its own choosing to any bank faced with a funding shortfall at the daily clearing. Beyond this the Hong Kong bank may, either on its own initiative or at the government's behest, provide emergency assistance on a longer-term basis or, where more protracted difficulties are evident, acquire the troubled bank (as happened with Hang Seng Bank in 1966). In November 1982 both the Hong Kong Bank and Chartered Bank announced their willingness to assist 'soundly based and well managed' deposit-taking companies that were unable to obtain credit elsewhere.[7]

The true lender of last resort is, however, the Hong Kong government, whose Exchange Fund has recently averaged around HK$35 billion (the precise figure is not disclosed), most of which is invested in US dollars. In 1965, the government exercised its lender of last resort role by depositing sterling funds in London for the use of the Hong Kong Bank and the Chartered Bank, which at the time were providing liquidity assistance to a number of other Hong Kong institutions.

The Hong Kong government has also indicated on several occasions that it would act as a direct lender of last resort to the Hong Kong Bank should the need ever arise.[8] Finally, at the height of the domestic financial crisis of September 1983 the government passed an emergency Bill enabling it to take over the Hang Lung Bank on the grounds that 'it would be unacceptable both domestically and internationally to allow this bank to fail, which would involve considerable loss to depositors'.[9]

Italy

The fact that over 50 per cent of bank deposits in Italy are placed with public sector institutions has had an important bearing on the Italian authorities' approach to deposit protection. The Bank of Italy's practice has been to encourage the merger of smaller banks facing financial difficulties or to arrange for support in other forms from larger institutions.[10] In October 1974 this procedure was formalised by a decree authorising the Bank of Italy to extend special low interest loans to banks willing to acquire failing institutions where liquidation proceedings had already been initiated. One consequence of this approach is that there have been no deposit losses with domestic banks in recent years. Foreign branches, though not subsidiaries, of Italian banks are in principle covered by the subsidised loan scheme, as are Italian subsidiaries and branches of foreign banks.

To accomodate temporary liquidity difficulties the central bank provides a line of credit to each bank, based on its balance sheet size; drawings may be made on this, backed by collateral in the form of public sector securities, at the official discount rate. The interest rate charged is subject to a graduated premium where frequent use is made of the facility.

Subsidiaries of foreign banks (of which there are very few) are not asked for letters of comfort from their parent banks, but branches of foreign banks are required to produce a declaration by their head office in a standard form, which asserts that under its own law the head office is liable to the full extent of its assets for the liabilities of its Italian branch. Under Italian law local branches of foreign banks are subject to separate liquidation proceedings, as in the case of Intra-Bank's failure, where the Italian branch's assets were used to pay off all branch creditors before remission of the surplus to the main liquidator.

The special procedures that were adopted to deal with the Banco Ambrosiano crisis in 1982 are discussed later in this Chapter (see pages 161–63).

Japan

Since 1971, Japan has had a deposit insurance scheme which is jointly capitalised by the government, the Bank of Japan and the banking industry.[11] The coverage is non-territorial in that all yen deposits held by residents and non-residents with Japanese banks and their overseas branches are insured, while Japanese branches of foreign banks are excluded. Neither foreign currency nor interbank deposits are covered. There is a maximum of yen 3 million (approximately US$13,000) payable to each depositor per institution. Participant banks contribute an annual levy (currently 0.008 per cent of their insured deposits) to the insurance fund which at the end of March 1984 amounted to around 180 billion yen or 0.067 per cent of total insured deposits. Given the modest size of the fund, the official intention is to raise the scale of contributions in stages over the next several years. The fund may, if necessary, be supplemented by borrowings from the Bank of Japan, although it has been officially stated that the system 'is not intended to cope with a general financial panic'.[12]

Routine liquidity assistance is provided on a day-to-day basis by the Bank of Japan at Bank Rate. For this purpose each bank, domestic or foreign, has a commercial bill discount quota based on the size of its yen assets. Foreign banks are given a proportionately higher quota because their yen assets are relatively small. Longer-term liquidity assistance may also be provided at Bank Rate, although such lending must (in the absence of a special Ministry of Finance waiver) be backed by adequate collateral. The Bank of Japan regards itself as a lender of last resort in yen only, although if a bank experiences a liquidity shortfall in foreign currency the Bank may, in principle, make yen available for conversion into foreign currency. During the international financial disturbances of 1974, when some Japanese banks experienced difficulties in securing dollar funds, the Bank of Tokyo provided large-scale liquidity assistance, borrowing dollars in its own name at a small margin over LIBOR and channelling funds to those banks in need.

Luxembourg

There is in Luxembourg no official or privately organised deposit protection scheme, despite the fact that an increasing proportion of the country's international banking business is retail rather than wholesale. The National Bank of Belgium, which has a branch in Luxembourg, provides liquidity support in respect of local currency banking and for this purpose is prepared to discount certain claims on or guaranteed by the Luxembourg government. The Luxembourg government itself would have the capacity to provide assistance if a local bank encountered difficulties. There is, however, no support facility for the Eurobanks, who must look to their parent institutions for liquidity assistance. The Luxembourg authorities do not demand letters of comfort for this purpose, but irrecoverable stand-by credit lines may be required on a case-by-case basis.

When the Banco Ambrosiano crisis broke in the summer of 1982, the six Italian banks in Luxembourg controlled by local holding companies were asked to provide unconditional guarantees from their parent banks in Italy. Guarantees were duly given pending the dismantling of the holding company structure by the banks concerned (which was completed in 1983).

The Netherlands

The revised Act on the Supervision of the Credit System provided that, in the absence of a voluntary deposit insurance scheme, a government scheme should be introduced. The voluntary (but comprehensive) scheme, which came into effect at the beginning of 1979, applies to all banks and credit institutions in the Netherlands, including branches of foreign banks; it guarantees all deposits by individuals (but not companies) up to DFl35,000 (index-linked) per depositor per institution;

and it makes no distinction between resident and non-resident depositors or between guilder and foreign currency claims.[13] However, deposits held with the foreign branches of Dutch banks are not covered. The scheme is not funded but is administered by the central bank which advances payments prior to apportionment of the burden among participant institutions. There is a maximum annual contribution per institution measured as a percentage of capital, designed to prevent contagious financial difficulties; any excess above this ceiling is funded by the central bank.

Section 15 of the Bank Act of 1948 gives the Nederlandsche Bank broad powers to provide liquidity assistance. However, section 16 of that Act states that 'the Bank shall grant no credit or advances without security', there being no further guidance on what constitutes security for this purpose.

The authorities are authorised to regulate interest rates on demand deposits if excessive competition is threatening the stability of the credit system. Other emergency provisions include, in the case of troubled banks, the appointment of receivers with full management powers where, for instance, an arranged merger may be considered preferable to conventional bankruptcy proceedings.

Singapore

Singapore has no deposit insurance scheme, although as a matter of record there have been no bank failures or deposit losses since the Monetary Authority of Singapore was established in 1970.

Routine liquidity assistance is provided to banks by the discount houses, which in turn may look to the MAS for any funding shortfall. While preferring to exercise its lender of last resort function through the discount houses, the MAS does have broad statutory powers in this area. In particular, under a 1972 amendment to the Monetary Authority of Singapore Act the MAS 'may, if it thinks such action is necessary to safeguard monetary stability, make a loan or advance to a bank carrying on business under the Banking Act or to such financial institutions or class of financial institutions as the Authority may from time to time approve against such forms of security as the Authority may consider sufficient'.[14]

The MAS does not, however, hold itself out as lender of last resort to foreign banks within its jurisdiction. Instead, the Singapore authorities rely on three kinds of protection. First, they have discouraged the local incorporation of foreign banks on the grounds that 'any bank of repute would be morally if not legally committed to give full support to its branch operations.'[15] Secondly, considerable importance is attached to letters of comfort demanded from the parents of foreign-owned banks.[16] And finally, under section 14 of the Banking (Amendment) Act 1984, the statutory order of priorities for paying off the deposits of failed banks gives preference to those deposit liabilities that are subject to reserve and liquidity requirements. In effect this means that offshore deposits (which are not subject to such requirements) are subordinated to onshore deposits in liquidation proceedings.

Switzerland

Switzerland does not yet possess a deposit insurance scheme, partly because central and other public sector banks have until recently attracted the major share of savings and other deposits from the general public. However, with the public's deposits now being dispersed more widely among commercial banks, proposals for such a scheme have been drafted by an expert committee and are now being considered in the context of broader banking reforms. The proposed system is mandatory, except for foreign banks having equivalent coverage from home-based schemes, and would be subject to a deposit ceiling equivalent to US$35,000. Protection would also be graduated so that only the first US$10,000 would be fully covered, with a progressively increasing proportion of loss borne thereafter by the depositor.[17] However, the proposed mandatory deposit insurance scheme was not included in a draft amendment to the Banking Law released in July 1984 and is therefore unlikely to be implemented at an early date.

The Swiss Bankers' Association has meanwhile approved its own voluntary deposit protection scheme which gives priority in bankruptcy proceedings to deposits of less than SFr30,000. Under this scheme the banks are to establish a special protection fund to ensure that priority deposits are paid out immediately bankruptcy proceedings are initiated, the fund assuming the depositors' claims against the failed bank.

The National Bank Law enumerates the Swiss National Bank's powers quite specifically but makes no reference to the lender of last resort function. On the other hand, this function may be viewed as an extension of the collateral-backed lending that the National Bank is authorised to undertake for monetary policy purposes. In any event, the National Bank confirmed its preparedness to act as lender of last resort when, in April 1977, it participated in a line of credit offered to Credit Suisse in the wake of the Chiasso Affair.[18]

United Kingdom

Sections 21–33 of the Banking Act 1979 provide for the introduction of a mandatory deposit insurance scheme which came into effect in February 1982. Under the new arrangements, 75 per cent of a depositor's 'protected deposit' is insured, a protected deposit for this purpose being limited to £10,000 per depositor per institution. Interbank and foreign currency deposits are excluded from the scheme, as are certificates of deposit, secured deposits and deposits with a maturity of over five years. Protection does not extend to sterling deposits made with an institution's branches or subsidiaries outside the United Kingdom, while UK offices of overseas banks may be exempted from participation if their sterling deposit liabilities are already as well protected as they would be under the UK scheme. A deposit protection fund has been established which is funded from flat rate contributions by participant banks, calculated on the basis of their sterling deposits (subject to maximum and minimum contributions that tend to favour larger institutions). The initial fund amounted to £5.4 million with power to borrow up to £10 million, and by June 1983 the Deposit Protection Board's total liability to depositors with failed institutions was estimated at around £4 million.[19]

The Bank of England has a broad discretion to assist banks experiencing liquidity difficulties and/or threatened with insolvency. During and in the immediate aftermath of the UK secondary banking crisis of 1973–75 this discretion was exercised in a variety of forms which included unilateral support arrangements, joint support operations with the clearing banks, the guaranteeing of a troubled bank's loan portfolio, the acquisition of another problematic loan portfolio and the acquisition of one institution as a subsidiary of the Bank.[20]

The Bank's view is that its lender of last resort function extends to the foreign network of parent banks under its jurisdiction and that, similarly, UK branches and subsidiaries of overseas banks are, for this purpose, the responsibility of the parent institution's supervisory authority. At the same time the Bank seeks non-legally-binding letters of comfort from shareholders of those UK banks which are overseas controlled, to the effect that they acknowledge a responsibility extending beyond strict legal liability to support their UK bank affiliates.[21]

The United States

The US Federal Deposit Insurance Corporation (FDIC) was established in 1933 as a direct result of the financial crash which, over a period of four years, witnessed 9,000 bank closures and aggregate deposit losses of $1.3 billion. The FDIC was designed to protect small depositors and in doing so to stabilise the financial system as a whole. This it has done with remarkable success, as reflected in average annual bank failures of less than four in 1942–71, rising to eight in 1971–80. In the three years 1981–83, however, failures increased sharply to an average of over 33 a year.[22]

With major exceptions, deposit insurance through the FDIC is a prerequisite to receiving a bank charter. US branches of foreign banks accepting retail deposits must also be insured, in which case, as a condition of insurance, the branch must pledge assets to the FDIC equal to 10 per cent of its total liabilities, representing security against any country or additional prudential risk beyond the US authorities' control. International Banking Facilities are not insured and foreign branches of US banks are currently outside the FDIC scheme. Insurance coverage is confined to non-bank deposits of residents and non-residents in any currency up to a ceiling of $100,000 per deposit. The FDIC is funded by member banks and at the end of 1982 it managed an insurance fund of $13.8 billion, equivalent to 0.9 per cent of insured deposits, with authority to borrow up to $3 billion from the Treasury.

The FDIC offers two kinds of protection to depositors. First, all eligible deposits under the statutory cut-off point are formally insured. Secondly, there is *de facto* protection for uninsured deposits arising from the FDIC's preferred method of dealing with failing banks – the so-called 'purchase and assumption' transaction. Under a 'P and A' transaction the FDIC replaces bad assets with cash while deposits and other non-subordinated liabilities are assumed by another bank. In such assisted mergers all depositors, insured and uninsured, are made whole. Thus, in the 620 bank failures during the period from 1934 to the end of 1982, 99.8 per cent of all depositors had their deposits paid in full, and 98.9 per cent of all deposits were recovered.

In recent policy statements the FDIC has suggested that the extent of *de facto* deposit insurance cover has tended to undermine financial discipline. Accordingly, the agency has formulated specific legislative proposals which would reduce the protection offered, in particular, to large depositors with large banks.[23] The first proposal would introduce a variable element into the present system of flat rate insurance premiums payable by banks. Under the second and more far-reaching proposal the FDIC would, in lieu of its usual 'P and A' approach to failed banks, combine a pay-off of insured deposits with a cash advance to uninsured depositors and other general creditors based on the present value of anticipated collections by the receivership. In other words, uninsured depositors would be exposed to losses arising out of the receivership in a way that does not happen when the FDIC organises assisted mergers.

The US Federal Reserve has broad powers to provide liquidity support to distressed banks. Section 10(b) of the 1913 Federal Reserve Act as amended states that any Federal Reserve Bank 'may make advances to any member bank on its time or demand notes having maturities of not more than 4 months and which are secured to the satisfaction of such Federal Reserve Bank'. The collateral requirement means, in effect, that the borrowing bank must be solvent since taking security from an insolvent institution would infringe the rights of unsecured creditors. Under section 7 of the International Banking Act 1978 the Federal Reserve may also make advances to any branch or agency of a foreign bank that holds reserves with the Federal Reserve 'in the same manner and to the same extent that it may exercise such powers with respect to a member bank'.

The Federal Reserve's Regulation A outlines the terms on which credit may be extended to eligible banks, as follows:

1. Short-term adjustment credit. This is available on a short-term basis

to meet temporary requirements for funds or to cushion more persistent fund outflows pending an orderly adjustment of the borrower's assets and liabilities. Credit under this heading is generally charged at the basic discount rate, although a variable surcharge may be applied to large, frequent borrowers.

2. Extended seasonal credit. This is available for longer periods to provide seasonal credit to smaller institutions lacking ready access to national money markets. Credit is generally charged at the basic discount rate.

3. Other extended credit. This may be provided to banks experiencing difficulties arising from exceptional circumstances or practices involving only that institution, if the needed funds are not available from other sources. Such credit may also be provided where liquidity strains are affecting a broad range of institutions. A special rate above the basic discount rate may be charged.

4. Emergency credit for others. In unusual circumstances, individuals, partnerships and non-financial corporations may obtain emergency credit from the Federal Reserve if failure to obtain such credit would adversely affect the economy.

Public statements by Federal Reserve spokesmen have made clear that US offices of foreign banks cannot expect to use the official discount window to meet the obligations of a foreign parent or head office.[24] Indeed, so far as subsidiaries are concerned, the US authorities expect the foreign parent to be a source of strength to its US offshoot, for which reason flows of funds between foreign parents and US subsidiaries are monitored through the confidential Y-8F report. The Federal Reserve's role as lender of last resort to foreign offices of US banks is less clear. However, support may be given to the foreign branch or subsidiary of a US bank by channelling funds through the US head office or parent, and where the US parent is itself insolvent, assistance can in principle be given directly to a foreign subsidiary, although special statutory procedures covering loans to non-bank entities would then have to be followed.

The Federal Reserve's lender of last resort function is designed to provide temporary liquidity to solvent institutions. Power to deal with insolvency is in the hands of the FDIC, which has three main options in such emergencies. First, it may pay off the depositors of a failed bank, although this has not been the preferred approach. Secondly, it may invite existing banks to bid to assume the deposit liabilities of the failed bank and to purchase certain of its assets (the 'P and A' transaction mentioned above). And, finally, under section 13(c) of the Federal Deposit Insurance Corporation Act the FDIC may provide direct financial assistance to a bank which is in danger of closing. At present this last capital infusion option is exercised only when the FDIC determines that the amount of assistance to be granted is less than the cost that would be incurred in the event of liquidation of the bank, or that the continued operation of the bank is essential to provide adequate banking services to its community.[25]

West Germany

There is no statutory scheme for deposit insurance but the banking associations for the private commercial banks, savings banks and credit associations have, with official encouragement, each set up their own voluntary deposit protection schemes. The Federal Association of German Banks has established a Deposit Protection Fund for the private commercial banking sector which protects non-bank deposits with member institutions up to a limit, per depositor, of 30 per cent of a bank's stated equity capital.[26] The scheme is funded by an annual membership levy, and in the case of German subsidiaries of foreign banks (whose licensing terms generally require participation) the Protection Fund seeks legally binding letters of indemnification from the parent bank requiring it to reimburse any payments made by the fund to the subsidiary's depositors.

The coverage of the Deposit Protection Fund extends to foreign branches of German banks, foreign currency deposits and deposits by non-residents. However, there are also some limitations: most but not all private commercial banks participate; the potential pay-out is limited by the size of the fund; and the pay-out is at all times discretionary, not mandatory.

In the aftermath of the Herstatt collapse, when a number of banks had to be given liquidity assistance on an *ad hoc* basis, the Bundesbank joined with the domestic banking industry in setting up, in September 1974, the Liquidity Consortium Bank (Liko-Bank).[27] The intended function of this institution is to give assistance to banks that have run into temporary liquidity difficulties but are otherwise sound, for which purpose it can engage in all normal banking transactions. As an exception to the general rule, the Liko-Bank did provide fully secured liquidity support to Schröder, Münchmeyer, Hengst when that bank was threatened with insolvency in late 1983 (see page 158 below). The Liko-Bank's equity capital, 30 per cent of which is subscribed by the Bundesbank, amounts in all to DM1 billion (DM250 million paid up, DM750 million unpaid). In addition it has been granted a special rediscount ceiling by the Bundesbank, a facility which reflects the central bank's continuing role as lender of last resort.

The Liko-Bank may offer support to any bank licensed to do business in Germany, including branches of foreign banks. Foreign branches, but not subsidiaries, of German banks are also eligible for support. There is no legal constraint on lending in foreign currencies, although such activity is not presently envisaged.

THE LENDER OF LAST RESORT FUNCTION IN PRACTICE: CASE STUDIES

The following survey of international bank failures occurring in the period 1973–84 offers some insight into the practical problems that may arise in such cases. The most important conclusion to emerge is that *ad hoc* co-ordination of national support arrangements might not be sufficient to contain the threatened collapse of a major multinational bank.

Bankhaus Herstatt

On 26 June 1974 Bankhaus Herstatt, with total assets of around US$800 million, was ordered by the West German authorities to close its doors after suffering foreign exchange and other losses which were eventually put at over $450 million.[28] Because of fraudulent book-keeping, Herstatt's losses could not be determined immediately, and attempts to launch a rescue operation involving the Big Three West German banks – Deutsche Bank, Dresdner Bank and Commerzbank – failed for lack of reliable information.[29] Legal claims arising out of the failure were settled in December 1974 on the basis that West German banks would receive 45 per cent of their claims, foreign banks 55 per cent and other creditors 65 per cent (the Association of German banks having already paid off small depositors with claims under the equivalent of US$8,000). These amounts were subsequently raised as assets were realised during the liquidation process.

The distinctive feature of the Herstatt failure was the way it disrupted the clearing mechanism for spot foreign exchange transactions (see page 74 above). This in turn had damaging effects on the international inter-bank market, where Italian and Japanese banks in particular suffered serious funding difficulties.[30] Indeed, during the latter part of 1974 the bank of Tokyo was obliged to borrow on behalf of smaller Japanese banks who were temporarily shut out of the Euromarkets. Within West Germany itself the shock to confidence led to large-scale deposit with-drawals from smaller banks, some of which could have been forced to close their doors in the absence of joint support operations by the Bundesbank and major commercial banks.[31]

Although Herstatt had a Luxembourg subsidiary, its international operations were conducted mainly from its head office rather than through a multinational banking network. The handling of the bank's collapse was therefore a matter primarily for West Germany and did not call for extensive international supervisory co-operation. The West German authorities' dissatisfaction with their own management of this affair is, however, reflected in their subsequent remedial actions. The so-called 'Lex Herstatt' that came into force in 1976 included, at the preventive level, new bank licensing requirements and limits on large loans, as well as restrictions on open foreign exchange positions. At the same time, new safeguard arrangements were put in place in the form of the Liquidity Consortium Bank (Liko-Bank), a strengthened deposit protection scheme and expanded powers for the Federal Banking Supervisory Office to deal with failing banks short of ordering immediate closure. These measures were insufficient in themselves, however, either to prevent or contain West Germany's next major bank failure – that of Schröder, Münchmeyer, Hengst (see below).

It may be argued that occasional banking traumas are an essential ingredient of financial discipline. That may well be so, but the Herstatt collapse failed to provide a therapeutic shock. In the very short term the market's reaction was to penalise not so much banks with known exposures to Herstatt but smaller West German banks, regardless of their financial condition, as well as Italian and Japanese banks whose own national authorities were at that time poorly placed to provide emergency dollar support.[32] In the longer run there was a reappraisal by banks of the counterparty risk in spot foreign exchange transactions, but otherwise there were few lessons the market could usefully learn from the Herstatt experience. Indeed, where, as in this case, fraud masks a bank's weaknesses from its own regulatory authorities, it is idle to suppose that market discipline will be sharpened by the losses suffered.

Schröder, Münchmeyer, Hengst

The rescue operation launched in early November 1983 to save Schröder, Münchmeyer, Hengst & Co. (SMH) from sudden collapse provides a remarkable contrast to the West German authorities' handling of Herstatt's failure. SMH, with assets of DM2.2 billion, was one of West Germany's most prestigious private banks and although the full details of its downfall have yet to be revealed, the chronology of events is straightforward enough.[33]

SMH's problems arose quite simply from massive over-exposure to a single borrower, IBH Holdings AG – Europe's biggest construction equipment maker – and its affiliated companies. When IBH got into difficulties, SMH, which had a shareholding of 7.5 per cent in the company, extended further loans to the point where its total risk exposure to the group reached some DM900 million. This was equivalent to over 800 per cent of SMH's DM110 million capital and 40 per cent of its total assets. A particular point of interest is that over half these loans were channelled through SMH's Luxembourg subsidiary, which commanded assets of DM1.1 billion and equity capital of DM29 million. In other words, the Luxembourg entity had exposure to IBH equivalent to some 50 per cent of its assets and 16 times its capital.

West Germany's bank regulations, enforced through the Berlin Supervisory Office, provide that no single loan should exceed 75 per cent of a bank's capital and also place restrictions on large loans exceeding 15 per cent of capital. These constraints proved useless in this instance, in part because they did not apply formally to foreign subsidiaries, while the gentlemen's agreement which required banks to keep their consolidated loan concentrations within the regulatory limits did not require them to report such exposures on a fully consolidated basis (all this will, however, change when the proposed new banking law comes into effect). In addition, SMH evidently misreported some of its lending to the IBH group as exposure to separate entities. Nor was the problem picked up in Luxembourg, where loan concentrations are not formally regulated.

While SMH's over-exposure to the IBH group may have highlighted deficiencies in West Germany's regulatory arrangements, the manner in which the crisis was handled reflected a remarkable degree of cohesion within the domestic banking industry as well as between banks, the domestic supervisory authorities and the Luxembourg authorities. When it became clear that SMH's prospective losses on its IBH exposure would far exceed its capital, an emergency meeting was held at the Bundesbank on 1 November 1983, at which representatives of some 20 domestic banks were present. The basic principles agreed at the outset were that SMH should not be permitted to collapse as Herstatt had done, that foreign banks with exposure to SMH should be fully protected and kept out of the support operation, and that the support provided should be to SMH as a whole, including its Luxembourg subsidiary.

The support operation itself took three main forms. First, the Liko-Bank provided liquidity assistance on a fully secured basis to offset deposit withdrawals from SMH. Secondly, the Deposit Protection Fund extended unsecured loans, thereby absorbing a proportion of SMH's losses. Thirdly – and this aspect of the rescue went beyond established protective arrangements – 20 or so major bank creditors converted some DM450 million of their claims on SMH into long-term subordinated debt, in effect meeting a major part of SMH's capital deficiency. Subsequently, another 18 creditor banks with claims on SMH of DM5–10 million participated in the rescue by, *inter alia*, keeping open their existing credit lines. Finally, in mid-December Lloyds Bank agreed to acquire the sound parts of SMH's business for an undisclosed sum, leaving the Luxembourg subsidiary to be liquidated. The Bundesbank played a key co-ordinating role throughout and was also indirectly involved in the support provided, both through its shareholding in the Liko-Bank and through more general liquidity assistance given to the domestic money market.

These are the bare outlines of a highly intricate operation. The SMH rescue was complex partly because it could not be handled through the machinery that had been put in place after Herstatt's collapse. The Liko-Bank was not designed to support an insolvent institution; the Luxembourg subsidiary, where a large proportion of the bad loans were booked, did not qualify for assistance from the Deposit Protection Fund, which covers only foreign branches (although assistance could be channelled through the parent bank so long as it remained afloat); and since the Deposit Protection Fund does not protect interbank deposits, there was no formal safeguard for foreign banks. The West German authorities were particularly anxious to protect the latters' interests in view of the outcry over foreign losses incurred when Herstatt collapsed and their desire to preserve Frankfurt's reputation as an international financial centre. The authorities were therefore faced with the need to put together in a matter of hours an *ad hoc* rescue package involving the direct support of the West German banking industry. In the event this was done with remarkable skill and despatch. The immediate impact on financial markets was thereby minimised, although some Luxembourg subsidiaries of West German banks had to resort to their parent institutions for liquidity assistance.

Apart from giving further impetus to West Germany's proposed banking law reforms, the longer-term significance of the SMH affair is two-fold. First, the Bundesbank, in common with several other European monetary authorities, is no longer prepared to contemplate major bank failures or deposit losses. Secondly, West Germany reversed the precedent established by the Ambrosiano collapse (see page 161) by taking full responsibility for the offshore activities of one of its banks – even though these activities are at present outside the West German authorities' control and viewed by them with considerable misgiving.[34] This action in part reflects commercial self-interest, but it also underlines the fact that central bankers, having endorsed the principle of parental responsibility in supervisory matters, are increasingly prepared to accept this principle in their lender of last resort capacity.

Franklin National Bank

On 8 October 1974 Franklin National Bank was declared insolvent after a prolonged official support operation. The failure of Franklin National is of particular interest because of the nature of the bank itself, the causes of its collapse, the way in which its failure was handled by the US authorities and its impact on financial markets.[35]

Franklin National was special first of all because of its size. At the end of 1973 it had total assets of $5 billion making it the twentieth largest bank in the United States. In addition it had extensive international operations which were conducted mainly through its London branch with assets of around $1 billion. Finally, although Franklin National had a well developed retail banking business in Long Island it had expanded both its domestic and international lending business by aggressively purchasing funds in the wholesale money market, its funding base being therefore heavily dependent on uninsured and potentially volatile deposits and placements.

The initial causes of Franklin National's difficulties, taken individually, are not remarkable. They may be summarised as excessive gearing, aggressive maturity mismatching and bond trading (reflecting speculation on interest rate movements), poor asset quality, over-dependence on purchased funds and foreign exchange losses.[36] The speculation in foreign exchange markets is especially significant because, as with Herstatt, losses were originally disguised through various book-keeping malpractices. The scale of speculation increased as the bank's situation deteriorated and the management felt compelled to adopt a 'go-for-broke' strategy in an attempt to restore the bank's fortunes. When the foreign exchange losses eventually came to light this contributed to a crisis of confidence that led directly to the bank's collapse. Indeed, it has been authoritatively stated that Franklin National never became 'insolvent' in a balance sheet sense and failed 'not because its net worth was eroded by poor credit judgement but rather because of a loss of confidence on the part of its funding sources'.[37]

The handling of Franklin National's failure also had a number of unusual features. First, the lender of last resort assistance provided by the Federal Reserve prior to the declaration of insolvency amounted to over $1.7 billion, representing nearly half Franklin National's assets at the time. Secondly, the Federal Reserve Bank of New York felt obliged to take over Franklin National's foreign exchange book to relieve the market's anxiety over uncompleted forward deals. Thirdly, much of the liquidity support provided by the Federal Reserve was used by Franklin National to plug the growing funding shortfall at its London branch (some $360 million of official assistance was absorbed in this way in the period May–July 1974). Fourthly, the official support operation was designed not so much to save Franklin National – which had suffered an irreparable collapse of confidence – as to buy time pending an orderly arrangement of the bank's affairs.[38] The solution that eventually emerged after five months of crisis management involved the appointment of the FDIC as receiver and the assumption of Franklin National's deposit liabilities and selected assets by an outside bidder (European-American Bank) – a familiar purchase and assumption transaction which protected the bank's 6,000 uninsured depositors.

Another aspect of the handling of Franklin National's failure deserves special mention. It has been suggested that by indirectly assisting the bank's London office the US Federal Reserve was taking a broad view of its international responsibilities and extending its traditional lender of last resort role to the Euromarkets.[39] In fact, the Federal Reserve had little choice in the matter since failure to support the branch would have brought down the whole bank. The real issue was not whether official funds should be used to support the London operation, but whether the assets of the London branch could be used as collateral for such support. The difficulty here was the threat of separate liquidation proceedings in

London and the possibility of legal proceedings by creditors of the London branch to seize branch assets and thereby secure their claims.[40] This danger was averted only by the co-operative intervention of the Bank of England,[41] which was presumably assured that branch creditors would not lose money in the event of the bank's failure and an ensuing purchase and assumption transaction. From a broader policy point of view, however, what this episode demonstrates is the formidable legal complexities that would face the Federal Reserve as lender of last resort if a large US bank with a global multinational banking network were to get into difficulties.

The impact of Franklin National's publicised difficulties on financial markets suggests that in times of uncertainty market participants view a bank's head office in its home jurisdiction as being more secure than its foreign branches. In this case Franklin National's London branch found that (in the wake of the Herstatt collapse) other banks were unwilling to enter into foreign exchange transactions which therefore had to be undertaken by the bank's head office.[42] More generally, in the disturbances that followed Herstatt's collapse and Franklin National's funding crisis, there was a tendency for depositors to shift their money out of the Eurodollar market into US-based banks.[43] Perhaps the most important lesson to be drawn from market reactions, however, is that a bank like Franklin National can purchase funds at will in the wholesale money markets (domestic and international) but that when confidence eventually breaks it may be abruptly cut off from its funding sources.[44] As pointed out in Chapter 3, the discipline of the market place operates in such cases not as a corrective mechanism or deterrent but as a means of killing off the offending institution.

Banco Ambrosiano

The scandalous circumstances surrounding the downfall of Banco Ambrosiano in the summer of 1982 have been widely reported and are not directly relevant to the present discussion. Suffice it to say that Banco Ambrosiano SpA, Italy's largest private bank with $6 billion of deposits, faced a major capital deficiency arising from $1.4 billion of doubtful foreign loans which were routed through its banking subsidiaries in Latin America. The Italian authorities were not prepared to contemplate a large-scale banking collapse that would involve losses for numerous small depositors. Accordingly, on the weekend of 10–11 July 1982 a rescue package was put together for the Milan-based parent bank involving a commitment by seven domestic banks (three state-owned) to provide all necessary liquidity support.

The scale of the refinancing required was increased by lurid reports concerning Banco Ambrosiano's business activities, and on 6 August the Italian government ordered a compulsory liquidation of Banco Ambrosiano SpA, thereby ensuring a complete break with the past. The net liabilities of the parent bank were put at around $540 million and those of the group as a whole, including the overseas affiliates, at over $1.4 billion.[45] In order to protect Banco Ambrosiano SpA's depositors the business of the parent bank was transferred to a new entity, Nuovo Banco Ambrosiano, whose initial capital of some $450 million was subscribed by the rescue consortium.

The ensuing controversy over the Italian authorities' handling of the affair focused on their refusal to offer parallel protection to depositors with Banco Ambrosiano's overseas subsidiaries – notably its 70 per cent owned Luxembourg unit, Banco Ambrosiano Holdings SA (BAH). BAH owed 88 Euromarket bank creditors some $450 million, these loans being declared in default on 19 July when payments of interest and principal became overdue. Subsequently, BAH was placed under judicial control and its operations frozen. The differentiation in the treatment of Banco Ambrosiano's onshore and offshore depositors led to accusations that the Italian authorities were not facing up to their international responsibilities. In addition, legal proceedings were initiated against Nuovo Banco Ambrosiano by the bank creditors of BAH who claimed, *inter alia*, that the Luxembourg subsidiary was a mere instrument of the parent bank and that the new bank was in breach of Article 54 of the 1936 Italian banking law which obliges a successor bank to take responsibility for the debts of its predecessor.[46]

For their part, the Italian authorities disclaimed any responsibility for the Luxembourg subsidiary, which was neither technically a bank nor wholly owned. One of the three Italian commissioners appointed to sort out Banco Ambrosiano's affairs, Mr Giovanni Arduino, was reported to have told creditors of BAH on 29 July that the Bank of Italy had no obligation to support overseas subsidiaries which 'are not under control of the Bank of Italy nor under Italian law or practice'.[47] In addition, it was pointed out that this was a case of insolvency not illiquidity and that if a central bank was obliged to support all institutions under its jurisdiction this would amount to a general guarantee of commercial bank loans.[48]

Luxembourg did not accept responsibility for BAH since it was licensed as a holding company and not a bank. The Luxembourg Banking Commissioner, Mr Pierre Jaans, felt that the Italian authorities should protect depositors with BAH and in order to limit damage to local confidence he sent on 9 August a stiffly worded telex to six major Italian banks with Luxembourg operations. This stated: 'The interposition of a holding company between an Italian bank and its foreign subsidiaries can be legally exploited to avoid what under standard banking practice are elementary responsibilities – with the agreement and complicity of the monetary authorities of your country'.[49]

In order to remedy this situation, Mr Jaans demanded that the Italian parent banks should transfer the controlling block of shares in the bank subsidiaries from the holding company directly into their own portfolios. Pending the dismantling of the holding company structure, the six Italian banks were asked to guarantee unconditionally the solvency of their Luxembourg subsidiaries, a request which was duly complied with by the stated deadline of 11 August.[50] In a separate message, Mr Jaans complained to the Bank of Italy over its role in the affair, commenting that 'the way in which matters have been handled is not easy to understand'.[51]

The Ambrosiano affair represented a serious breakdown in international supervisory co-operation. From the point of view of preventive regulation a glaring loophole in international supervisory arrangements had emerged. Furthermore, since no regulatory authority accepted supervisory responsibility for BAH, it was not surprising that official support for this entity was also lacking – underlining the point that regulatory loopholes are likely to be accompanied by lender of last resort gaps. In this instance, too, there were conflicting pressures between the jurisdiction where damage to confidence was likely to be felt (Luxembourg) and the jurisdiction which had the capacity to provide support (Italy). Of particular concern to offshore financial centres generally was not so much the default of BAH but the fact that the Italian authorities were seen to be giving preference to onshore depositors, thereby casting doubt on the stability of the Euromarket. More fundamentally, therefore, the Ambrosiano episode highlighted underlying tensions within the international financial system between jurisdictions that host Eurocurrency banking business and jurisdictions whose regulations may be bypassed through domestic banks' Euromarket operations.

Nevertheless, the failure of international co-operation on this occasion did provide a stimulus to further initiatives through the Basle Committee on Bank Regulations and Supervisory Practices (see Chapter 7).

The UK Secondary Banking Crisis

Where a banking crisis is confined within a single country's borders, skilful and determined action by the monetary authorities can generally stabilise the situation. This is the lesson to be drawn from the UK secondary banking crisis of 1973–75 which was characterised by severe disturbances in the wholesale deposit market. A Bank of England director who was instrumental in setting up an emergency lender of last resort facility (the 'Lifeboat') to deal with this crisis has commented on the experience as follows:

'In the first eight months of 1974 about thirty secondary banks had to be taken into communal support by the Lifeboat . . . and outside the Lifeboat at least as many required support under individual arrangements from their clearing bankers or from the Bank of England itself or from parent companies and other large shareholders. Without these supporting operations virtually all of them would have collapsed and the cumulative effect of those collapses would have spread much more widely through the banking system. Undoubtedly many of the primary banks would have been swept away in the maelstrom.'[52]

The Bank of England was able to contain this potentially disastrous situation because it had virtually unlimited authority to handle matters within its own jurisdiction. The international repercussions were minimal, although some foreign banks were obliged to provide support to their London affiliates (including consortium banks) and the Bank of England was induced to take over one secondary bank, Slater Walter Ltd, partly because it had a Eurobond issue outstanding, default on which could have undermined confidence in London as an international financial centre.[53]

Significantly, one of the most intractable difficulties that arose during this crisis involved the subsidiary of a foreign bank. On 11 July 1974 the London subsidiary of Israel-British Bank of Tel Aviv closed its doors following seizure of the parent bank's assets by the Israeli authorities. The Bank of Israel stated that it would guarantee all deposits held in the parent bank's eight branches in Israel but was prepared to take no action to safeguard deposits with the London subsidiary. The Bank of England, on the other hand, took the view that the Bank of Israel had an obligation to support the wholly-owned foreign subsidiary of one of its banks. The final outcome of a dispute that persisted for over a year has been described by Joan Spero: 'Eventually, under pressure from the United States, Israel agreed to pool the assets of the parent bank and the British subsidiary while the Bank of England, in a concession it insisted was not a precedent but a magnanimous gesture, contributed £3 million to the pool of assets.'[54]

The important lesson of this troublesome episode, which took place in the context of a much graver UK domestic banking crisis, is that banking problems become far less manageable when they acquire a cross-border and inter-jurisdictional dimension.

Continental Illinois

In the spring and early summer of 1984, the United States experienced its biggest post-war banking crisis, involving the near collapse of Continental Illinois National Bank and Trust Company, the country's seventh largest bank with assets of over $41 billion. At the time of going to press the detailed circumstances surrounding Continental's sudden funding crisis, the underlying condition of the bank and the shape of the long-term rescue package had yet to be determined. Nevertheless, this episode in US banking history is too important to be omitted from consideration.[55]

Continental Illinois had suffered a serious erosion of confidence in the summer of 1982 as a result of losses arising out of loan participation arrangements with Penn Square Bank of Oklahoma and heavy exposure to troubled borrowers in the energy sector. Yet having survived the events of 1982, Continental was by the beginning of 1984 widely supposed to be on the road to gradual recovery. In the spring of that year, however, confidence was again shaken by the revelation that in the first quarter Continental's non-performing loans had risen to $2.3 billion – equivalent to 7.7 per cent of the bank's total loan portfolio and well in excess of its stated $1.8 billion equity capital (excluding loan loss reserves). At the same time rising US interest rates were increasing the cost of holding non-earning assets and aggravating more general concerns about the stability of the US banking system and its exposure to third world borrowers.

Against this background Continental suffered a sudden and devastating run on deposits in the two weeks ending 18 May 1984, amid widely circulating rumours of its imminent collapse, focusing in particular on reports that a number of other institutions had been approached as potential merger partners. During this two-week period Continental lost some $6 billion of deposits, $2.5 billion of which was incurred through its London Euromarket operations. The total represented no less than 20 per cent of Continental's deposit liabilities and amounted to a funding crisis on the grand scale, going far beyond a conventional liquidity squeeze of the kind that might be resolved through access to the Federal Reserve's discount window.

The US authorities at first tried to shore up confidence in Continental Illinois, the Comptroller of the Currency issuing an unusual statement on 10 May to the effect that his agency was 'not aware of any significant change in the bank's operations as reflected in its published financial statement that would serve as a basis for these rumors'. This statement failed to reassure financial markets and by 11 May Continental was reported to be borrowing $4 billion daily from the Federal Reserve Bank of Chicago. Faced with a rapidly deteriorating situation the Federal Reserve was instrumental in arranging a rescue consortium of 16 banks, led by Morgan Guaranty Trust, which on 14 May announced that it had formed a $4.5 billion safety net for Continental. Even this was insufficient to stop the slide in confidence, which by now was threatening to develop into a generalised banking crisis as investors switched from bank certificates of deposit to Treasury bills. On 17 May the US authorities arranged an unprecedented package of initiatives which offered to continue open-ended liquidity support while providing a federal guarantee for depositors with Continental Illinois.

Under the 17 May emergency measures the rescue consortium was increased to include 24 banks, and the standby facility was raised to $5.5 billion; the Federal Deposit Insurance Corporation provided a $1.5 billion capital infusion in the form of subordinated note purchases, which was supplemented by a $500 million contribution from other banks; the Federal Reserve undertook to meet any extraordinary liquidity requirements faced by Continental pending the restoration of normal market funding; and, most crucially, the FDIC gave an unprecedented undertaking that 'in any arrangements that may be necessary to achieve a permanent solution, all depositors and other general creditors of the bank will be fully protected, and service to the bank's customers will not be interrupted'.[56] In effect, therefore, the US authorities, faced with a grave threat to the US banking system, decided to extend deposit insurance to all deposits, beyond the $100,000 statutory cut-off point. At the same time, $7.5 billion of additional funding was made available to Continental, over and above whatever support might continue to be provided by the Federal Reserve. This was by far the biggest bank rescue operation in financial history.

The most remarkable feature of the Continental crisis is that a major multinational bank with substantial net worth ($2.3 billion including loan loss reserves) should have fallen victim to unsubstantiated rumours within a matter of a few trading days. A further noteworthy aspect of the crisis is the manner in which it threatened to envelop not merely the rest of the US banking system but multinational banks headquartered outside the United States – the contagion in this case being evidenced by a widening gap between yields on bank certificates of deposit and on US Treasury bills of comparable term, as well as by sharp declines in the share prices of multinational banks. The Continental episode therefore underlines the importance of the confidence factors outlined in Chapter 3 of this book. It also provides a clear illustration of the dangers of relying on market mechanisms to discipline excessive risk-taking by banks – mechanisms which tend to operate indiscriminately once confidence is shaken and which also have the dire effect of depriving the victim bank of funds rather than imposing a premium on funding costs.

The Continental affair also underlines the dangers associated with multinational banks' funding techniques. As an Illinois bank, Continental had no regional branching network and was therefore unusually dependent on funds purchased through the domestic and international wholesale markets, no less than two-thirds of its deposits being purchased from abroad. The absence of a captive deposit base and the consequent need to roll over large-scale borrowings in the money market left Continental particularly vulnerable to a liquidity crisis. More generally, however, Continental's difficulties have highlighted the growing volatility of banks' deposit liabilities, associated (in the United States) with the abolition of interest rate ceilings and the increasing volume of Euromarket funding. Such volatility lends support to proposals for comprehensive deposit insurance coverage as discussed in Chapter 3.

Finally, the handling of the Continental crisis has illustrated the limitations of the lender of last resort function. Knowledge that the Federal Reserve was providing open-ended liquidity assistance to Continental failed to reassure financial markets in a situation where there were doubts about Continental's solvency. Indeed, reports (subsequently denied) that the bank rescue consortium had demanded and obtained some form of security for their initial $4.5 billion standby facility appear to have accentuated the collapse of confidence. The lesson is that a lender of last resort, however liberal the assistance given, may be unable to stabilise financial markets when confidence is severely shaken and that the availability of liquidity support cannot be viewed as a substitute for comprehensive deposit insurance.

The Continental Illinois crisis will undoubtedly have far-reaching regulatory consequences. Already the momentum in the direction of financial deregulation in the United States has been broken; the innate fragility of wholesale deposit markets (including the Euromarkets) has been clearly demonstrated; and the FDIC's proposals for imposing losses on large depositors with failed banks – proposals that were implemented on an experimental basis from March 1984 – will very likely be reviewed as part of a general reassessment of US deposit insurance arrangements.

CONCLUSIONS

Recent experience suggests that international banking crises are, for a variety of reasons, much more difficult to handle than domestic financial disturbances. First, the shock waves that may be transmitted through the Euromarkets are more unpredictable and less easily contained than local confidence effects, as the repercussions of the Herstatt collapse clearly demonstrated. Secondly, the capacity of national authorities to handle international financial problems is necessarily uncertain in a situation where some major offshore banking centres lack lender of last resort facilities and where international banking business is typically denominated in currencies foreign to the local jurisdiction. Third, conflicts between different jurisdictions are liable to arise where troubled banks conduct their business through foreign banking establishments – as exemplified by the failures of Banco Ambrosiano and Israel-British Bank. Finally, technical legal problems can jeopardise cross-border support operations, a danger illustrated by the difficulties encountered during the Franklin National rescue effort.

Following the eruption of the world debt crisis in 1982, national authorities, in conjunction with the IMF, organised a holding operation, which appeared, until US interest rates began to rise sharply in early 1984, to be at least temporarily effective. This may have encouraged the belief that co-operation among the major central banks was adequate in the area of crisis management. It needs to be stressed, however, that the debt crisis was initially focused on the assets side of banks' balance sheets and that all those involved in restructuring loans to debtor countries had ample time in which to conduct their negotiations. In contrast, disturbances on the liabilities side, arising from precautionary deposit withdrawals, may occur within a far shorter time-scale that demands instantaneous corrective action. This was clearly demonstrated by the Continental Illinois affair, where the US authorities' initial rescue

168   *The Regulation of International Banking*

efforts were swamped by massive withdrawals of money market funds. The general conclusion, therefore, is that emergency support facilities, like preventive regulation, should be the subject of careful co-ordination and pre-planning between national monetary authorities – a matter discussed in the next and final chapter.

NOTES

1. The IRG was established by Royal Decree No. 175 of 13 June 1935.
2. For details see *Revue de la Banque*, 1981, No. 3, pp.337–63.
3. Canada Deposit Insurance Act, 1966–67, c.70s.1, as amended.
4. Article 11 of the Canada Deposit Insurance Corporation Act.
5. 'Mécanisme de solidarité de la profession; règles adoptées par l'Association Francaise des Banques' (Paris, Association Française des Banques, 1981).
6. *Financial Times*, 10 March 1983.
7. *Wall Street Journal*, 22 November 1982.
8. See, for instance, the UK Monopolies and Mergers Commission, 'The Hong Kong and Shanghai Banking Corporation, Standard Chartered Bank Ltd, The Royal Bank of Scotland Ltd: A Report on the Proposed Mergers' (London, 1982), p.69; and 'Report of the Superintendent of Banks of New York State on the Proposed Acquisition by the Hong Kong and Shanghai Banking Corporation of Marine Midland Bank', New York State Banking Department, 29 June 1979, p.31.
9. Statement by the Financial Secretary, cited in the *Wall Street Journal*, 28 September 1983.
10. See Felice Scordino, 'The Bank Supervisory Department's experience in the detection of banks in financial difficulties and relative intervention', paper presented to the International Conference of Banking Supervisors, Washington DC, 24–25 September 1981.
11. See 'The Deposit Insurance Law and the related Cabinet Order and Regulation', Deposit Insurance Corporation, Tokyo, undated. The relevant laws are Law No. 34 of 1 April 1971, Cabinet Order No. 111, promulgated on 1 April 1971 and Ministry of Finance Ordinance No. 28, promulgated on 1 May 1971.
12. 'The Deposit Insurance Law and the related Cabinet Order and Regulation', p.27.
13. Decree of 27 December 1978, to give binding force to the collective guarantee scheme by virtue of section 44 of the Act on the Supervision of the Credit System.
14. Article 24A of the Monetary Authority of Singapore Act (added by MAS Amendment Act No. 31 of 1972).
15. Remarks by Michael Pakshong, then Managing Director of the MAS, in 'Supervision of a Regional Financial Centre', International Conference of Banking Supervisors, London, 5–6 July 1979, *Record of Proceedings*, p.17.
16. A specimen copy of the kind of letter of comfort demanded by the MAS reads as follows: We [name of parent bank] accept full responsibility for the operation of Y [name of subsidiary]. In addition to our legal responsibility deriving from our 100% shareholding of Y, we will ensure that Y maintains a sound liquidity and financial position at all times, and we will, on demand, provide adequate funds to make up for any liquidity shortfall in the merchant bank as well as to continue to meet all the obligations of the merchant bank. This undertaking applies to the total operations of Y covering both the Asian Currency Unit and Domestic Banking Unit.'
17. See Bernhard Müller, 'Deposit Insurance', paper presented to the International Conference of Banking Supervisors, Washington DC, 24–25 September 1981.
18. See statement by Mr Aeppli, Chairman of Crédit Suisse, at extraordinary meeting of shareholders, 24 June 1977.
19. Deposit Protection Board, Report and Accounts for the year to 28 February 1983, 17 June 1983.
20. See Brian Gent, 'The Secondary Banking Crisis of 1973/74', paper presented to the International Conference of Banking Supervisors, Washington DC, 24–25 September 1981.
21. On this point see address by the Governor of the Bank of England, The Rt Hon.

Gordon Richardson, 'International Co-operation in Banking Supervision', to the International Conference of Banking Supervisors, London, 5–6 July 1979, pp.8–9.

22. For a general review of the FDIC's activities and policies see 'Deposit Insurance in a Changing Environment' (Washington, DC, FDIC), 15 April 1983.

23. For an explanation of these proposals, see address by William Isaac before the Management Conference of the National Council of Savings Institutions, New York, 6 December 1983.

24. See remarks by Henry C. Wallich, 'Perspectives on Foreign Banking in the United States', speech issued as Press Release by Federal Reserve Board, Washington, DC, 1 March 1982, p.5.

25. See FDIC Report Bulletin No. 5, 2 November 1983.

26. See 'By-laws of the Deposit Protection Fund of the Federal Association of German Banks (May, 1976)' in Schneider, Hellwig and Kingsman, *The German Banking System* (Frankfurt, Fritz Knapp Verlag, 1978).

27. Gesellschaftsvertrag der Liquiditäts: Konsortialbank GmbH. For a brief description of the Liko-Bank's activities as well as other protective measures, see Ekkehard Bauer 'Dealing with Problem and Failing Banks – Experience in the Federal Republic of Germany', paper presented to International Conference of Banking Supervisors, Washington, DC, 24–25 September 1981.

28. See Andrew Brimmer, 'International Finance and the Management of Bank Failures: Herstatt vs Franklin National', paper prepared for presentation before the American Economic Association and the American Finance Association, Atlantic City, 16 September 1976.

29. Bauer, 'Dealing with Problem and Failing Banks', p.4.

30. J. W. Bachman, 'Euromarket Still Tiered', *Money Manager*, 7 September 1976, pp.9–10.

31. Bauer, 'Dealing with Problem and Failing Banks', p.10.

32. See Jack Guttentag and Richard Herring, *The Lender of Last Resort Function in an International Context*, Princeton Studies in International Finance, No. 151, May 1983, p.16.

33. The following comments on the SMH crisis are based on press reports in the *Financial Times*, the *Wall Street Journal* (Europe) and the *International Herald Tribune* covering the period 3 November to 14 December 1983, as well as on discussions with the West German supervisory authorities.

34. A Bundesbank director has commented as follows on the question of liquidity assistance to Luxembourg subsidiaries of West German banks: 'The central bank that is responsible for the parent bank cannot be under any obligation to provide foreign subsidiaries with liquidity so long as this central bank has no means of exerting any influence on the foreign subsidiaries, for instance by fixing reserve requirements.' Panel contribution by S. Burger at the International Conference of Banking Supervisors, London, 5–6 July 1979, pp.31–32.

35. For a full description of the events surrounding Franklin National Bank's collapse, see: Joan Spero, *The Failure of the Franklin National Bank* (New York, Columbia University Press, 1980); Andrew Brimmer, 'International Finance and the Management of Bank Failures', pp.34–54; and Cantwell Muckenfuss, 'Handling Distressed Banks in the United States', paper presented to the International Conference of Banking Supervisors, Washington DC, 24–25 September 1981, pp.25–45.

36. See Spero, *The Failure of the Franklin National Bank*, pp.69ff.

37. Muckenfuss, 'Handling Distressed Banks', p.42. Interestingly, it appears that when the drawn-out liquidation proceedings that followed Franklin National's collapse are eventually completed, there will be some positive 'net worth' left after all creditors are paid off. See 'Special Report on the Receivership of Franklin National Bank, New York City', FDIC News Release, 11 June 1982.

38. Spero, *The Failure of the Franklin National Bank*, p.125.

39. Brimmer, 'International Finance and the Management of Bank Failures', p.2.

40. Spero, *The Failure of the Franklin National Bank*, pp.151–52.

41. Spero, *The Failure of the Franklin National Bank*, pp.151–52.

42. Spero, *The Failure of the Franklin National Bank*, p.131.

43. Brimmer, 'International Finance and the Management of Bank Failures', pp.52–54.

44. In fact, by early 1974 Franklin National was having to pay a risk premium over LIBOR for its Eurodollar borrowings, but by then the events leading to the bank's downfall

had already been set in motion. See Spero, *The Failure of the Franklin National Bank*, pp.91–92.

45. See *Financial Times*, 9 August 1982, p.1.
46. See *Financial Times*, 31 March 1983, p.18.
47. Quoted in *New York Times*, 30 July 1982, p.D1.
48. See *New York Times*, 11 August 1982, p.D1.
49. Quoted in *Financial Times*, 12 August 1982, pp.1,18.
50. *Financial Times*, 12 August 1982, pp.1,18.
51. *Financial Times*, 12 August 1982, pp.1,18.
52. Cited in Margaret Reid, *The Secondary Banking Crisis, 1973–75* (London, Macmillan, 1982), p.90.
53. Reid, *The Secondary Banking Crisis*, p.116.
54. Spero, *The Failure of the Franklin National Bank*, p.157.
55. The following discussion is based on press reports in the *American Banker*, the *Wall Street Journal* and the *Financial Times* during May and June 1984, and on press releases from the US regulatory agencies during this period.
56. Press Release from the Comptroller of the Currency, the Federal Deposit Insurance Corporation and the Federal Reserve Board, 17 May 1984.

7 *International Supervisory Co-operation*

It should be clear from the previous two Chapters that even among the more mature financial centres there is a wide variety of regulatory and protective arrangements designed to ensure the safety and soundness of banks. Because of the scope for what has been described as regulatory arbitrage it is also clear that this is an area that calls for the closest possible co-operation between national regulatory authorities, if not actual harmonisation of regulatory practice. Before describing the various co-operative initiatives that have been taken, however, it is necessary to emphasise once more the conflicts of national interest that present such a serious obstacle to progress on this front.

Chapter 2, in examining the regulatory framework of multinational banking and the Eurocurrency market which sustains it, highlighted the competitive tensions that exist among rival financial centres. This tension is most acute between those countries whose currencies are used in the Euromarkets (notably the United States) and the centres through which such Eurocurrency business is routed. As the Deputy Governor of the Bank of England has put it: 'Offshore centres are, after all, to a greater or lesser extent, competing with each other and with the centres where the parent banks are located to attract business and . . . their interests and concerns appear to be rather different.'[1]

Put simply, host financial centres typically seek to attract international banking business by offering a permissive regulatory climate, but at the same time try to secure the implicit support of foreign parent banks (and their central banks) through letters of comfort and other means. This approach is, of course, aimed at off-loading risks incurred within the host jurisdiction on to home country authorities. For their part, countries which do not host Euromarket business but whose banks operate offshore will wish either to extend their regulatory reach to such operations or else to limit the extent of their lender of last resort assistance to banks' offshore entities. Otherwise, the home authorities will be offering support to banks whose activities are not only beyond their control but which have been deliberately

171

located offshore for that very purpose. These considerations may, however, be outweighed by another competitive concern – namely, that by interfering with its banks' freedom of operation in offshore centres, the home country might undermine these institutions' competitive position in international markets.

It can be argued, therefore, that within a multi-jurisdictional regulatory regime there is an inbuilt tendency towards competitive deregulation. Not surprisingly, therefore, the history of international co-operation in this area is one of 'after the event' initiatives, with short bursts of co-operative activity following hard on the heels of successive financial crises. Against this background, the following sections provide a brief description of the history of international supervisory co-operation, followed by an examination of alternative ways of handling the regulatory problem at the international level.

HISTORY OF SUPERVISORY CO-OPERATION

Until the Herstatt crisis of 1974 there was no formal machinery for co-ordinating national regulatory arrangements. As Peter Cooke of the Bank of England has stated, 'supervisors were still very much domestically orientated within the framework of different national banking systems'.[2] The disturbances that followed in the wake of Herstatt's collapse focused attention on the interdependence of national banking systems and led, in the following year, to the creation of a standing committee of bank supervisors, under the auspices of the Bank for International Settlements, comprising the Group of Ten countries plus Switzerland. This Committee on Banking Regulation and Supervisory Practices (now called the 'Cooke Committee', after its chairman) seeks not to harmonise national laws and practices but rather to interlink disparate regulatory regimes with a view to ensuring that all banks are supervised according to certain broad principles.[3]

One of the earliest and most far-reaching initiatives of the Cooke Committee was to develop broad guidelines for the division of responsibilities among national supervisory authorities. These guidelines, which were approved by the central bank governors of the Group of Ten in December 1975, became known as the 'Basle Concordat' and were described by Peter Cooke as 'a most important cornerstone of international supervisory co-operation'.[4] The following key principles were embodied in the original Concordat:[5]

1. The supervision of foreign banking establishments is the joint responsibility of parent and host authorities.
2. No foreign banking establishment should escape supervision.
3. The supervision of liquidity should be the primary responsibility of the host authorities.
4. The supervision of solvency is essentially a matter for the parent authority in the case of foreign branches and primarily the respon-

sibility of the host authority in the case of foreign subsidiaries.

5. Practical co-operation should be promoted by the exchange of information between host and parent authorities and by the authorisation of bank inspections by or on behalf of parent authorities on the territory of the host authority.

Although the Concordat represented a significant step towards greater international supervisory co-operation, it suffered from a number of defects which began to become apparent from 1978 onwards. In the first place, the primary supervisory responsibility accorded to host authorities for the solvency of foreign subsidiaries ran counter to another important initiative of the Cooke Committee. This was the recommendation, endorsed by the central bank governors of the Group of Ten in 1978, that supervision of banks' international business should be conducted on a consolidated basis, the object being to limit the opportunities for regulatory evasions of the kind described above.[6] There was a clear danger here that host countries would look to parent authorities to supervise locally incorporated subsidiaries of foreign banks under the principle of consolidated supervision, while home authorities would rely on host countries to exercise their responsibilities under the Concordat. Indeed, subsequent events (see below) suggest that there was considerable confusion about the allocation of responsibilities in this area.

Another weakness of the original Concordat was its failure to address the question of differing supervisory standards, although it did recommend that supervision should be judged adequate by both host and parent authorities. Because national supervisory standards vary, some countries were more reluctant than others to share or delegate supervisory responsibilities. The US approach, for instance, appears to have been based on the view that 'bank supervision in foreign countries, at least from an examination standpoint, is generally non-existent or far inferior to that in the US'.[7] The US perception of supervisory inadequacies in other countries led to a serious dispute in 1979 when the US Federal Reserve formulated proposals for imposing extensive reporting requirements on the US offices of foreign banks relating to their parent institutions' structure and condition.[8] Several foreign supervisory authorities felt that these reporting requirements were in breach of the Concordat and, following a succession of strong representations to this effect, certain modifications were made to the US proposal – although these did not fully satisfy all concerned.

This episode underlines the difficulties that can be created by uneven supervisory standards. The correspondence between supervisory authorities relating to the dispute also revealed a variety of interpretations as to the allocation of responsibilities laid down in the Concordat. For instance, the Swiss National Bank, in a letter to the US Federal Reserve Board dated March 1980 stated:

'According to the principles worked out by the [Basle] Committee and approved by the Governors in 1975, primary responsibility for the supervision of a foreign branch, subsidiary or agency, doubtlessly lies with the host authority.'[9]

On the other hand, the Bank of England, in a letter to the Federal Reserve Board dated January 1980, adopted the following interpretation:

'In their present form these proposed requirements seem to us to imply an approach to supervision which runs counter to a basic principle agreed to by the Governors of the G-10 countries and Switzerland in 1975 – namely that the primary responsibility for supervising banks incorporated in a particular country rests with the central bank or other regulatory authorities of that country.'[10]

A third interpretation of the Concordat's responsibility guidelines was provided, *inter alia*, by the Netherlands Bank which made the following comments in a letter to the Federal Reserve Board dated February 1980:

'The Concordat entails that the primary responsibility for the prudential super- vision of the banks established in a particular country both as to solvency and – to a lesser degree – as to liquidity, rests with the supervisory authorities of the country of the head-office or parent bank.'[11]

The remarkable confusion regarding an agreement which was supposed to have been a cornerstone of international supervisory co-operation also underlines the unnecessary secrecy surrounding official initiatives in this area – the precise terms of the original Concordat were not released to the public until March 1981, more than five years after their adoption by the central bank governors.

The original Concordat also led to a widespread but mistaken belief among commercial bankers that the supervisory and lender of last resort responsibilities of national authorities necessarily went hand in hand. In fact it was never intended that the Concordat should establish guidelines for lender of last resort purposes, but it was difficult for financial markets to resist the inference that a central bank should be responsible in a lender of last resort sense for banking establishments falling within its supervisory jurisdiction. This was an understandable source of confusion. It is indeed hard to envisage a generally acceptable allocation of regulatory responsi- bilities which does not take account of the responsibility for emergency support, there being a natural reluctance on the part of central banks to extend financial assistance to institutions whose activities are beyond their control and a corresponding reluctance to yield supervisory control over institutions for which they remain financially responsible.

Finally, experience with the 1975 Basle Concordat illustrates the weak- nesses of a co-operative regime based on informal and broadly drawn guidelines. Under such non-binding arrangements countries are free to interpret agreements as they see fit, to implement only those parts which suit their purposes and to defer action indefinitely on other recommen- dations. Above all, where the stability of the international banking system is at stake it seems inappropriate to accept a policy of gradualism that is characterised by slow progress towards regulatory targets without any specified timetable. This is particularly true in a situation where the explosive growth of multinational banking is tending to out-distance the individual capabilities of national regulatory authorities.

Most of these regulatory weaknesses, and some others in addition, were amply illustrated by events surrounding the collapse of Banco Ambrosiano's Luxembourg subsidiary in the summer of 1982. At that time both the Luxembourg and Italian authorities disclaimed responsibility for either supervising or providing lender of last resort assistance to the Luxembourg entity, in part because it was technically a holding company rather than a bank. Ensuing discussions between national authorities revealed differing views on: the proper division of supervisory and lender of last resort responsibilities; the precise circumstances under which the lender of last resort function should be exercised; and the nature of a parent bank's legal and moral responsibilities towards its foreign subsidiaries. In particular, the Italian authorities felt limited responsibility for a foreign subsidiary whose activities were beyond their control, while the Luxembourg authorities held to the view that the local subsidiary of a foreign bank trading under its parent's name should be supported by the parent and, if necessary, the parent's central bank.[12]

The controversy surrounding the handling of Banco Ambrosiano's collapse was one factor prompting a reappraisal of the original Concordat and the emergence of a revised version, which was approved by the central bank governors in June 1983 (see Appendix 1). The authors of the new Concordat clearly had the Ambrosiano case in mind when they introduced more precise guidelines for the supervision of holding companies. Apart from closing such supervisory gaps, the new Concordat contains two major innovations: it addresses directly the question of adequacy of supervision and it embodies the principle of consolidated supervision.

In the absence of harmonised prudential rules governing international banking operations, it is clearly impossible to ensure that national supervisory arrangements will conform to an appropriate standard – even where there is full agreement on the division of supervisory responsibilities. However, the new Concordat attempts to deal with this problem by introducing what might be described as a 'dual key' approach to the operation of foreign banking establishments. Under the revised guidelines, if a host authority considers that the supervision of parent institutions of foreign banks operating on its territory is inadequate, it should prohibit or discourage the continued operation of such offices, or alternatively impose specific conditions on the conduct of their business. This provision clearly represents an important concession to the US authorities, whose attempts to monitor the condition of foreign parent banks with US offices has hitherto met with strong resistance from foreign supervisory authorities, as mentioned above. In addition, where the parent authority considers that the host authority's supervision is inadequate it should 'either extend its supervision, to the degree that it is practicable, or it should be prepared to discourage the parent bank from continuing to operate the establishment in question'. (This recommendation is, however, qualified by a presumption that host authorities are in a position to fulfil their supervisory obligations adequately.) Each national supervisory authority must therefore satisfy itself that its banks' foreign operations are being conducted in jurisdictions with sound supervisory practices and that foreign banks to which it is host are subject to adequate supervision within their home jurisdiction. Evidently the intention here is to reverse the tendency for banks to gravitate to the least regulated jurisdictions with resulting competition in regulatory laxity between financial centres competing for foreign banking business. Under the 'dual key' system, supervisory standards should, in theory, be aligned on those of the most stringently regulated centres, rather than *vice versa*. For this to happen, however, national authorities in the major banking centres must be prepared to lock out foreign banks originating from permissive jurisdictions and to prevent their own banks from conducting their international operations from poorly regulated centres.

CONSOLIDATED SUPERVISION

The attempt to ensure adequacy of supervision is buttressed by the other major innovation of the new Concordat, namely, incorporation of the principle of consolidated supervision. The idea is that host authorities' supervisory responsibilities should in no way be downgraded by this principle, but that overall supervision should be strengthened by having parent authorities supervise risks on the basis of banks' global operations. Accordingly, whereas under the original Concordat primary responsibility for supervising the solvency of foreign subsidiaries was accorded to the host authorities, under the new guidelines this becomes a joint responsibility of host and parent authorities. The division of responsibilities here reflects the view that foreign bank subsidiaries should, as legally separate entities, be financially sound in their own right, while also being supervised as integral parts of the group to which they belong. Primary responsibility for supervising the liquidity of both foreign branches and subsidiaries remains with the host authorities on the grounds that the latter are more familiar with local money markets.

Consolidated supervision is the most important principle to emerge from a decade of international supervisory co-operation. On this issue the EEC Commission has followed the Cooke Committee's lead and, in collaboration with the EEC Advisory Banking Committee, formulated proposals for a Directive on the Supervision of Credit Institutions on a Consolidated Basis. This Directive was adopted in June 1983 and will take effect from 1 July 1985.[13]

Under the provisions of the Directive, EEC member states are obliged to supervise banks headquartered in their own jurisdiction on a consolidated basis, including for consolidation purposes majority-owned or effectively controlled subsidiaries in other member states. Consolidated supervision is to be without prejudice to supervision on an unconsolidated basis by host authorities; the flow of information between parent and subsidiary banks as well as between supervisory authorities themselves should be permitted to the extent necessary for consolidated supervision; and home country authorities may appoint auditors from the host country in order to verify information received from a subsidiary located in that country.

Because of the central role played by consolidated supervision it is worth considering more fully its merits as a supervisory technique. It is certainly easier to reach international agreement on consolidated supervision than on regulatory harmonisation. Indeed, it may be said that consolidated supervision is a partial substitute for regulatory co-ordination in that it permits each country to impose its own regulatory regime on domestic banks' global operations. However, consolidated supervision that is not accompanied by regulatory co-ordination carries with it a number of dangers. First, there is the danger that regulatory arbitrage will simply be diverted into new channels. Instead of banks routing their international business through unregulated centres, international business will be attracted to the least regulated banks (since these will enjoy a competitive advantage over more tightly regulated institutions).

Secondly, banks that are supervised on a consolidated basis may themselves engage in regulatory arbitrage of the type described in Appendix 2, from which it will be seen that Citibank (quite legitimately) employed not only its own multinational banking network but also transactions with third party banks to escape regulatory constraints on its activities. Interbank, as distinct from intra-bank, dealings of this kind would not be picked up by consolidated supervision.

Thirdly, so long as one or more major offshore banking centres retain secrecy laws that prevent on-site inspections by outsiders as well as the transmission of information to other jurisdictions, the principle of consolidated supervision cannot be fully implemented. Furthermore, it takes only one blind spot within the supervisory process to allow banks to bypass official constraints on excessive risk-taking. Less than full implementation of the consolidation principle is no implementation at all, so that regional consolidation arrangements such as those prescribed by the EEC have limited value – except as a first step towards world-wide consolidation of banks' activities.

Finally, consolidated supervision does not take account of local laws and practices that seek to 'untie' foreign subsidiaries and branches from their parent banks. For instance, the US authorities have made clear that they do not expect the resources of US subsidiaries of foreign banks to be used in support of their parent institutions; some jurisdictions, notably New York State,[14] require special asset pledges from branches of foreign banks to protect branch depositors in the event of the parent's insolvency; and several offshore centres require not merely separate liquidation proceedings for local offices of foreign banks but give priority in such proceedings to repayment of onshore deposits. In these circumstances consolidated accounts cannot provide a true picture of the capital resources available to protect deposits. In recognition of this fact the revised Concordat states that consolidation 'should not be applied to the exclusion of supervision of individual banking establishments on an unconsolidated basis by parent and host authorities'.

The overall conclusion, therefore, is that consolidated supervision does not in itself constitute an adequate substitute for regulatory co-ordination. Before considering the broader policy implications of the need for closer international supervisory co-operation, it is first necessary to describe the various initiatives that have been taken to co-ordinate lender of last resort arrangements in international financial markets.

LENDER OF LAST RESORT

There have been few public declarations relating to the lender of last resort function in an international context. The 1975 Basle Concordat did not deal with this issue, which was reserved to the central bank governors themselves rather than to the Cooke Committee; and the revised Concordat states explicitly that 'it does not address itself to the lender of last resort aspects of the role of central banks'. The central bank governors of the Group of Ten did, however, have discussions about possible liquidity assistance to the Euromarkets in the immediate aftermath of the Herstatt collapse in 1974. This resulted in an official statement from Basle to the effect that the governors were 'satisfied that means are available for the provision of temporary liquidity to the Euromarkets and will be used if and when necessary'.[15]

There have been a number of reports about what was actually agreed at Basle.[16] From some of these it appears that there were serious differences of view and that in particular the United States objected to the idea that it should be expected to provide assistance to foreign subsidiaries (as distinct from branches) of US banks.[17] This attitude would be consistent with the US authorities' sceptical view of the Euromarkets and might also reflect their disinclination to act as lender of last resort to institutions beyond their control. Five years later Edward Frydl, a senior officer of the Federal Reserve Bank of New York, stated that the emergence of the extraterritorial Euromarket had created ambiguities about which central bank would be responsible for providing lender of last resort support for overseas operations and that 'no final resolution of those ambiguities has yet been reached'.[18] Subsequently, Mr Frydl commented that the Basle Concordat, together with the 1974 declaration on emergency assistance, had 'contributed to the continuing erosion of perceived risk in the Euromarket, prompting more deposits and faster growth'[19] – a development that was clearly unwelcome to the US authorities. Significantly, when the Deputy Governor of the Bank of England reiterated the Basle declaration on emergency support in May 1982, the US authorities remained silent on the subject.[20]

The revision of the Basle Concordat in 1983, which involved some significant concessions to the US point of view, appears to have been accompanied by some softening of the US position on its lender of last resort responsibilities. Such a shift is suggested by the following statement from Governor Wallich of the Federal Reserve Board: 'By the nature of relationships in international banking, the principle of parental reponsibility applies. Branches *and subsidiaries* of foreign parents must first look to those parents in case of liquidity needs, while the parents look to their own central banks' (emphasis added).[21] From this it is clear that the Federal Reserve is prepared under appropriate circumstances to provide support to foreign subsidiaries of US banks, using the parent institution as a conduit for the infusion of liquidity. It seems, therefore, that despite their customary reticence on the subject, leading central banks may have a closer understanding than previously of their lender of last resort responsibilities based on the principle of parental responsibility.

PROPOSALS FOR REFORM

In considering proposals for regulatory reform, this section focuses on the broad policy implications of the growth of multinational banking and the Eurocurrency market, rather than on specific problems associated with the third world debt crisis.[22]

It has been suggested that because the Eurocurrency market is part of a closed system, funds can always be recycled back to banks experiencing deposit withdrawals and that prudential regulation of banking in this area is therefore superfluous.[23] Such a view is, however, difficult to accept, if only for the reason that automatic recycling, in whatever form it may occur, to banks which are suffering liquidity problems must be expected to undermine market discipline and thereby give rise to the familiar moral hazard problems that underlie the modern theory of bank regulation.

More typically, the Eurocurrency market has attracted the critical attention of those who believe that supervision of international banking is seriously deficient, particularly in the current disturbed financial environment. Among the many proposals for reform, which have tended to focus on emergency arrangements rather than preventive regulation, the following are prominent:

An International Deposit Insurance Corporation (IDIC)

Professor Grubel has proposed[24] that an IDIC should be established to insure deposits placed with the foreign offices of multinational banks, since such deposits, at least when denominated in non-local currencies, are generally unprotected by national insurance schemes. Apart from questions of funding and membership, the major difficulty with such a scheme is that participating countries would be required to protect deposits in banks subject to widely differing regulatory standards. Professor Grubel suggests that this problem might be overcome by authorising the IDIC to impose uniform regulatory standards on the foreign banking establishments concerned and also by setting variable insurance premiums related to risk class. However, since the risks incurred by parent banks cannot at present be severed from those incurred by their foreign offshoots (see below), this must be regarded as an incomplete solution to the problem.[25]

An International Lender of Last Resort

There have been a number of proposals for a supranational lender of last resort backed by the major central banks. However, precisely the same difficulties arise here as with the IDIC proposal. Above all, no central bank can be expected to underwrite the activities of banks outside its own regulatory purview, given the present wide variations in regulatory practice.

Private International Safety Net

Dr Guth, a chief executive of Deutsche Bank, has floated the idea of a private safety net jointly organised by international banks and designed to provide prompt liquidity assistance on a reciprocal basis.[26] Dr Guth has evidently had second thoughts about the practicality of such a proposal on the grounds that a broad-based scheme would necessarily involve considerable risks for the creditor banks, who could not be assured of the solvency of the institutions to which they were lending, while a narrowly based scheme would have undesirable consequences for those seen to be excluded from the magic circle.[27] Here again, it may be supposed that commercial banks, like central banks, would be unwilling to enter into open-ended commitments *vis-à-vis* institutions subject to widely differing regulatory standards.

An Inter-Bank Commitment Network

Professors Dean and Giddy have suggested[28] that central banks should encourage the establishment of a network of formal, guaranteed credit commitments among commercial banks by charging an annual fee for acting as lender of last resort. The fee, which would be based on the amount of each bank's uninsured deposits less the amount of any guaranteed commitments obtained from other banks, would be set high enough to induce banks to switch to interbank commitments to back up the bulk of their interbank liabilities. This ingenious proposal presents a number of difficulties. If the unconditional commitments are valid for any length of time, the committed bank risks being embroiled in insolvency problems as a result of deterioration in the potential borrower's condition during the period of the commitment, while if the commitments are rolled over at frequent intervals, the protection afforded may be correspondingly limited. In any event, the scheme would presumably only work if all major countries participated, since commitment fees, by adding materially to the cost of financial intermediation, would impose a competitive penalty on the banks concerned. Furthermore, an international agreement along these lines presupposes agreement also on lender of last resort responsibilities.

THE OUTLOOK FOR THE FUTURE

A common characteristic of these and other proposals for reform is that they attempt to isolate one aspect of the regulatory problem without giving due consideration to the broader policy dilemma posed by the presence of multinational banking networks operating in various jurisdictions. Accordingly, before examining possible improvements in the safeguarding of the multinational banking system, it is necessary to identify the contradictions implicit in the present fragmented regulatory structure.

The most flagrant contradiction lies in the fact that 'soft' financial centres (i.e., those adopting permissive regulatory standards) are able to free-ride at the expense of 'hard' centres. More specifically, a financial centre which seeks to attract banking business by offering a permissive regulatory environment does not bear any prudential cost in the form of a risk premium payable on locally placed deposits. The additional risks attaching to banking business transacted within the centre are not separately 'priced' for the simple reason that any difficulties encountered by foreign banks established there are transferred, whether by law, convention or commercial necessity, to the respective parent institutions in their countries of origin. To put it another way, because parent banks are generally obliged to absorb the financial strains experienced by their foreign subsidiaries and branches, deposits placed with a loosely regulated foreign banking establishment can be no more risky in a *credit* sense[29] than deposits placed with its more tightly regulated parent bank. The net result is that financial centres at best have little incentive to control the risks incurred by foreign banks to which they are host, and at worst may be induced to attract banking business by engaging in what has been described by a former Chairman of the US Federal Reserve Board as 'competition in laxity'.[30]

The obvious dangers in this situation are aggravated by the likelihood, during periods of financial stress, of large and destabilising movements of funds both between financial centres and between banking groups. This latent instability is explained by a number of related factors. First, whereas in normal conditions depositors with offshore banks look primarily to the parent institution for security, in times of crisis they can be expected to look beyond the parent bank to the protection afforded by national authorities.[31] Secondly, the principle of parental responsibility which applies to commercial banks is not necessarily followed by central banks in their lender of last resort capacity (that is to say, foreign subsidiaries cannot automatically look to their parent banks' central bank for emergency assistance) and is typically rejected in favour of the territorial principle by national deposit insurance schemes. Finally, official support facilities of both kinds may be available in the national authorities' local currency only. Under these circumstances depositors may reasonably perceive that their funds will, *in extremis*, be better protected if placed as local currency deposits in the domestic banks of a 'hard' financial centre than they would be if held as Eurocurrency deposits with foreign banking establishments in a 'soft' financial centre. A major collapse of confidence could therefore trigger an exodus of funds not merely from 'soft' centres themselves but from banking groups headquartered in such jurisdictions.[32]

It should be noted that three regulatory principles combine to bring about this state of affairs. First, there is the principle of national autonomy in regulatory matters which permits wide variations in national regulatory practice. Secondly, there is the neutrality principle, which requires that all banks resident in a particular country should be subject to regulatory parity under that country's laws. Thirdly, there is the principle of parental responsibility, which asserts that parent institutions are financially responsible for their foreign establishments. In order to correct the destabilising tendencies implicit in the present regulatory structure it is necessary to reverse at least one of these principles. Conceptually the simplest but in practical terms the most far-reaching reform would be to harmonise national regulatory arrangements through a binding international agreement. Central bankers have consistently rejected such an idea, although Governor Wallich of the US Federal Reserve Board has spoken of the need for greater co-ordination of national laws in the following terms:

> 'Growing integration across national boundaries makes it important for us to attain a better insight into banking laws and practices elsewhere. These laws and practices, which increasingly affect the condition and competitiveness of the banks we supervise, differ enormously across nations. Probably most of us believe that there are good reasons for doing things the way we do. We are not proposing to change each other's ways. But there is a need to individually adapt our national laws and practices into an international framework so that they will accommodate and support each other instead of creating gaps or even conflicts that could pose a threat to the worldwide system.'[33]

Clearly, one of the major problems of harmonisation would be to secure the participation of all countries having financial centre status, although this might be achieved if participating countries refused both to host banks headquartered in non-participating countries and to permit their own banks to establish offices in such jurisdictions. Financial centres which declined to co-operate might then find themselves left out in the cold, or at the very least relegated to fringe banking status. The 'dual key' principle embodied in the revised Concordat, involving reciprocal monitoring of regulatory standards by host and home authorities, could mark an important step in the direction of common regulatory standards, if not regulatory harmonisation.

An alternative approach would be to reverse the neutrality (or national) principle which currently governs regulatory practice, in favour of the so-called equity principle.[34] This would mean that all foreign branches and/or subsidiaries of a single group would be subject to the same regulatory regime as the parent bank in its country of origin. Under the equity principle, 'soft' centres could no longer free-ride on 'hard' centres, since the foreign banks they host would not be permitted to engage in activities riskier than those of their parent institutions. The adoption of consolidated supervision as a key regulatory guideline may be viewed as a shift towards the equity principle. However, a regime based on strict adherence to the equity principle would present numerous practical problems, among which would be the possible adverse competitive implications of banks conducting business on unequal terms within the same jurisdiction and the likelihood that many countries would not wish to host banks subject to external regulation.

The third approach to reform is to abolish the principle of parental responsibility by preventing risk transfers from foreign banking establishments to their parent institutions. As matters now stand, parental responsibility rests on legal, conventional and commercial constraints: banks are committed to their foreign branches legally[35] and to their foreign subsidiaries through letters of comfort extracted by host authorities,[36] persuasive pressure from home authorities,[37] and commercial self-interest arising from the fact that the credit standing of a bank would be seriously damaged by the demise of a subsidiary.[38] The legal and conventional commitments could presumably be severed by confining foreign operations to the subsidiary form and limiting financial dealings between parent banks and their foreign subsidiaries. More problematical is the commercial interdependence of banks within a single group, although this difficulty might be mitigated by, for instance, prohibiting foreign subsidiaries from trading under their parent bank's name. In any event, further consideration might be given to ways of fragmenting risks within the multinational banking network.[39] If such fragmentation were achieved, 'soft' financial centres would have to bear the burden of risks incurred within their jurisdiction, a consideration which would presumably be reflected in a risk premium on locally placed deposits. Regulatory diversity would therefore no longer give rise to free-rider problems.

The reluctance hitherto of the US authorities to offer lender of last resort assistance to foreign subsidiaries of US banks can be interpreted as an attempt to sever risks within a multi-jurisdictional regulatory regime. Equally, it may be regarded as a way of bringing pressure to bear on offshore banking centres in the debate over regulation of the Euromarkets. Edward Frydl has pointed out that denial of emergency support to unco-operative banking centres would reduce these centres' share of international banking business. He has also suggested that the withdrawal of lender of last resort facilities from the Euromarkets could conceivably be used as a means of curbing their expansion:

> 'A final approach to regulation of the Euromarket would be to increase the perceived riskiness of the Euromarket, making Eurodollar deposits less attractive for any given yield differential. In practice, this would involve limiting the guarantee of lender-of-last-resort assistance to the Euromarket in a way that would have a convincing effect on market views of risk.'

Any one of the above three approaches to reform – harmonisation, adoption of the equity principle or risk severance – would provide an incentive for soft financial centres to put their house in order. Alternatively, those centres which failed to respond to the new arrangements would experience a loss of banking business based on the perception among depositors that their funds would, even during periods of financial stability, be safer elsewhere. Furthermore, initiatives of the kind proposed would help to reduce the risk of a sudden movement of funds from 'soft' to 'hard' centres during times of crisis. Under harmonised rules there would be no basis for such a movement; the equity principle would, by facilitating the extension of parent authority support arrangements to all foreign banking establishments, remove the incentive for shifts between centres (though not necessarily between different banking groups); and the risk severance approach would contribute to the same objective by obliging depositors to focus on the risks of the local jurisdiction while encouraging offshore centres to strengthen their own financial support schemes.

As noted above, the present international regulatory regime, based on the revised Basle Concordat and undisclosed lender of last resort arrangements, combines in some degree all three approaches to regulatory reform. Formal harmonisation of national regulatory arrangements is not on the agenda but there is a prospect of further gradual convergence, encouraged perhaps by the Concordat's new provisions on the adequacy of supervisory standards. The equity principle is also to be applied in a limited way in so far as consolidated supervision will require foreign banking establishments to account to their home country authorities for the risks they incur abroad. Finally, risk transfers will continue to be affected by various cross-currents as host authorities try to bind in parent banks via letters of comfort (while discouraging risk transfers in the opposite direction through local asset pledges and liquidation proceedings) and home authorities such as the United States remain purposefully ambivalent on cross-border lender of last resort facilities.

In the absence of any single coherent co-ordinating principle, further regulatory upsets and difficulties may lie ahead. In particular, home country authorities may not be in a position to curtail the activities of their banks in permissive banking centres any more than such centres will feel obliged to respond to pressures for more stringent supervision. The overall conclusion, therefore, is that the Basle approach to international supervisory co-operation is not an adequate substitute for a formal legal framework covering the regulation of multinational banking. The revised Concordat represents a significant improvement on previous guidelines, and no doubt the process of regulatory convergence will continue. But where the stability of the international banking system is concerned progress does not suffice: it is necessary to arrive.

NOTES

1. C. W. McMahon, 'Offshore Financial Centres', *Bank of England Quarterly Bulletin*, June 1982, p.267.
2. Peter Cooke, 'Developments in Co-operation among Bank Supervisory Authorities', *Bank of England Quarterly Bulletin*, June 1981, p.238.
3. Cooke, 'Developments in Co-operation', p.239.
4. Cooke, 'Developments in Co-operation', p.240.
5. 'Report to the Governors on the Supervision of Banks' Foreign Establishments', Committee on Banking Regulations and Supervisory Practices, Basle, 26 September 1975. This document was approved by the central bank governors in December 1975, released to the public in March 1981 and published in IMF Occasional Paper No.7, August 1981, pp.29–32.
6. See 'Consideration of Banks' Balance Sheets: Aggregation of Risk-Bearing Assets as a Method of Supervising Bank Solvency', Committee on Banking Regulation and Supervisory Practices, Basle, October 1978.
7. *FINE: Financial Institutions and the Nation's Economy*, a compendium of papers prepared for the Fine Study, Book I; evidence submitted by the Comptroller of the Currency, 94th Congress, Second Session, 1976, p.385.
8. These requirements are embodied in the Federal Reserve's Reporting Forms FRY-7 and FRY-8 which were first proposed in October 1979 and finally introduced in modified form in February 1981. See Federal Reserve Press Releases, 29 October 1979 and 9 February 1981.
9. Comments regarding Federal Reserve Docket No. R-0256 (Proposed Form FRY-7) and Federal Reserve Docket No. R-0257 (Proposed Form FRY-8F), 3 March 1980.
10. Comments regarding Proposed Forms FRY-7 and FRY-8F, 11 January 1980.
11. Comments regarding Proposed Forms FRY-7 and FRY-8F, 22 February 1980.
12. See *Aspects of the International Bank Safety Net*, International Monetary Fund, Occasional Paper 17, March 1983, pp.4–5.
13. *Official Journal*, Legislative Series, 18 July 1983.
14. See Parts 322 and 323 of the Superintendant's Regulations regarding asset pledge and asset maintenance requirements of foreign banks licensed to do business in New York.
15. Cited by Henry C. Wallich in 'Central Banks as Regulators and Lenders of Last Resort in an International Context: a View from the United States', Key Issues in International Banking Series, No.18 (Federal Reserve Bank of Boston, October 1977), p.95.

16. See, for instance, Brimmer, 'International Finance and the Management of Bank Failures: Herstatt vs Franklin National', paper prepared for presentation before the American Economic Association and the American Finance Association, Atlantic City, 16 September 1976, pp.28–29, and *What Was Agreed in Basle* (London, Euromoney, October 1974, p.5.).
17. See *New York Times*, 3 September 1974, pp.31–32.
18. Edward Frydl, 'The Debate over Regulating the Eurocurrency Markets', *Federal Reserve Bank of New York Quarterly Review*, Volume 4, No. 4, Winter 1979–80, p.17.
19. Edward Frydl, 'The Eurodollar Conundrum', *Federal Reserve Bank of New York Quarterly Review*, Volume 7, No.1, Spring 1982, p.14.
20. Speech by C. W. McMahon, Mansion House, London, 26 May 1982, p.5.
21. Speech by Henry C. Wallich, 'Institutional Co-operation in the World Economy', Chicago, 5 May 1983, issued as Press Release by Federal Reserve Board, Washington, DC, p.7.
22. For an appraisal of the policy issues arising out of the debt crisis see Richard Dale and Richard Mattione, *Managing Global Debt* (Washington, DC, The Brookings Institution, 1983).
23. '. . . If a large depositor withdraws funds from a bank, the bank can borrow readily in the inter-bank market, for the [Euro-currency] market is a closed system. Withdrawals from a particular bank come back into the market or can be brought back into the market one way or another – provided, of course, that the key central banks and in particular the Federal Reserve do not withdraw funds from the system altogether. That feature marks a big difference from national banking where there is the possibility that the public will withdraw deposits in favour of holding currency . . . so the usual modes of government intervention – deposit insurance, reserve requirements and close surveillance over portfolios of banks – would not seem applicable to the Euro-currency market, whatever their merits may be today in national banking systems.' Summary remarks by Richard N. Cooper in Gary Hufbauer, ed., *The International Framework for Money and Banking in the 1980s* (Washington, DC, Georgetown University Law Centre, 1981), p.9.
24. Herbert Grubel, *A Proposal for the Establishment of an International Deposit Insurance Corporation*, Princeton Studies in International Finance, No. 133, July 1979.
25. A foreign branch may, for instance, be brought down by the activities of the parent institution in its country of origin. Given such interdependence, an acute free-rider problem would arise from the co-existence of (a) national regulatory regimes embracing parent banks and (b) a seperate international regulatory regime covering foreign establishments.
26. 'Guth Underlines Microeconomic Risks for Private Banks in Recycling Funds', *International Herald Tribune*, 16 June 1980.
27. See Dr Wilfried Guth, 'Trends in International Banking,' Speech given at the 34th International Banking Summer School, Timmendorfer Strand, 31 August 1981, pp.12–13.
28. James Dean and Ian Giddy, *Averting International Banking Crises*, Monograph Series in Economics and Finance, 1981-1 (New York University, Salomon Brothers Center).
29. Foreign currency deposits placed in offshore banking centres may, however, be subject to 'country risk' in that the host authorities could apply exchange controls preventing the transfer of such funds to other centres. This transfer risk was demonstrated when the Philippines imposed exchange controls in October 1983 and Citibank's Manila office was prevented thereby from meeting its dollar interbank obligations. See *Wall Street Journal* (Europe), 28 February 1984, p.9.
30. Arthur F. Burns, *Reflections of an Economic Policy Maker*, (Washington, DC, American Enterprise Institute, 1978), p.365.
31. This proposition is supported by the behaviour of Eurobank deposit rates during periods of uncertainty such as 1974: See Guttentag and Herring, *The Lender of Last Resort Function in an International Context*, Princeton Essays in International Finance, No. 151, May 1983, p.16. It is also consistent with the argument advanced by Guttentag and Herring that financial markets tend to ignore low-probability events; see their 'Financial Disorder and the Eurocurrency Markets', mimeograph, University of Pennsylvania, March 1981.

32. During the 1974 Euromarket crisis funds moved both between banking groups and from the Euromarkets into the United States. The latter move was partly compensated for by the recycling of funds from American parent banks to their foreign branches but there is, of course, no saying that in such a situation individual parent banks will necessarily gain what their foreign branches lose. See Brimmer, 'International Finance and the Management of Bank Failures: Herstatt vs Franklin National', paper prepared for presentation before the American Economic Association and the American Finance Association, Atlantic City, 16 September 1976, pp.52–54.
33. Remarks by Governor Wallich at the International Conference of Banking Supervisors, Washington, DC, 24–25 September 1981, p.2.
34. The equity principle has been advocated by a former Director of Financial Institutions in the EEC Commission. See H. R. Hutton, 'The Regulation of Foreign Banks – A European Viewpoint', *Columbia Journal of World Business*, Winter 1975, p.113.
35. For a full analysis of this relationship under US law see Patrick Heininger, 'Liability of US Banks for Deposits Placed in their Foreign Branches', *Law and Policy in International Business*, Volume 11, No. 3, 1979.
36. The legal status of letters of comfort is examined in Jacques Terray, 'La Lettre de Confort', *Banque*, No.393, March 1980.
37. Official pressure was, for instance, brought to bear on United California Bank of Los Angeles to support its majority owned Basle affiliate when the latter incurred large commodity trading losses in 1970. See Francis Lees, *International Banking and Finance*, (New York, John Wiley and Sons, 1974), pp.42–43.
38. See, for instance, views of the Board of Governors of the Federal Reserve presented in compendium of papers prepared for the FINE Study, Book I, p.499 and comments by Rt Hon. Gordon Richardson, Governor of the Bank of England at the International Conference of Banking Supervisors, London, 5–6 July 1979, pp.8–9.
39. For an analogous proposal to fragment risk within the US domestic banking system by 'building a wall' between bank holding companies and their bank subsidiaries, see Fischer Black, Merton Miller and Richard Posner, 'An Approach to the Regulation of Bank Holding Companies', *Journal of Business*, Volume 51, No.3, July 1978, pp.400–402. Section 23a of the US Federal Reserve Act is designed to limit risk transfers between banking affiliates: see John Rose and Samuel Talby, 'The Banking Affiliates Act of 1982: Amendments to Section 23a', *Federal Reserve Bulletin*, November 1982, pp.693–99.

Appendix 1:
The Revised Basle Concordat
Principles for the Supervision of Banks' Foreign Establishments

I. INTRODUCTION

This report sets out certain principles which the Committee believes should govern the supervision of banks' foreign establishments by parent and host authorities. It replaces the 1975 'Concordat' and reformulates some of its provisions, most particularly to take account of the subsequent acceptance by the Governors of the principle that banking supervisory authorities cannot be fully satisfied about the soundness of individual banks unless they can examine the totality of each bank's business worldwide through the technique of consolidation.

The report deals exclusively with the responsibilities of banking supervisory authorities for monitoring the prudential conduct and soundness of the business of banks' foreign establishments. It does not address itself to lender-of-last-resort aspects of the role of central banks.

The principles set out in the report are not necessarily embodied in the laws of the countries represented on the Committee. Rather they are recommended guidelines of best practices in this area, which all members have undertaken to work towards implementing, according to the means available to them.

Adequate supervision of banks' foreign establishments calls not only for an appropriate allocation of responsibilities between parent and host supervisory authorities but also for contact and co-operation between them. It has been, and remains, one of the Committee's principal purposes to foster such co-operation both among its member countries and more widely. The Committee has been encouraged by the like-minded approach of other groups of supervisors and it hopes to continue to strengthen its relationships with these other groups and to develop new ones. It strongly commends the principles set out in this report as being of general validity for all those who are responsible for the supervision of banks which conduct international business and hopes that they will be progressively accepted and implemented by supervisors worldwide.

Where situations arise which do not appear to be covered by the principles set out in this report, parent and host authorities should explore together ways of ensuring that adequate supervision of banks' foreign establishments is effected.

II.   TYPES OF BANKS' FOREIGN ESTABLISHMENTS

Banks operating internationally may have interests in the following types of foreign banking establishment:

1. *Branches*: operating entities which do not have a separate legal status and are thus integral parts of the foreign parent bank.
2. *Subsidiaries*: legally independent institutions wholly owned or majority-owned by a bank which is incorporated in a country other than that of the subsidiary.
3. *Joint ventures or Consortia*: legally independent institutions incorporated in the country where their principal operations are conducted and controlled by two or more parent institutions, most of which are usually foreign and not all of which are necessarily banks. While the pattern of shareholdings may give effective control to one parent institution, with others in a minority, joint ventures are, most typically, owned by a collection of minority shareholders.

In addition, the structure of international banking groups may derive from an ultimate holding company which is not itself a bank. Such a holding company can be an industrial or commercial company, or a company the majority of whose assets consists of shares in banks. These groups may also include intermediate non-bank holding companies or other non-banking companies.

Banks may also have minority participations in foreign banking or non-banking companies, other than those in joint ventures, which may be held to be part of their overall foreign banking operations. This report does not cover the appropriate supervisory treatment of these participations, but they should be taken into account by the relevant supervisory authorities.

III.   GENERAL PRINCIPLES GOVERNING THE SUPERVISION OF BANKS' FOREIGN ESTABLISHMENTS

Effective co-operation between host and parent authorities is a central prerequisite for the supervision of banks' international operations. In relation to the supervision of banks' foreign establishments there are two basic principles which are fundamental to such co-operation and which call for consultation and contacts between respective host and parent authorities: firstly, that no foreign banking establishment should escape supervision; and secondly, that the supervision should be adequate. In giving effect to these principles, host authorities should ensure that parent authorities are informed immediately of any serious problems which arise in a parent bank's foreign establishment. Similarly, parent authorities should inform host authorities when problems arise in a parent bank which are likely to affect the parent bank's foreign establishment.

Acceptance of these principles will not, however, of itself preclude there being gaps and inadequacies in the supervision of banks' foreign establishments. These may occur for various reasons. Firstly, while there should be a presumption that host authorities are in a position to fulfil their supervisory obligations adequately with respect to all foreign bank establishments operating in their territories, this may not always be the case. Problems may, for instance, arise when a foreign establishment is classified as a bank by its parent banking supervisory authority but not by its host authority. In such cases it is the responsibility of the parent authority to ascertain whether the host authority is able to undertake adequate supervision and the host authority should inform the parent authority if it is not in a position to undertake such supervision.

In cases where host authority supervision is inadequate the parent authority should either extend its supervision, to the degree that it is practicable, or it should be prepared to discourage the parent bank from continuing to operate the establishment in question.

Secondly, problems may arise where the host authority considers that supervision of the parent institutions of foreign bank establishments operating in its territory is inadequate or non-existent. In such cases the host authority should discourage or, if it is in a position to do so, forbid the operation in its territory of such foreign establishments. Alternatively, the host authority could impose specific conditions governing the conduct of the business of such establishments.

Thirdly, gaps in supervision can arise out of structural features of international banking groups. For example, the existence of holding companies either at the head, or in the middle, of such groups may constitute an impediment to adequate supervision. Furthermore, particular supervisory problems may arise where such holding companies, while not themselves banks, have substantial liabilities to the international banking system. Where holding companies are at the head of groups that include separately incorporated banks operating in different countries, the authorities responsible for supervising those banks should endeavour to co-ordinate their supervision of those banks, taking account of the overall structure of the group in question. Where a bank is the parent company of a group that contains intermediate holding companies, the parent authority should make sure that such holding companies and their subsidiaries are covered by adequate supervision. Alternatively, the parent authority should not allow the parent bank to operate such intermediate holding companies.

Where groups contain both banks and non-bank organisations, there should, where possible, be liaison between the banking supervisory authorities and any authorities which have responsibilities for supervising these non-banking organisations, particularly where the non-banking activities are of a financial character. Banking supervisors, in their overall supervision of banking groups, should take account of these groups' non-banking activities; and if these activities cannot be adequately supervised, banking supervisors should aim at minimising the risks to the banking business from the non-banking activities of such groups.

The implementation of the second basic principle, namely that the supervision of all foreign banking establishments should be adequate, requires the positive participation of both host and parent authorities. Host authorities are responsible for the foreign bank establishments operating in their territories as individual institutions while parent authorities are responsible for them as parts of larger banking groups where a general supervisory responsibility exists in respect of their worldwide consolidated activites. These responsibilities of host and parent authorities are both complementary and overlapping.

The principle of consolidated supervision is that parent banks and parent supervisory authorities monitor the risk exposure – including a perspective of concentrations of risk and of the quality of assets – of the banks or banking groups for which they are responsible, as well as the adequacy of their capital, on the basis of the totality of their business wherever conducted. This principle does not imply any lessening of host authorities' responsibilities for supervising foreign bank establishments that operate in their territories, although it is recognised that the full implementation of the consolidation principle may well lead to some extension of parental responsibility. Consolidation is only one of a range of techniques, albeit an important one, at the disposal of the supervisory authorities and it should not be applied to the exclusion of supervision of individual banking establishments on an unconsolidated basis by parent and host authorities. Moreover, the implementation of the principle of consolidated supervision presupposes that parent banks and parent authorities have access to all the relevant information about the operations of their banks' foreign establishments, although existing banking secrecy provisions in some countries may present a constraint on comprehensive consolidated parental supervision.

IV.   *ASPECTS OF THE SUPERVISION OF BANKS' FOREIGN ESTABLISHMENTS*

The supervision of banks' foreign establishments is considered in this report from three different aspects: solvency, liquidity, and foreign exchange operations and positions. These aspects overlap to some extent. For instance, liquidity and solvency questions can shade into one another. Moreover, both liquidity and solvency considerations arise in the supervision of banks' foreign exchange operations and positions.

1. Solvency

The allocation of responsibilities for the supervision of the solvency of banks' foreign establishments between parent and host authorities will depend upon the type of establishment concerned.

For branches, their solvency is indistinguishable from that of the parent bank as a whole. So, while there is a general responsibility on the host authority to monitor the financial soundness of foreign branches, supervision of solvency is primarily a matter for the parent authority. The 'dotation de capital' requirements imposed by certain host authorities on foreign branches operating in their countries do not negate this principle. They exist firstly to oblige foreign branches that set up in business in those countries to make and to sustain a certain minimum investment in them, and secondly, to help equalise competitive conditions between foreign branches and domestic banks.

For subsidiaries, the supervision of solvency is a joint responsibility of both host and parent authorities. Host authorities have responsibility for supervising the solvency of all foreign subsidiaries operating in their territories. Their approach to the task of supervising subsidiaries is from the standpoint that these establishments are separate entities, legally incorporated in the country of the host authority. At the same time parent authorities, in the context of consolidated supervision of the parent banks, need to assess whether the parent institutions' solvency is being affected by the operations of their foreign subsidiaries. Parental supervision on a consolidated basis is needed for two reasons: because the solvency of parent banks cannot be adequately judged without taking account of all their foreign establishments; and because parent banks cannot be indifferent to the situation of their foreign subsidiaries.

For joint ventures, the supervision of solvency should normally, for practical reasons, be primarily the responsibility of the authorities in the country of incorporation. Banks which are shareholders in consortium banks cannot, however, be indifferent to the situation of their joint ventures and may have commitments to these establishments beyond the legal commitments which arise from their shareholdings, for example through comfort letters. All these commitments must be taken into account by the parent authorities of the shareholder banks when supervising their solvency. Depending on the pattern of shareholdings in joint ventures, and particularly when one bank is a dominant shareholder, there can also be circumstances in which the supervision of their solvency should be the joint responsibility of the authorities in the country of incorporation and the parent authorities of the shareholder banks.

2. Liquidity

References to supervision of liquidity in this section do not relate to central banks' functions as lenders of last resort, but to the responsibility of supervisory authorities for monitoring the control systems and procedures established by their banks which enable them to meet their obligations as they fall due including, as necessary, those of their foreign establishments.

The allocation of responsibilities for the supervision of the liquidity of banks' foreign establishments between parent and host authorities will depend, as with solvency, upon the type of establishment concerned. The host authority has responsibility for monitoring the liquidity of the foreign bank's establishments in its country; the parent authority has responsibility for monitoring the liquidity of the banking group as a whole.

For branches, the initial presumption should be that primary responsibility for supervising liquidity rests with the host authority. Host authorities will often be best equipped to supervise liquidity as it relates to local practices and regulations and the functioning of their domestic money markets. At the same time, the liquidity of all foreign branches will always be a matter of concern to the parent authorities, since a branch's liquidity is frequently controlled directly by the parent bank and cannot be viewed in isolation from that of the whole bank of which it is a part. Parent authorities need to be aware of parent banks' control systems and need to take account of calls that may be made on the resources of parent banks by their foreign branches. Host and parent authorities should always consult each other if there are any doubts in particular cases about where responsibilities for supervising the liquidity of foreign branches should lie.

For subsidiaries, primary responsibility for supervising liquidity should rest with the host authority. Parent authorities should take account of any standby or other facilities granted as well as any other commitments, for example through comfort letters, by parent banks to these establishments. Host authorities should inform the parent authorities of the importance they attach to such facilities and commitments, so as to ensure that full account is taken of them in the supervision of the parent bank. Where the host authority has difficulties in supervising the liquidity, especially in foreign currency, of foreign banks' subsidiaries, it will be expected to inform the parent authorities and appropriate arrangements will have to be agreed so as to ensure adequate supervision.

For joint ventures, primary responsibility for supervising liquidity should rest with the authorities in the country of incorporation. The parent authorities of shareholders in joint ventures should take account of any standby or other facilities granted as well as any other commitments, for example through comfort letters, by shareholder banks to those establishments. The authorities in the country of incorporation of joint ventures should inform the parent authorities of shareholder banks of the importance they should attach to such facilities and commitments so as to ensure that full account is taken of them in the supervision of the shareholder bank.

Within the framework of consolidated supervision, parent authorities have a general responsibility for overseeing the liquidity control systems employed by the banking groups they supervise and for ensuring that these systems and the overall liquidity position of such groups are adequate. It is recognised, however, that full consolidation may not always be practicable as a technique for supervising liquidity because of differences of local regulations and market situations and the complications of banks operating in different time zones and different currencies. Parent authorities should consult with host authorities to ensure that the latter are aware of the overall systems within which the foreign establishments are operating. Host authorities have a duty to ensure that the parent authority is immediately informed of any serious liquidity inadequacy in a parent bank's foreign establishment.

3.   Foreign exchange operations and positions

As regards the supervision of banks' foreign exchange operations and positions, there should be a joint responsibility of parent and host authorities. It is particularly important for parent banks to have in place systems for monitoring their group's overall foreign exchange exposure and for parent authorities to monitor those systems. Host authorities should be in a position to monitor the foreign exchange exposure of foreign establishments in their territories and should inform themselves of the nature and extent of the supervision of these establishments being undertaken by the parent authorities.

Committee on Banking Regulations and Supervisory Practices
Basle
May 1983

Appendix 2:
Citibank's 'Rinky Dink Deals':
A Case Study in Regulatory Arbitrage

Chapter 2, in describing the regulatory arrangements prevailing in major financial centre countries, underlined the close connection between multinational banking activity and differential regulation. This case study illustrates the connection in greater detail using as its material a recent investigation into Citibank's offshore banking operations.

Following allegations made in 1977 by a Citibank employee, David Edwards, to the effect that Citibank had devised various schemes to circumvent other countries' tax and currency laws, the US Securities and Exchange Commission (SEC) carried out an extensive investigation into Citibank's international dealings covering the period 1973–80. In January 1982 the SEC overruled its enforcement staff and declined to bring a civil action against Citicorp (Citibank's holding company), but in subsequent Congressional hearings the SEC report on this matter, together with related documentary evidence, was made publicly available, thereby providing a rare insight into a leading US multinational bank's global financial activities.[1] This material provides documentary support for several key propositions advanced in this book: namely, that differences in national regulatory arrangements generate large-scale financial transactions that have no underlying economic justification; that such disparities both reflect and contribute to competition between national regulatory authorities; and that fragmented supervision and regulation are largely ineffective when applied to multinational banks operating across national frontiers.

The evidence assembled by the SEC shows that during the period 1973–80 Citibank used its multinational banking network, including offshore operations in Nassau, Monaco, the Channel Islands and Panama, to engage in what one of its officers described as 'rinky dink deals' designed explicitly to circumvent a variety of national bank regulations.[2] These included monetary regulations, in the form of minimum reserve requirements, exchange controls designed to limit capital outflows and/or inflows and tax laws applicable both to the bank

195

itself and to its clients, and prudential controls such as capital adequacy and liquidity requirements, limits on foreign exchange exposure and local norms limiting the extent of maturity mismatching.

The techniques employed by Citibank to circumvent these regulations were mainly of two kinds: 'parking' and 'round-tripping'. 'Parking' involves booking a position at a branch or subsidiary other than that which initiates and controls the position. For instance, if Citibank's Frankfurt branch were to incur an open foreign exchange position which it wished to transfer to Citibank's Nassau branch it could achieve this simply by undertaking an offsetting transaction with Nassau. Depending on where Citibank wished to book the profit or loss arising from this exposure, the parked position could be reversed either at the original exchange rate (with no loss/profit to Nassau), at the subsequent prevailing market rate (leaving the loss/profit with Nassau) or at a contrived off-market rate. A 'round-trip' transaction, on the other hand, refers to a situation where the funds of one branch are deposited in another branch which then re-deposits them with the first branch. Such operations, which are also referred to as 'back-to-back loans', may involve deposits with matched or unmatched maturities and interest rates.

During the period covered by the SEC investigation, Citibank engaged extensively in parking, round-tripping and other similar transactions. The following account of these activities focuses on Citibank's main operating banks in Europe, although there are indications that parallel techniques were employed in Latin America (where Panama was used as a booking centre) as well as in the Far East. In considering the tax implications of these manoeuvres it should be borne in mind that although Citibank's profits in Nassau and other tax havens were subject to US corporation tax, the bank was earning such large profits abroad that it had more foreign tax credits than it could use. Accordingly, the overall tax burden could be reduced by shifting profits from high to low (or zero) tax centres.[3]

LONDON

During a 2½ year period covering 1975–77 Citibank's London branch engaged in large-scale maturity mismatching or 'gapping' by borrowing dollars at call and lending them back on the interbank market at a fixed term of six months.[4] So long as call rates remained significantly below the returns on six month deposits Citibank was able to earn large profits on such transactions, although there was always the risk that funding costs would rise suddenly, thereby resulting in a loss on the mismatched position. The Bank of England actively monitors the extent of maturity mismatching by London banks because of the risks involved, and partly for this reason, but also as a means of reducing its overall tax burden, Citibank determined that its gapping operations should not show up on the UK returns but instead be transferred to Nassau.[5] This was achieved through a series of round-trip transactions whereby London borrowed from Nassau at six months and re-lent at call, the effect being to shift not merely the mismatched position but also the resulting profits onto Nassau's books. At the peak of these transactions in 1976 Citibank's London branch had a mismatched position of $1.5 billion booked to Nassau while over a $2\frac{1}{2}$ year period an average of $1 million per month in profits was transferred from London to Nassau by this means.

In addition to initiating round-trip transactions, London was also used as a passive agent in round-trip transactions initiated by other Citibank branches in both Europe and the Far East. Furthermore, because the UK Inland Revenue had adopted the practice of taxing fund transfers between related entities (intra-bank deposits) on the basis of a notional $5/64$ funding 'spread', it paid Citibank to route some transactions through its UK finance subsidiary, which, by charging a margin of $1/8$ over LIBOR, was able to secure an element of tax-free profit.[6]

During the period considered by the SEC the Bank of England limited Citibank London's overnight position against sterling to $1 million. This restriction prompted Citibank to park short sterling positions ranging from $2 million to $4 million with its Nassau branch, beginning in April 1976 and extending (at least) through May 1978.[7] However, the parking of foreign exchange positions by London was on a relatively modest scale when compared with the activities of Citibank's operations in Switzerland and Frankfurt, mainly because the UK authorities did not then (as they do now) limit foreign exchange positions against currencies other than sterling.

GERMANY

Citibank's operations in Germany were conducted through a branch, Citibank NA, and a wholly owned subsidiary, Citibank AG, which held investments in two other German subsidiaries, Trinkaus and Burkhardt and Kunden Kreditbank. Citibank NA, being a foreign bank, was subject to a higher tax rate than Citibank AG and was therefore mainly responsible for the funding of other Citibank branches and subsidiaries at low profit margins. In contrast, Citibank AG handled the more remunerative business of foreign exchange and domestic lending, while the two other German subsidiaries were managed autonomously and had few dealings with either NA or AG.[8]

Following the Herstatt collapse of 1974, the German authorities had introduced a prudential limit on each bank's overnight foreign exchange position equivalent to 30 per cent of capital, which for Citibank AG and NA translated into an aggregate exposure limit of some DM28 million.[9] In order to bypass this restriction Citibank routinely parked excess positions in Nassau, either directly or through Switzerland, the stated frequency being two to three times per week at an average of some $40 million per transaction.[10] The profits arising from this activity were often booked to Nassau, too, partly because it would have raised suspicions if disproportionately large foreign exchange profits had been reported in the context of modest overnight trading limits.

Citibank's Frankfurt offices also engaged in elaborate round-trip transactions with a view to circumventing a variety of local regulations. The centrepiece of these arrangements was the 'Jersey Pool', consisting of some DM1.5 billion of offshore funds, DM1.3 billion of which was provided through Citibank Channel Islands (CI) Ltd and DM200 million through Citibank Luxembourg SA.[11] The scheme operated in the following way:

1. Citibank NA Frankfurt solicited interbank Euro-Deutschmark deposits which were booked to Nassau. Nassau in turn made a deposit with Citibank CI Ltd which advanced a long-term (over four years) loan to Citibank AG Frankfurt. Nassau made a small funding profit and Citibank CI Ltd charged a margin of ⅛ per cent which was taxed at 4 per cent.

2. Citibank NA Frankfurt solicited interbank Euro-Deutschmark deposits which were booked to Nassau (as above). Nassau forwarded the money to Citibank Brussels which in turn made a deposit with Citibank Luxembourg SA. The Luxembourg subsidiary completed the circle by making a long-term (over four years) loan to Citibank NA Frankfurt. Nassau again made a small funding profit while the Brussels and Luxembourg offices split between them a lending margin of ⅛ per cent.

These circuitous transactions offered several advantages to Citibank. First (although this was not the primary concern), profits were in some measure transferred from Germany to the Nassau and Channel Island tax havens. Secondly, having the borrowed funds booked initially to Nassau rather than to Frankfurt enabled Citibank to employ low-cost Euro-Deutschmark deposits rather than high-cost domestic deposits. Thirdly, having the funds returned to Frankfurt in the form of long-term loans provided a double benefit: under the Bundesbank's regulations, deposit liabilities of four years or more were exempt from minimum reserve requirements, while long-term funding of this kind also reduced the amount of capital Frankfurt was required to hold against its loan portfolio.[12] Finally, by interposing other Citibank branches and subsidiaries between Frankfurt and Nassau, Citibank evidently hoped to cover its tracks so far as the German regulatory authorities were concerned.

One Citibank officer described the benefits of the Jersey Pool as follows:

'Upon reflection, the advantages of the 'Jersey Pool' become clear:
–it provides funds that the bank could not obtain domestically.
–it is a higher leveraged and consequently less expensive funding source since a smaller volume of funding supports a larger volume of lending.

–it is less expensive to borrow Euro-marks rather than domestic funds which are subject to higher reserve costs.

–it avoids the marketing and operation exposures necessary to capture and process a commercial deposit base.'[13]

Quite apart from the Jersey Pool, deposits solicited by Frankfurt were routinely booked through Nassau, which could then lend directly to Citibank's German customers without incurring the cost of holding interest-free reserves with the German monetary authorities. When Frankfurt solicited loans from other Citibank sources the funds could be booked either directly to Nassau or through Frankfurt's own books (since in the latter case the deposits would be free of reserves as intra-bank 'clearance' transactions). The scale of these operations is reflected in Nassau's Frankfurt-funded loan portfolio which at mid-1977 stood at DM3.8 billion, an amount broadly equivalent to the combined assets of Citibank NA and AG.

It should be understood that 'Nassau' in the present context means simply a separate set of books in Frankfurt called the Nassau/Germany unit. All confirmations and agreements for this unit's lending and funding operations were signed and mailed by the 'Nassau representative' in London, so the unit's connection with Nassau, from both a management and communications point of view, was remote; so remote, indeed, that the German tax authorities eventually came to the conclusion that the management of the Nassau/German unit remained effectively in Frankfurt and that Nassau's earnings were therefore subject to German tax.[14]

Citibank's response to this tax threat was to wind down Nassau/Germany's operations and, with effect from 1977, to shift the unit's business to an alternative booking centre in Monaco. Under the new arrangements, Frankfurt's traders again undertook all the funding and lending on behalf of Monaco, the novel feature being that in return for this service and in order to satisfy the German tax authorities, Citibank AG received from Monaco a ¼ per cent brokerage commission on loans and a ¹/₁₆ per cent commission on deposits.[15] In this way Citibank was able to retain the benefits of a tax shelter while also continuing to circumvent the Bundesbank's reserve requirements, although the danger of having Monaco's profits attributed to Frankfurt was not wholly eliminated.[16]

SWITZERLAND

Citibank's Swiss operations were conducted through four branches located in Geneva, Zurich, Lugano and Lausanne. The most lucrative activity in Switzerland was foreign exchange trading which, according to internal records, yielded Citibank $83 million in profits during the period 1974–78.[17] However, Citibank had to contend with the following regulatory constraints introduced by the Swiss authorities in 1974–75 in an attempt to clamp down on foreign exchange activity:

1.   A net long overnight position in Swiss francs was not permitted (a restriction designed to discourage capital inflows).
2.   There was a general position limit, comprising all long and short positions, equivalent to 40 per cent of each bank's capital. For Citibank this translated into a $16 million ceiling on open positions.
3.   In response to the Herstatt collapse, a counterparty limit was imposed on deals with other banks which in effect restricted the Swiss branches' transactions with Citibank's offices abroad to $20 million.[18]

Limits 1 and 2 posed no particular problem to Citibank since positions could be routinely parked in Nassau. The record shows that Switzerland took dollar/Swiss franc positions (both short and long) two or three times per week in amounts typically ranging between $10 million and $50 million.[19] Citibank's internal foreign exchange exposure limit for Switzerland ranged between $50 million and $75 million, the latter figure representing a multiple of nearly five times the official ceiling of $16 million,[20] and at one point in 1978 Switzerland had a $90 million position parked in Nassau.[21]

Limit 3 presented a minor problem because it meant that Zurich, for instance, could not do a large deal in its own name and subsequently off-book the position to Nassau (the normal parking technique) without breaching its $20 million counterparty limit. On the other hand, booking the deal directly to Nassau might have raised official suspicions and would in any case probably have been unacceptable to the Swiss counter-parties. Accordingly, deals were often booked in the name of other European branches (for instance London or Frankfurt) before being passed through to Nassau. By such means Citibank was able to circum-vent the Swiss regulations, although the scale of its foreign exchange lending in Swiss francs eventually attracted the attention of the Swiss National Bank and resulted in a severe reprimand, including the threat that its licence might be withdrawn.[22]

In addition to bypassing local foreign exchange regulations, Citibank's Swiss branches (in common with other Swiss banks) engaged in extensive 'window-dressing' operations designed to improve reported liquidity on relevant quarterly closing dates. For instance, the Geneva branch would borrow $25 million at over 30 days from Citibank London and place the funds with Westdeutsche Landesbank at short maturity. Zurich would also borrow $25 million from London and place it with Société Générale, while Lugano and Lausanne would undertake similar transactions in amounts of $5 million and $7 million, respectively.[23] These deals were possible because the Swiss reporting requirements were based on Citibank's fiscal closing (20th of the month) whereas, for instance, liquidity reports to the French authorities were prepared as of the calendar end of the month.

Citibank's Swiss branches were in effect prohibited from making deposits with sister branches outside Switzerland since this would be regarded by the regulatory authorities as repatriation of capital. However, since Swiss management felt that it was sufficient to conform to this requirement on reporting dates only, the constraint was more apparent than real. For instance, Zurich normally kept 'substantial' placements with Citibank London, where maturities were arranged to fall due just before closing dates at which time the funds would be placed for one day with other (non-Citibank) institutions. These placements would be re-deposited with Citibank London the following day, with the maturity dates again falling due just before the next closing date.[24]

Finally, the Swiss branches engaged in round-trip transactions in order to provide a currency hedge against Citibank's capital exposure in Switzerland. In essence, Nassau would deposit dollars with the Swiss branch (this represented the branch's capital endowment for regulatory purposes) which would then be converted into Swiss francs. Simultaneously, Nassau would secure a Swiss franc deposit, solicited through the Swiss branch, which would be converted into dollars, thereby matching Citibank's dollar/Swiss franc exposure.[25]

PARIS

The French authorities required that 60 per cent of a bank's short-term (under three months) deposits be held in the form of specified low-yielding liquid assets. Initially Citibank's Paris branch met this liquidity requirement on relevant reporting dates by engaging in a round-trip transaction with Brussels, placing with Brussels at seven days and simultaneously receiving funds back from Brussels at 93 days.[26] However, following objections from the Belgian Banking Commission, an alternative round-trip was adopted, whereby Paris placed with London, London with Amsterdam and Amsterdam with Paris, all deposits being at one-day call and subject to the same interest rate. These transactions, which involved amounts of around £250 million on each occasion, had the effect of improving reported liquidity by increasing both short-term assets and liabilities *pro rata*.[27]

Paris did on occasion park foreign-exchange positions with other Citibank branches but more often was used by Brussels, Milan, Zurich and Frankfurt to off-book their own positions. In addition, Paris avoided a special 17.6 per cent tax on foreign exchange profits by converting such profits into interest income. In essence this was achieved by having Paris take a deposit in a low interest currency and swap it into a high interest currency which was then placed with another bank. When the deposit, the placement and the forward contract covering the swap transaction all matured, the net result was a gain in interest earnings (from the interest rate spread between the two currencies) and a loss on foreign exchange (arising from the forward discount on the high interest currency).[28]

Finally, Paris undertook round-trip transactions with Nassau and Jersey in order to transfer profits to the tax haven centres. Under this scheme Nassau or Jersey would deposit dollars at three or six months with a (non-Citibank) French bank, the French bank would re-deposit at two days' notice with Citibank Paris at a lower interest rate, and Citibank Paris would complete the circle by re-depositing short-term with Nassau or Jersey at a still lower interest rate.[29] A refinement here was that the deposit by the first French bank was, for liquidity purposes, dressed up contractually as a three or six month placement but since the funds could, under the terms of the contract, be withdrawn at 48 hours' notice without penalty, the interest payable was equivalent to that on a two-day deposit.[30]

MILAN

Citibank Milan, in common with the bank's other offices, made a regular habit of parking its foreign exchange positions with other centres, the amounts typically being $5 million to $10 million and the frequency two or three times per week.[31] Parking was considered necessary because under Italy's exchange control regulations a bank's position in dollars, EEC currencies together and other currencies (taken separately) had to be broadly matched. On occasion, when parked positions in Nassau resulted in a loss, the deficit would be discreetly repatriated to Milan through a series of small deals, thereby ensuring maximum tax relief for Citibank. As a separate matter, futures contracts between bank residents in Italy were subject to a special stamp duty designed to discourage speculation. To avoid this Milan would close a futures contract with another Citibank branch or subsidiary in Europe and instruct the latter to close an off-setting contract with another Italian bank.[32]

BELGIUM

Brussels parked modest foreign exchange positions in excess of official limits with Amsterdam while larger positions of between $5 million and $10 million were parked with Nassau.[33] Although arbitrage between the Convertible and Financial Belgian francs was prohibited by the authorities, Brussels was able to circumvent this restriction by using a non-resident counterparty and an intermediate currency (dollars).[34] For instance, Brussels might buy dollars against Convertible francs and sell them against Financial francs, the resulting net position in Financial francs being parked in Nassau.

Customers of Belsa Antwerp, a Citibank financial subsidiary, were enabled to avoid the Belgian withholding tax on interest by having their deposits routed through accounts opened on their behalf at Citibank's Geneva branch. The funds were placed back with Belsa Antwerp as fiduciary deposits, thereby avoiding liability to Swiss withholding tax.[35]

THE FAR EAST

It appears that Citibank's European banking and round-tripping transactions were duplicated in its Far East operations, albeit on a more modest scale. Singapore 'gapped' for the whole of south-east Asia[36] and there were extensive back-to-back loans, involving Indonesia, Brunei, Malaysia, Singapore, Hong Kong and Tokyo, the main aim of which was to improve reported liquidity in the centres concerned.[37] For instance, Hong Kong would place perhaps US $88 million on demand with Singapore, which in turn re-deposited the funds with Hong Kong on eight days' call, Hong Kong's placement counting towards its first tier liquidity requirement under local regulations.[38]

OTHER ACTIVITIES

Apart from the activities described above, which in effect transferred positions between different financial centres, Citibank also devised a scheme for keeping certain positions off the books of *any* centre – at least for a period of time. This could be achieved, quite simply, by making use of centres located in different time zones, with positions being passed from one centre to another overnight. In the extreme, deals could be kept off the closing books of any centre by passing them through successive time zones. As one Citibank officer put it, 'eventually we will be securing our major positions around the world and selling them by contract to the next centre to the West when we close for the day'.[39] This kind of manoeuvre has special significance from a supervisory point of view, since unlike parking and round-tripping exercises it would not necessarily be picked up by regulatory authorities even if they were monitoring the bank's activities on a fully consolidated basis.

CONCLUSIONS

The main purpose of the SEC investigation into Citibank's international activities was to determine whether or not there had been breaches of the law which warranted disciplinary action. In this event the SEC decided not to pursue matters further, although there can be little doubt that Citibank did infringe certain local regulations. For instance, the Swiss National Bank evidently took the view that the parking of foreign exchange positions was illegal and wrote to the US Comptroller of the Currency making it clear that 'the behaviour of the bank and its persons in charge was not in full accordance with the Swiss laws and practice'.[40]

However, the real significance of Citibank's activities in the context of this book relates not so much to the question of illegality and wrongdoing as to the ease with which deals can be booked to any part of the world that happens to be convenient and the possibilities presented thereby for regulatory circumvention. Nassau purportedly undertook large-scale transactions for its own account ('our deals with Nassau are like their

GNP')[41] despite the fact that it had no foreign exchange dealer and no independent trading capacity. Similar shadow transactions were routed through Citibank's offshore offices in Monaco, Jersey and Panama, as well as though operational branches and subsidiaries in the main European centres. Furthermore, there are numerous indications in the SEC documentation that these activities, far from being confined to Citibank, are endemic to multinational banking. Indeed, widespread regulatory arbitrage of the kind practised by Citibank would help to explain why, as noted in Chapter 4 above, interbank (including intra-bank) placements account for an estimated 70 per cent of the Eurocurrency deposit market, far above the comparable figure for domestic interbank activity.[42]

NOTES

1. The Citibank hearings were held before the Subcommittee on Oversight Investigations, House of Representatives Committee on Energy and Commerce, 17 September 1982. The documentation released includes the following: 'in re Citicorp', Division of Enforcement, Securities and Exchange Commission, February 1981 ('von Stein Report'); 'Citibank Foreign Exchange Investigation', Report by the Comptroller of the Currency, December 1980; Report by Peat, Marwick, Mitchell & Co on the German tax treatment of Citibank's offshore lending and funding, August 1977; 'Memorandum Relative to the Tax Review of the Paris Branch of Citibank', Report by Peat, Marwick, Mitchell & Co, September 1977; and extensive internal Citibank memoranda which are identified by the SEC's page references for this material. Finally, the Subcommittee on Oversight Investigations itself commissioned staff studies of the Citibank material under the headings of 'Capital Hedges', 'Citicorp's German Operations', 'Gapping and Bank Liquidity', 'London Roundtrip' and 'Roundtrip Transactions'.
2. Citibank memoranda (7930).
3. 'Von Stein Report', p.19.
4. 'Von Stein Report', pp.48–53a.
5. One of Citibank's officers commented as follows on the Bank of England's surveillance of its London operation: 'B of E has never come to check up in the actual dealing room or operating departments. It is possible that they have gone to other banks, but it is felt unlikely that they could adequately staff a thorough investigation of a bank of our size.' Citibank memoranda (02076).
6. Report by Peat, Marwick, Mitchell, August 1977, Attachment, p.5.
7. 'Von Stein Report', p.79a.
8. See Subcommittee on Oversight Investigations, staff study on 'Citicorp's German Operations'.
9. Citibank memoranda (01710).
10. Citibank memoranda (01710).
11. On the Jersey Pool arrangements, see Report by Peat, Marwick, Mitchell, August 1977, Attachment, p.4–9.
12. See Principles II and III in 'Principles Concerning the Capital and Liquidity of Banks', Deutsche Bundesbank, 1980.
13. Citibank memoranda (1804).
14. Citibank memoranda (1789).
15. Citibank memoranda (1791).
16. Report by Peat, Marwick, Mitchell, August 1977, p.8.
17. 'Von Stein Report', p.13.
18. Citibank memoranda (01721).
19. Citibank memoranda (01726).
20. 'Von Stein Report', p.22.
21. 'Von Stein Report', p.94.
22. Citibank memoranda (02201).

23. Citibank memoranda (10D).
24. Citibank memoranda (10D).
25. Citibank memoranda (02295).
26. Citibank memoranda (01973).
27. Citibank memoranda (01702).
28. Citibank memoranda (01702).
29. 'Memorandum Relative to the Tax Review of the Paris Branch of Citibank', Peat Marwick, Mitchell, September 1977, p.8.
30. 'Memorandum Relative to the Tax Review of the Paris Branch', p.9.
31. Citibank memoranda (01747).
32. Citibank memoranda (01703).
33. Citibank memoranda (02192).
34. 'Von Stein Report', p.70.
35. Citibank memoranda (01973).
36. Citibank memoranda (02388).
37. Citibank memoranda (01942–57).
38. Citibank memoranda (019942).
39. Citibank memoranda (02191).
40. 'Von Stein Report', p.133.
41. Citibank memoranda (01710).
42. See J.G. Ellis, 'Eurobanks and the Inter-bank Market', *Bank of England Quarterly Rewiew*, September 1981, pp.351–64. Whereas Ellis estimates the interbank proportion of the Eurocurrency market at around 70 per cent, Stephen Clarke of the Federal Reserve Bank of New York has calculated (in a memorandum given to the author) that the interbank proportion of US banks' domestic liabilities is approximately 12 per cent.

Index

206